SOCIAL WORK AND HUMAN SERVICES RESPONSIBILITIES IN A TIME OF CLIMATE CHANGE

This book provides an accessible, research-informed text for students, social workers and other social service workers and community development workers focused on practically linking climate change to social justice.

The book is designed for:

- Those who want to embed an understanding of climate change and its social justice impacts in their everyday practice.
- Those keen to explore the explicit but also often invisible ways we see injustice playing out and exacerbated by climate change.
- Those interested in embarking on research and action which addresses climate change in an inclusive, creative and fair way.

Utilising existing and current research with organisations, government and communities, it examines key themes and contexts where work has been done and where more work is needed to design and implement inclusive and just action on climate change.

With a core position revolving around the idea and practice of justice – for earth and everything that lives here, it draws on First Nations worldviews, critical analysis, community-led approaches and complexity theory, to outline some practical ways to adapt to and mitigate the impacts of climate change as well as a strategy to reshape our life and work for the longer term.

It will be required reading for all scholars, students and professionals of social work, social welfare, community development, international development, community health and environmental and community education.

Amanda Howard (Professor) is part of the Social Work and Policy Studies team at the University of Sydney and is the Director of Undergraduate Programs.

Areas of research include community development, disasters and climate change, inclusion and participatory action research.

Margot Rawsthorne works as an Associate Professor at the University of Sydney in the Social Work and Policy Studies team. Areas of research interest include the lived experience of social disadvantage, community development, housing and disasters.

Pam Joseph (PhD) is a Lecturer at the University of Sydney in the Social Work and Policy Studies team. Her research includes a focus on community-led disaster resilience and the impacts of climate change, the intersection of health and disability, and is particularly interested in processes of transition.

Mareese Terare (PhD) works at the University of Sydney in the Social Work and Policy Studies team. Her research focus includes decolonising practice, First Nations knowledges and epistemologies, interpersonal trauma, social justice, children's rights and human rights.

Dara Sampson (PhD) works as the Academic Research Manager in the School of Medicine and Public Health at the University of Newcastle. Research interests include using fiction in social work teaching, disasters, mental health and social justice.

Meaghan Katrak Harris (PhD) works at the University of Sydney as part of the teaching and research teams in Social Work and Policy Studies, and as a freelance researcher, writer and practitioner. Meaghan's areas of research focus include decolonising practice, disasters, social justice and community practice.

Routledge Advances in Social Work

https://www.routledge.com/Routledge-Advances-in-Social-Work/book-series/RASW

SOCIAL WORK AND HUMAN SERVICES RESPONSIBILITIES IN A TIME OF CLIMATE CHANGE

Country, Community and Complexity

Amanda Howard, Margot Rawsthorne, Pam Joseph, Mareese Terare, Dara Sampson and Meaghan Katrak Harris

Routledge
Taylor & Francis Group

LONDON AND NEW YORK

Cover image: Created by Margot Rawsthorne

First published 2023
by Routledge
4 Park Square, Milton Park, Abingdon, Oxon OX14 4RN

and by Routledge
605 Third Avenue, New York, NY 10158

Routledge is an imprint of the Taylor & Francis Group, an informa business

© 2023 **Amanda Howard, Margot Rawsthorne, Pam Joseph, Mareese Terare, Dara Sampson** and **Meaghan Katrak Harris**

The right of **Amanda Howard, Margot Rawsthorne, Pam Joseph, Mareese Terare, Dara Sampson** and **Meaghan Katrak Harris** to be identified as author[/s] of this work has been asserted in accordance with sections 77 and 78 of the Copyright, Designs and Patents Act 1988.

British Library Cataloguing-in-Publication Data
A catalogue record for this book is available from the British Library

Library of Congress Cataloging-in-Publication Data
Names: Howard, Amanda, 1967- author.
Title: Social work and human services responsibilities in a time of climate change : country, community and complexity / Amanda Howard, Margot Rawsthorne, Pam Joseph, Mareese Terare, Dara Sampson and Meaghan Katrak Harris.
Description: Abingdon, Oxon ; New York, NY : Routledge, 2023. | Series: Routledge advances in social work | Includes bibliographical references and index. |
Identifiers: LCCN 2022024013 (print) | LCCN 2022024014 (ebook) | ISBN 9780367704483 (hbk) | ISBN 9780367704391 (pbk) | ISBN 9781003146339 (ebk)
Subjects: LCSH: Social service—Environmental aspects. | Community development. | Social justice. | Climatic changes. | Human ecology.
Classification: LCC HV40 .H675 2023 (print) | LCC HV40 (ebook) | DDC 361.3/2—dc23/eng/20220902
LC record available at https://lccn.loc.gov/2022024013
LC ebook record available at https://lccn.loc.gov/2022024014

ISBN: 978-0-367-70448-3 (hbk)
ISBN: 978-0-367-70439-1 (pbk)
ISBN: 978-1-003-14633-9 (ebk)

DOI: 10.4324/9781003146339

Typeset in Bembo
by codeMantra

CONTENTS

ACKNOWLEDGEMENT

This book draws on extensive research through which a diverse range of community knowledge, insight, action and reflection has been shared with us over many years. We want to acknowledge and thank all those we have been privileged to research alongside and collaborate with as we make sense of and act for climate justice.

How we name and use key concepts throughout the book

Mother Earth/Earth

Throughout the book we refer to the planet which gives us life using a capital letter. We do this to name Earth rather than describe the planet generically. In parts of the book, we use the term Mother Earth. Where we use this term, it is connected to First Nations Worldviews and is explained in further detail in Chapter 3.

First Nations/Aboriginal/indigenous

We make use of these three terms in different parts of the book to refer to the continuous culture of people who have lived in Australia for over 50,000 years. We use First Nations to refer also to Worldviews and cultures of communities who were the custodians of lands across the globe which have been colonised by others.

Risk management paradigm

We use the concept of a 'risk management paradigm' to refer to the increasing formalisation of practice through techniques of audit, metrics, administrative and bureaucratic processes. It involves planning and controls to reduce the probability of adverse events. The growth of this paradigm has been accompanied by a reduction in discretion.

Craftivism

This concept captures the re-claiming of so-called 'domestic arts' such as sewing and knitting and the mobilising of these crafts for political and campaigning purposes. It is a play on the words crafts and activism. There is a growing movement of craftivism in relation to climate change.

1

STARTING THE CONVERSATION

When Summer comes and I read that the temperature for tomorrow will be above 45 degrees Celsius, I feel a surge of worry and fear. I know that at my place that means it will be close to 50 degrees. I water the garden, but I know some of the plants will die tomorrow. I put out water and create as much shade as I can and will watch the animals (wild and domestic) that share the surrounding environment with me because I know those temperatures are at the edge of their tolerance. I am thankful and worried for the big White Cedar and the Blue Gums which will be bearing the brunt of the heat to protect us all below. We will probably all survive one day at 50 degrees, but what if there are more days? I think about the places where life already has to survive when it is that hot for long periods.

Listening to the air-conditioning pumping as hard as it can to keep things inside below 40 degrees, I know that I am part of the problem. The life I live is contributing to the rising temperatures which may lead to extinction.

I wonder about how other people are faring, who have nowhere cool to go. Where are the cool places in the community? Have we thought about creating these places? What do we need to do differently and together to care for the environment that cares for us? Am I responsible? Are we all? Why didn't we think of things earlier?

At work, I am usually seeing the crisis end of this story. Is this what we can expect in the future? More people, more animals, more environments in crisis. I know that I am not enough, and my individual effort will not do what is needed. I think we need to do something different, to change where and how we do our work. I know we need to act together. What can we do, what do we need to change, how can we act now?

Climate change is here, now. It is no longer something that will happen sometime in the future, although what the future looks like for diverse forms of life, including humans, may be very different depending on how we act now. The practicalities of working on climate change dramatically and fundamentally bring into question how work and life have been organised during the

DOI: 10.4324/9781003146339-1

Anthropocene – the era when we became powerful enough to impact the climate with our actions. We, who work in the world of people, in social work and human services, are, like everyone else, compelled into a time of uncertainty, questioning and change. We say we work for social justice, but is this really possible without environmental justice? Is it really possible for us to work anymore in single fields and professions when we are in the midst of a change in existence which encompasses all aspects of life?

For us, working in the purely social world is no longer possible because it is no longer enough. We want to invite you in this book to work with us through exploring and imagining what might be possible for those of us working currently in social work and human services as we shift our paradigm towards action where social and environmental justice coalesce. For us climate change and the transition to a new era offer us a critically important moment to recalibrate what we do in ways which connect social, environmental, cultural, scientific and economic knowledge. Social work emerged in the city from the modernist industrial world drawing attention to the unfair and unequal consequences of industrial capitalism. As this project comes to an end and our relationship with the environment changes fundamentally, what does this work look like?

We hope that what you will read here will be a starting point for you in imagining a different way of thinking and working. We offer possibilities throughout the book to support changes to systems, to the way we frame our knowledge and to practice. We want to start conversations which lead to action, and we invite you to come along with us, hoping we can work with you into a future where climate change can be addressed in ways which are fair and equitable.

About this book

We see the primary audience for this book to be *social work and human services workers*. In the definition of 'social work', we include those studying or graduated from a formal social work degree. The term 'human services worker' is a broader term, including those with social work qualifications but also other disciplinary backgrounds such as youth work, welfare, community services, aged care, criminology, community development, psychology, nursing and allied health. What both groups have in common is their direct involvement in supporting individuals and communities in relation to their social and economic welfare. This may be in a range of settings (government, non-government, private) and roles (family support, youth work, case management, community development). In essence, we are inviting everyone who works with people to walk with us in connecting that work with life on Earth at its most encompassing. We are also hopeful that educators will find the book of use in their efforts to support student learning.

We approach the task of writing this book with both a sense of trepidation and urgency. Trepidation is due to the complexity of the task of thinking through how and why people in social work and human services might be usefully involved in action around climate change. Trepidation is also due to a sense of inadequacy about our 'scientific' expertise, although this is overcome by our growing unease about our collective futures. We write this book with urgency due to the slow (but speeding up) catastrophe we see unfolding all around us. Over recent years, we have individually and collectively spent time subject to natural disasters of fire, flood and storms as well as undertaking research with communities likewise affected by disasters. These experiences have highlighted the intersections and contours of disadvantage that lead to uneven impacts of climate change. These intersections are pivotal to the question of social justice and will, therefore, be interwoven throughout the entire book, rather than presented as a 'stand-alone' feature. Like other social scientists in this book, we argue that

> disasters [and broader climate change] impact on different groups within communities in varying ways. In other words, social marginalisation, and economic inequity as experienced in 'everyday' life will also define the experience of disaster for many.
>
> *(McKinnon & Cook, 2020, p.13)*

Unfortunately, climate change has become very politicised particularly in Australia as it has in many parts of the world. Hochachka (2021) describes one of the fundamental roadblocks for action on climate change stems from our struggle to develop shared meaning on the issue. Taking a critical theory perspective, this should not come as a surprise as demands for change challenge existing social, economic and political power arrangements. It is unfortunate though as it can contribute to a paralysis: many people feel powerless in the face of the complexity whilst others feel any change is pointless given the enormity of the challenges. Taking action, such as generating or using renewable power, may be subject to strong critique by others as other parts of the system have not been addressed. This can result in further disengagement. A key aim of this book is to provide some ideas that enable people to act, at different scales.

The start

In this chapter, we lay out the framework for the book as a whole. The chapter introduces our motivations and fears in writing the book, as well as the key theoretical ideas. Many of the ideas we introduce in this chapter will be explored in much greater depth in later chapters, in other writing and by other scholars. We anticipate that individual readers will be looking for different things from this text. For some, it will contribute to an exploration of ideas at the beginning of a career. For others, it may involve revisiting and extending ideas that have developed over years of practice. We hope that this book provides opportunities for dialogue, debate and a catalyst for action.

We write this book deliberately in the Australian context. Firstly, we all live and work in the Australian context. Secondly, we believe our First Nations

Peoples' Worldviews offer a unique, enduring, perspective on climate change and justice for Mother Earth. And finally, we find ourselves at the frontline of climate change impacts:

> Australia is experiencing higher temperatures, more extreme droughts, fire seasons, floods and more extreme weather due to climate change. Rising sea levels add to the intensity of high-sea-level events and threaten housing and infrastructure. The number of days that break heat records has doubled in the past 50 years.
>
> *(Australian Museum, 2022)*

We bring to the task of writing this book several key desires: to learn from the First Nations Peoples of the land we now share about caring for the earth; to demand that those people whose everyday injustices place them at the margins of society do not carry the burden of climate change; and to bring this work to the core of social work and human service practice. Rather than present answers, this book adopts a position of cultural humility and is guided by a need to know more and to understand more deeply. We hope to offer to readers some useful ideas to shape action on climate change bringing together spiritual, theoretical and research knowledges. These knowledges include Aboriginal Worldviews (ways of knowing, ways of being and ways of doing), complexity theories and community development practice. All these knowledges centre on concepts of justice: for Mother Earth, for humans and for all life on the planet. We join our voices to the many, many other people calling for a just response to climate change. In doing so, we aim to bring a particular social work and human service lens to this call.

First Nations Worldviews – the first sunrise

Australia is home to the longest continuous culture in human history. Pre-1788, the invasion and its consequential doctrine of Terra Nullius, some 300 tribal nations (Tindale et al., 1974) lived in harmony with their environment in a relational way for over 65,000 years. This way of knowing, being and doing provides hope for life on this land. Through a process of decolonisation, First Nations groups, communities and individuals across Australia are reclaiming our tribal essence and rightful epistemology by re-committing to protect our mother. They are reconnecting to country and therefore reconnecting to honour centuries of traditions, knowledges and ceremonies. They are re-imagining these Worldviews and are being guided by their ancestors through circle gatherings and yarning circles. The old knowledge that guides traditional values and underpin the principles of survival are essential to the ongoing cycle of life for Mother Earth and her entities and for humans. The rekindling of these values requires commitment to understand as well as commitment to making changes to current ways of knowing, being and doing.

First Nations people are guided by a commitment to tribal values and Lores of reciprocity. Reciprocity informs relational lore – our responsibility was to care for our mother – 'Mother Earth' – and her entities (Martin, 2009). Epistemic Worldviews encompassed ways of knowing, ontological understandings ways of being and axiological ways of doing. First Nations Worldviews were guided by each Nations' Lores. Lores evolved from tribal responsibilities through which the circle of life continues. Lores are bodies of knowledge that guide us through every sunrise and through every sunset. Therefore, Lore defines our tribal responsibilities, and these are embedded within relational ways with the environment. Historically, Elders guided children on ways of knowing and ways of being and ways of doing – to protect and care for Mother Earth – these are sacred stories of hope, love and creation, in essence the circle of life (Terare, 2020). Children learn and grow as one with the environment, children and the environment are raised as equals where the children learn to care and protect their country and the entities. The very nature and characteristics of totems are principal to their epistemology and the responsibilities of care and protection and are significant to their ontological understandings. Children grow with these principles that guide their life and support their survival. The circle of life continues.

Decolonisation, a process for all who live on this land, must guide our personal journeys. For First Nations people, decolonisation enables a declaration of tribal/nation identity that enacts a responsibility to care and protect our Mother Earth. Once we connect to our Country, we instantly are obligated to protect her. This process of reclaiming our place on Country protects our mother and re-empowers by ensuring we follow ceremonial practice including cultural burns and ceremonial dance stomping which energises our mother. For non-Indigenous people, decolonisation enables you to demonstrate your understanding of the importance of our mother, not just people. Through Acknowledgement of Country, you are obligated to respect and honour her. The Lore of relational responsibilities becomes an essence belonging to you.

In this book, we seek to privilege First Nations Worldviews and voices (Rigney, 1999). The non-Indigenous writers of this book have been guided by our Indigenous colleague, mentor and friend Mareese Terare, a Bundjalung Goenpul woman.

Complexity theory

Complexity theory enables us to imagine, analyse, track and make change in the interconnected and entangled systems in which life and our work unfolds. Changes in complex systems are non-linear, dynamic and evolving (Wolf-Branigin, 2014). Complexity theory provides a conceptual framework and language to make sense of phenomena such as climate change and social justice where uneven impacts, disproportionate relationships between initial and end point changes and densely interconnected relationships shape both every day and long-term experiences. In its attention to interaction within and between diverse systems, in contexts that shift and change over time, complexity theory offers a conceptual landscape that can accommodate multiple ways of knowing, being and doing and so allows us to explore ideas through both Western and Indigenous lenses. Throughout the book, we use complexity theory to analyse current systems and to recommend promising action.

In our work across a range of fields, we have observed the increasingly ineffective and often detrimental effects of under-estimating complexity and of an adherence to fixed regulatory systems which fail to account for changing dynamics or people outside their remit. In emergency management, we see the persistence of rigid hierarchical paradigms operating in both planning and practice. These ongoing attempts to impose a linear logic on the management of complex events such as bush fires, floods, cyclones and earthquakes are having increasingly adverse impacts due to the poor fit of the paradigm which excludes considerable community effort mobilised through informal networks. In human services, we have also seen an increase in linear programme logics, reductive measurement regimes and prescribed practice driven by risk management approaches. Here also we see the application of simple problem-solving on complex problems in complex systems, which provides an illusion of control by overlaying a limited set of parameters that exclude critical elements. The impact of such thinking is exacerbated by policy development that actively seeks simplified, quantified information, even when responding to issues that are neither simple nor easily quantifiable.

Complexity theory invites us to draw knowledge from what we see and experience as climate change impacts increase and develop new paradigms to describe the dynamic relationships and configurations inside and between systems. Key concepts such as emergence, convergence, self-organisation, feedback loops and adaptation help us make sense of what is happening and offer a number of practical processes for shaping and mobilising new ideas, relationships and action. For us complexity theory and complex systems thinking provide both a metaphorical frame and language with the dimensions and intersections to assist us in understanding and planning action and also a framework for mapping and analysing the ways in which Earth, climate and social justice might coalesce.

In thinking through complexity and how it might assist us in making sense of the systems in which we live and work, we do not want to succumb to a view that the complexity of climate change equates to an overwhelming array of problems which are impossible to work through. Jonathan Beacham and colleagues (2018), in their ethnographic research on alternative food systems, hit the nail on the head here, encouraging us to move from what they describe as 'anxious and pessimistic politics of the Anthropocene' (p.535) to a 'new, hopeful, more than human ethics of care' (p.535).

Community development

Community development provides both conceptual ideas and practice tools for those interested in social and climate justice. Unfortunately, there is a lot of confusion about the concept of community development in the literature, with some seeing it as a job, some as a qualification and others as a theory. It has also become far less popular among mainstream funders, policymakers and governments as the pervasive spread of neo-liberal individualism has successfully reshaped us as consumers and entrepreneurs. In the social work field, it has struggled to keep a 'toe hold' in education programmes across Australia as individual case work has been positioned as 'real social work' (Hugman, 2015). It will come as no surprise to those familiar with our collective work that we reject this positioning. For us community development provides a hopeful (and possibly the only) approach to shifting cultural and structural power to confront and challenge inequality and disempowerment (Rawsthorne & Howard, 2011). For us, people should be treated with respect, be able to exercise their rights and have opportunities in life, but these rights and opportunities are fundamentally interdependent, entangled and collective. Adopting a community development approach to our work on climate change encourages cultural humility, generosity, dialogue, inclusion and action. On a day-to-day practice basis, this means working in ways which increase people's skills, knowledge and confidence and instil in them a belief that they can make a difference; promote collective action; confront discrimination; enable learning from, and celebration of, difference; create organisations and groups that are open and democratic; link and build bridges across differences; and enable communities to influence decisions affecting their lives (Howard & Rawsthorne, 2019).

Working with communities, in the context of the everyday, we have room to include experiences of people in all aspects of life. This perspective shifts us from compartmentalised thinking and practice, where particular aspects of life are amplified, while others are ignored or even silenced. Where we become defined only by how we relate to service systems, regulatory regimes or financial need, a process which underpins much of the human service system, we succumb to applying simple approaches which hide many of the aspects of life needed to survive and to thrive. Taking a community development approach opens up ways to see people as part of a broader ecology, as connected to places, to animals and the natural world and to a wide range of other people. This approach disrupts power relations in human services through building momentum for change which is not solely reliant on individuals but is assertively collective and takes its starting point as small, local, lateral and reciprocal community relationships. Throughout the book, we explore examples where this approach is being practised, and in Chapter 7, we think through the role of collective action in transforming our work in social justice and climate change.

We are witnessing a turn towards each other as we realise the scale and depth of the work required to recalibrate the ways in which we live on Mother Earth as human-induced climate change takes hold. We do not argue naively that community development is 'the answer' or that working in a community way is without challenges. We are interested, however, in what is possible when we turn our gaze from *me* to *us* and how support for action through very different relationships between people focused on what can be done/grown/created together starting from the ground and working out and up may change the way we organise our work.

A note on context – neo-liberalism

Neo-liberalism is a term so widespread in discussions across social work and human services that it is easy to assume we share a common understanding of its meaning and implications. Connections between neo-liberalism and climate change may not be immediately clear, but for us, the historical, current and future impacts of this ideology are important to talk through. The pervasive character of neo-liberal policy in action means that it will shape how climate change is addressed in obvious and also indirect ways. Neo-liberalism, with its emphasis on markets as the most effective way to organise resources, on small and hands-off government approaches, and on individualised approaches to service provision and support, has very intentionally recast our relationships with each other, with organisations and with government as ones of consumers or customers and producers or providers. This reduction of everyday life to a series of market transactions and everyday relationships to those which are purely economic provides a powerful example of compartmentalised and oversimplified worldviews. The reductive work of neo-liberalism is a very effective siren call reassuring us that we don't need to worry about the messy, complex and overwhelming tangle of threads in our lives as community members and citizens of Earth. All we need to worry about is our rights as customers and our individual choices. The market will organise resources efficiently, and all we need to do is participate according to its parameters. Government intervention and proactive policy are seen as distorting the market and as a result are to be discouraged. In a recent example of neo-liberalism in action, Scott Morrison, the Australian Prime Minister, having behaved at the Glasgow COP21 talks in a way which brought ill will on Australia due to its poor commitment to emissions reduction, welcomed the rapidly growing interest and investment in renewable energy, low-emission technologies and other innovations led by the private sector (Eckersley, 2021). Framing Australia's lack of action to reduce global warming as a triumph providing the market with opportunities to furnish the answers needed and reinforcing the idea that small government and policy were the most effective way to address human-induced climate change, Morrison provided us with a perfect example of neo-liberal ideology in practice (Joy & Vogel, 2021). So, neo-liberalism is triumphant and the community is provided with a simple answer to a complex problem which omits as much as it includes.

In this book, we draw attention to what is missing from this victory narrative outlining the long-term lack of clear policy, uncertainty regarding government investment and inconsistent decision making which has underpinned Australia's lack lustre approach to climate change and created frustration in the markets. In Chapter 8, we discuss the critical role of policy at all levels, looking closely at the mythology surrounding neo-liberalism and unpacking the connected role of public and private sector collaboration where climate change is being effectively acted on.

For us, neo-liberalism runs counter to and undermines First Nations Worldviews, an understanding of complexity and the creation of climate justice as it frames the individual in the market as the foundation of society. Collective action, consideration of factors outside the market such as the natural world and value systems which are focused on ethics of care rather than economic profit are viewed with antipathy by neo-liberal thinkers. A growing body of research argues that individualised approaches will not be enough to ensure climate change impacts are mitigated and that the burden of these impacts is not felt disproportionately by those with least economic power (Bravo, 2009; Cameron, 2012; Hetherington & Boddy, 2013; Klepp & Chavez-Rodriguez, 2018; Taylor, 2015). Neo-liberalism, for us, must be considered as part of our process for understanding the current shapers of human-induced climate change and strategies for mitigation and adaptation which will deliver social and environmental justice.

Social work and human services: what's climate change got to do with it?

We are not climate scientists, and this book is not about the science of climate change although we engage with and draw on scientific, social, political and cultural ideas and research as we make sense of where social and environmental justice coalesce and how we as people who work in social work and human services might contribute to reversing the terrible impacts of human-induced climate change.

For us, this book is an opportunity to ask and explore questions about what we do in social and human services work and social justice work with people more broadly if we centre justice and care for Mother Earth and all who depend on her for life. We are curious about the founding social work idea of a *person in environment* which shapes the work we do and wonder whether a different understanding of the complex relationships between environments, non-human and human inhabitants might provide a more meaningful paradigm for just, respectful and equitable action on climate change. These questions are emerging in the field of social work as the impacts of COVID-19 reshape the parameters of practice (McDermott, 2021) and are equally important as we make sense of what climate change means for future work in human services. We come from workplaces which pay close attention to the experiences of people, and our work is focused on the different systems through which justice, fairness and inclusion for people are conveyed. It can be easy to lose sight of the broader systems of earth (ecology, climate and weather, plant and animal species, land and water) when human-centric issues are always pressing in our everyday work and lives.

Research and its roles

We draw on our research, knowledge and practice as well as that shared by others interested in supporting social justice as a core element in climate change action. We are all researchers as well as practitioners and community members. As researchers, we do not take a position of neutrality or objectivity. Knowledge and information, for us, is constructed and shaped by power relations, histories, norms and structures. We support the position of Cameron and Hicks (2014) who argue that:

> As a performative practice, academic research is activism; it participates in bringing new realities into being. Our role as academics has thus dramatically changed. We are less required to function as critics who excavate and assess what has already occurred, and more and more pushed to adopt the stance of experimental researchers, opening to what can be learned from what is happening on the ground.
>
> *(p.53)*

Cameron and Hicks see engagement in 'climate politics of hope' (p.55) as essential work for researchers and see this work as resisting the efforts of neo-liberalism to marginalise or trivialise the impact of grassroots community-led initiatives. Instead, they argue that shaping a different future where such initiatives can be transforming is critically important. Following the work of Anderson (2006), Massumi (2002) and Solnit (2004), they see these politics of hope as underpinning action by experimenting with real and detailed alternatives to the way we currently live in the world.

Possibilities

Taking this invitation seriously, in the last chapter of the book, we engage in some detail in a hopeful research experiment. We work through some alternative scenarios, to engage in some speculation about what we might need to change, what we might need to give up and what we might need to share if the way we organise human services and social support systems were altered at their core. Through the book, we will be walking through a range of possible scenarios which experiment with fundamental change. In doing this, we will be starting with the local, the particular, the everyday and working outwards to large-scale systems change. We have chosen to write this way because some of the fundamental changes are already here in small, quiet, largely unrecognised practices. Some are being enacted under the radar or as resistance to dominant systems. Some are waiting to be imagined and brought into existence. In doing some of this speculative work, we want to invite you, as you read the book, to think about and maybe start this practice yourself. This is not a practice of naivety or wishful thinking, but rather one which takes seriously the notion that change requires a paradigm shift in the social sciences as it does in science (Kuhn, 1996) and drawing on community development, that an effective place to start change is by looking differently at what you already have to work with. Isabelle Stengers writes in relation to the practices of science:

> If learning to think is learning to resist a future that presents itself as obvious, plausible, and normal, we cannot do so either by invoking an abstract future, from which everything subject to our disapproval has been swept aside, or by referring to a distant cause that we could and should imagine to be free of any compromise. To resist a likely future in the present is to gamble that the present still provides substance for resistance, that it is populated by practices that remain vital even if none of them has escaped the generalised parasitism that implicates them all.
>
> *(2010, p.10)*

This quote seems apt for inviting resistance in the practices of the social world, of social work and human services. It moves us from a stance where climate change is an adjunct to slightly changed business as usual (social work and climate change, social work and the environment) to a set of practices which are founded on justice and care for Earth and from which whatever we might come to call social work is shaped. Even the term 'human services' speaks to an existing paradigm, set of power relations and organising principles for support. Whilst this paradigm shift compels us to consider all life on earth, not just human, we acknowledge that non-human justice is deserving of much more attention than has been possible in this book. Where possible we will point you to other writers and sources to support a more complete exploration of these issues.

The guiding question for us in this book is how do we shift our focus from social problem-solving and work on socio-economic systems to a system of work which centres ideas and practices on custodianship, stewardship?

The layout of this book

Chapter 1 – Starting the conversation sets the context, outlines key ideas, locates us as a collective of researchers and starts to set up the foundations for our thinking.

Chapter 2 – Ideas in action invites the reader to question, investigate, ponder and think through some of the ways in which very particular ideas in discussions on climate change have been constructed and then enacted as truth. It explores some core concepts informing current thinking about climate justice. These core concepts are responsibility, risk and resilience.

Chapter 3 – First Nations Worldviews – the first sunrise privileges First Nations Worldviews to guide our thinking about social and climate justice. This focuses our attention to ways of knowing about climate change (epistemology), beliefs during these often-tumultuous times where, internationally, natural disasters are common events (ontology) and finally ways of going forward, what action do we need to undertake to support better understanding and respect for the environment (axiology).

Chapter 4 – Complexity explores complexity theory as a framework that, while having roots in Western scientific traditions, offers a way for us to draw on Indigenous, Western and other traditions of knowledge and meaning making and, in doing so, to grapple with wicked problems – those problems that resist simplified, superficial and de-contextualised solutions. Understanding complex social and environmental systems concepts such as convergence, emergence, self-organising systems, feedback loops and adaptation are particularly useful.

Chapter 5 – The basics brings focus to the basic elements of everyday life which fundamentally drive the ways in which we impact on climate change (*Sections Food; Energy; Water*). How we produce, access and consume food, where we source energy and how much we use, how we utilise water and act in relation to water systems, reflect both directly and indirectly our relationship with the environment as well as the contours of social (in)equity.

Chapter 6 – Acting for change is the first of three chapters interested in acting for change. We commence by outlining key community development practice theories that we have found useful in supporting action for change. In this chapter, we also ask how might a social work and social justice lens contribute to thinking about action at home, in the office and in our neighbourhoods.

Chapter 7 – Acting for change together: collective action notes that increasingly dominant discourses which locate competition at the core of human survival are being questioned. Attention is being paid to collaboration as key to human as well as planetary futures. It celebrates the human capacity to create, grow and sustain ideas through collaborative processes centred on imagination and story.

Chapter 8 – Acting for change: mobilising policy pays attention to the core aspect of social and human service practice of understanding, influencing and implementing policy. A range of tools are detailed, including Carole Bacchi's methodological approach to interrogating policy as discourse called 'What's the Problem Represented to Be?' (WPR). Lessons from previous campaigns and hopeful change are also highlighted.

Chapter 9 – Emergent moments: when it all goes wrong shifts our attention to those moments when climate change impacts bubble up into daily life to disrupt and destroy, often referred to as 'natural disasters'. These moments provide us with a window into possible futures and opportunities to learn and make change in the here and now.

Chapter 10 – Emergent moments: the future returns to our conversations about possibilities, about the impetus climate change provides for us to shift paradigms, recognising the complex dimensions in which life unfolds. To bring some form to our ideas about a paradigm shift, in this chapter, we want to imagine social work and human services differently through a series of speculations (or backcasting).

Chapter 11 – Case studies concludes the book through a series of contextualised case studies with the aim of assisting students and educators unpack the complexities of working towards climate justice.

The authors

So, who are we as authors of this book?

Mareese

I bring to this book a sense of re-empowerment, confidence and social justice. Re-empowered to critique the powerful and insidious nature of colonisation, whilst reflecting and reclaiming my tribal epistemes and applying actions to re-lational responsibilities, that is to care, nurture and protect our Mother. The academic role broadens my scope to collaborate and develop meaningful and purposeful alias ship to action social justice for Mother Earth, as expected by Ancestors.

Professionally, I define myself as a human services/welfare worker. I have worked in the women's services sector reflecting my personal and professional responsibilities regarding advocacy, social justice and empowerment. I was a frontline worker for 25 years, responding to women and children in crisis, as a counsellor, group worker and community development worker. The past 16 years I have worked in the education sector starting out in RTO and currently in higher education of academia. The bane of my professional existence directed me to explore Aboriginal Worldviews and how to apply these, to social work and human services theory and practice – which ultimately led to my PhD.

Margot

I bring to this book what I hope I bring to other aspects of my life and work: a desire to learn and an obligation to speak out against what feels wrong. I am not offering answers but want to feel uplifted by the optimism, passions and intelligence of others. It is clear there are thousands of people making small meaningful changes each day around the globe. I want to celebrate these acts and to belong to a movement built on respect for Mother Earth. My family have lived for eight generations on Wiradjuri lands, and I want to embrace their phi-losophy of Yindyamurra: to show respect, to give honour, to go slow and to take responsibility.

Professionally, I describe myself as an applied sociologist, interested in not only understanding but changing people's experiences. Prior to my time in academia, I was employed as a planner in State and Local governments, community development worker and researcher in South Western Sydney and manager of community legal centres. In academia, my focus has been on the lived experi-ence of social disadvantage particularly with residents living in social housing, women who have experienced violence and those living in rural settings. Since 2005, I have taught community development theory and practice on the social work programme at the University of Sydney.

Pam

My understanding of diverse communities and cultures has been shaped by multiple intertwining identities: as a fifth-generation descendant of British settlers, as a 'third culture kid' in Papua New Guinea during its transition to Independence in the 1970s, as a community health nurse in metropolitan Australia and now as a social worker, academic and resident of a small rural community. My qualifications and professional experience in nursing, midwifery and community health, and subsequently a Bachelor of Social Work and a PhD centred around issues of complex care, confronted me with the way environments shaped people's experiences and opportunities, not only individually but across successive generations. In recent years, teaching and research roles have opened up new possibilities to explore these themes, inspired by the energy of colleagues, students and research participants.

Throughout my life, I have benefited from family, friends and colleagues who have walked beside me as I gradually deepen my understanding of justice and care of Earth and her inhabitants. Now that I am a grandmother and in the later phase of my professional career, my commitment to finding a way towards a caring, just and sustainable world has sharpened. This book represents, for me, an opportunity to continue in my own learning, as well as to make a contribution to ongoing conversations.

Dara

Inequity was one of the reasons I became a social worker. Through my own, and observational experience, came an early realisation that social and economic disadvantage is so often randomly allocated by virtue of gender, culture, class, ableism and so many other factors. This intersectional inequity is compounded by political policies and governance. For people already marginalised, the impact of climate change will be greater than the impact on people with more power and resources. This informed my involvement with this venture, along with a belief that language can create change.

In terms of my professional background, I worked for 20 years in Department Human Services, Centrelink, initially as a social worker and then as a business manager. I have taught social work at both University of Newcastle and University of Sydney. My research areas include fiction and its capacity to transform, mental health, disasters and education.

Meaghan

My work as a social worker has always been informed by my commitment to working alongside communities: listening, learning and the responsibility of making what contribution I can. I have worked in community and social work for almost 35 years and lectured and researched for more than 15. It has been my great privilege to have spent much of that time working alongside my local Aboriginal community. My first human services job was in family services programmes at our local Aboriginal Cooperative, and this context of self-determination, advocacy and activism has shaped my social work career ever since. My work has encompassed a range of front line and management roles including kinship and out of home care, women's services, community development, programme planning and development, counselling and group work. This work informed my PhD, which provided an historical perspective of social and welfare work and the local Aboriginal community. Home for me is Tati TatiMutti Mutti and Latji Latji Country, where we are at the forefront of water and environmental crisis. My involvement in this book is motivated by optimism that in sharing ideas and collaborations, we can collectively create change. My work at Sydney University has given me the privilege to connect with and make a contribution to this project with Amanda, Margot, Mareese, Dara and Pam.

Amanda

For a long time, I have been thinking about, working with and trying to understand communities and why they are so important to life. For just about as long I have been a gardener. The intersections between the work I have been involved with and my life learning patience and observation in the garden and in nature more broadly have always had a porous boundary. I am a social worker by training and work now at Sydney University where I have been able to connect and collaborate with Margot, Mareese, Pam, Dara and Meaghan in connecting the different parts of life as we think together about climate and change. Living in Australia, the need for healing and justice which stems from the ongoing destructive action of colonialism is visible in all aspects of life. Climate change brings injustice even more sharply in focus and invites a fundamental change for the profession I am part of and for us all. This book, I hope, makes a contribution to that change by sharing ideas and practices that have emerged from collaboration, dialogue and experience. I live on Awabakal Country.

I worked in community development and community planning for 20 years before I returned to study. My PhD was the culmination of two decades making sense of how language shapes practice and how power travels through community life. For the past 10 years, I have been teaching and researching at the Universities of Newcastle and Sydney working to connect an understanding of environment in its broadest and deepest terms with the experiences of people, of communities and society.

In this chapter, we have set the scene of the book, provided context and key ideas and introduced ourselves, the authors. In Chapter 2, we will explore some of the current thinking around climate change and invite the reader to critically reflect on the ways ideas around climate change have been constructed.

References

Anderson B (2006) "Transcending without transcendance": Utopianism and an ethos of hope. *Antipode, 38*(4), 691–710.

Australian Museum. (2022) Impacts of climate change. Retrieved April 5, 2022 from: https://australian.museum/learn/climate-change/climate-change-impacts/

Beacham, J., Nyberg, D., Wright, C., Freund, J., & Rickards, L. (2018). Organising food differently: Towards a more-than-human ethics of care for the Anthropocene. *Organization, 25*(4), 533–549. https://doi.org/10.1177/1350508418777893

Bravo, M. T. (2009). Voices from the sea ice: The reception of climate impact narratives. *Journal of Historical Geography, 35*(2), 256–278. https://doi.org/10.1016/j.jhg.2008.09.007

Cameron, E. S. (2012). Securing Indigenous politics: A critique of the vulnerability and adaptation approach to the human dimensions of climate change in the Canadian Arctic. *Global Environmental Change, 22*(1), 103–114. https://doi.org/10.1016/j.gloenvcha.2011.11.004

Cameron, J., & Hicks, J. (2014). Performative research for a climate politics of hope: Rethinking geographic scale, "impact" scale, and markets. *Antipode, 46*(1), 53–71. https://doi.org/10.1111/anti.12035

Eckersley, R. (2021, November 15). *"The Australian way": How Australia's stubbornness on climate change is damaging our international reputation.* ABC Religion & Ethics. https://www.abc.net.au/religion/robyn-eckersley-australian-stubbornness-on-climate-change/13631814

Hetherington, T., & Boddy, J. (2013). Ecosocial work with marginalized populations: Time for action on climate change. In M. Gray, J. Coates, & T. Hetherington (Eds.), *Environmental social work* (1st ed., pp. 46–61). Routledge.

Hochachka. (2021). Integrating the four faces of climate change adaptation: Towards transformative change in Guatemalan coffee communities. *World Development, 140*, 105361. https://doi.org/10.1016/j.worlddev.2020.105361

Howard, A., & Rawsthorne, M. (2019). *Everyday community practice.* Allen & Unwin

Hugman, R. (2015). *Social development in social work: Practices and principles.* Routledge. https://doi.org/10.4324/9781315780337

Joy, M., & Vogel, R. K. (2021). Beyond neoliberalism: A policy agenda for a progressive city. *Urban Affairs Review, 57*(5), 1372–1409. https://doi.org/10.1177/1078087420984241

Klepp, S., & Chavez-Rodriguez, L. (Eds.). (2018). *A critical approach to climate change adaptation: Discourses, policies and practices.* Routledge.

Kuhn, T. S. (1996). *The structure of scientific revolutions* (3rd ed.). University of Chicago Press.

Martin, K. L. (2009). *Please knock before you enter: Aboriginal regulation of Outsiders and the implications for researchers* [Doctoral thesis, James Cook University]. https://researchonline.jcu.edu.au/4745

Massumi, B. (2002). Navigating moments. In M Zournazi (Ed.), *Hope: New philosophies for change* (pp. 210–243). Sydney: Pluto.

McDermott, F. (2021). Impact of a global pandemic on scope and diversity of social work research and practice: Complexity theory a lens to review current thinking. *Australian Social Work, 74*(3), 261–263. https://doi.org/10.1080/0312407X.2021.1908876

McKinnon, S., & Cook, M. (Eds.). (2020). *Disasters in Australia and New Zealand: Historical approaches to understanding catastrophe.* Palgrave Macmillan.

Rawsthorne, M., & Howard, A. (2011). *Working with communities: Critical perspectives.* Common Ground Publishing. ISBN: 978-1-86335-934-4

Rigney, L. (1999) Internationalisation of an indigenous anti-colonial cultural critique of research methodologies: A guide to Indigenist research methodology and its principles, in HERDSA Annual International conference proceedings. *Research and Development in Higher Education: Advancing International Perspectives, 20*, 629–636.

Solnit R (2004) *Hope in the dark: Untold histories, wild possibilities.* Nation Books.

Stengers, I. (2010). *Cosmopolitics.* University of Minnesota Press.

Taylor, M. (2015). *The political ecology of climate change adaptation: Livelihoods, agrarian change and the conflicts of development.* Routledge.

Terare, M. (2020). *It hasn't worked so we have to change what we are doing: First Nations worldview in human service practice* [PhD doctoral thesis, University of Sydney]. University of Sydney Repository. https://hdl.handle.net/2123/23499

Tindale, N., Jones, R., & Jones, R. (Rhys M). (1974). *Aboriginal tribes of Australia: Their terrain, environmental controls, distribution, limits and proper names.* Australian National University Press.

Wolf-Branigin, M. (2014). Complexity and the emergence of social work and criminal justice programmes. In A. Pycroft & C. Bartollas (Eds.), *Applying complexity theory: Whole systems approaches to criminal justice and social work* (pp. 79–96). Polity Press.

2

IDEAS IN ACTION

Connecting social and ecological justice: exploring frames and ideas

In thinking through, shaping and writing this book, we want to start conversations, work our way curiously through existing research and knowledge, draw on and make sense of what we are learning in our own research and recalibrate our work in ways which intimately link social and environmental justice. In this chapter, we want to walk with you through some of this process, outlining how and why we have included particular knowledge, research, reflections and examples. We do this for two reasons. Firstly, to mark out a possible pathway for you, the reader, in finding a meaningful and practical way through what we found often to be an overwhelming array of issues, debates and information. Secondly, to encourage and support everyone working in social work and human services to connect with issues of climate change in ways which have the potential to expand our thinking and practice into the future.

Let's start, then, in a very practical way. We want to invite you, at the beginning of the book, to question, investigate, ponder and think through some of the ways in which very particular ideas in discussions on climate change have been constructed and then enacted as truth. The ideas covered here do not amount to an exhaustive list but hopefully will start the ball rolling as we engage in the ongoing process of making sense of the entangled and complex relations contributing to social and environmental justice.

From our practice and research with communities, we have learned that the ways in which knowledge is *framed* shapes our decisions, our perception of possibilities and the direction of our action (Rawsthorne & Howard, 2011). Drawing from the seminal work of Lakoff and Johnson (1981) on the power of metaphorical frames, we see the framing of climate change debates and discussions as

DOI: 10.4324/9781003146339-2

critical in opening up or closing down parameters for action on climate change. This is no more evident than in scientific discourse on global warming and provides a useful starting example for us in this chapter as we think through some possible ways in and through the dimensions of climate change and social justice.

Increasingly, research is linking more detailed and urgent scientific explanations of climate change and its impacts with less engagement and impetus for action in audiences worldwide (Markam, 2018; Xiang et al., 2019). It feels counter-intuitive that the more we know, the less we are willing and able to act. Surely, more factual explanation provides us with the information we need for effective mitigation and adaptation. Making sense of this trend, however, is familiar ground for those of us who work every day with people overwhelmed and paralysed by increasingly detailed narratives of their own and their community's deficits. Information is useful, but without space and parameters to act and clarity about the strengths we have to draw on to address problems, we know people become despondent, disengaged and distressed (Saleebey, 2002). Put simply, the way in which we frame our circumstances directly and indirectly creates and limits the possibilities for action.

Although we have, at times, felt overwhelmed with the scale and intensity of climate change and social justice challenges, what we have come to, and what we offer here, is not only a discussion of problems but some thoughts, suggestions and approaches which we have found offer both every day and long-term support for the kind of paradigm shift, we argue, provides hopeful and impactful climate justice action. Returning to the decreasing impacts of increasingly concerning and detailed scientific reports on climate change, we wonder about the unintended consequences of framing what is vital and critical information using binary arguments (do this or bad things will happen) and metaphors of war and apocalypse. Ahamer (2013) draws attention to some of the dead ends created by using fight metaphors to encourage action on climate change. He argues this metaphor fails to recognise the complexity of climate change arguing instead that this is only part of a broader landscape of global change and that a game, rather than a fight metaphor, offers much more promise as a strategy for action. His description of the 'intercomplex (i.e. both interdisciplinary and intercultural) argumentative landscape' (p.275) through which we must walk to understand and address climate change (as part of global change) provides a more helpful perspective for understanding the dynamics of change being experienced.

In a similar way, we are interested in what kind of approaches and framing of issues are more likely to precipitate action. Bain and colleagues (2013) in their research on collective futures offer an interesting perspective on this in the context of social work and human services. They were interested in the links between the ways in which people imagine the future and possible factors existing in society now that may drive a change towards that future. In one of their studies, they asked research participants who reported agreeing that human-induced climate change was real, to imagine how things would be in 2050 if action had been taken in Australia to address climate change. In this study and the others, they conducted, they found benevolence (defined as 'warmth and morality', p.526) was consistently important in shaping an imagined future. In addition, they found that participants were more likely to act for change based on information about crises or decline in society than they were by scientific or technological development. Their results indicated a strong community orientation in responses. Interdependence between people was seen as important. This is consistent with broader research which shows altruism and warmth have not only a positive impact on their recipient but also on the person undertaking the altruistic act (Hu et al., 2016). Bain et al. (2013) argue that messages about climate change may be more effective if they frame the issue in line with increased warmth, compassion and connection as a result of climate change action, than emphasising catastrophic impacts if no action is taken.

Peter Tangney (2019), tapping into this discussion, argues that the polarising and bogged down debate in Australia about climate change requires a change of focus away from assumptions made in climate science communication that if we have more information, the truth of the situation will become obvious to everyone, and that scientific expertise is agreed upon, and only ignorance and a lack of information are preventing consensus. For Tangney, what is described as the 'deficit model of science communication' (p. 136), where it is posited that a better and more detailed understanding of the scientific explanation of the problem is all that is required to trigger action, is ineffective. Appeals to neutral evidence-based information in relation to climate change have been caste within an ideological frame by climate sceptics including many conservative politicians in Australia, effectively rendering the power to convince those who are inclined to question the validity of climate change null and void. Tangney argues for a move away from this style of argument towards a focus on tangible alternatives such as renewable energy which are already gaining support in the community and with business, thus answering to the values of those interested primarily in jobs and economic prosperity and those wanting action on climate change. In a similar way, Tangney argues, Australia's ongoing experiences of disaster create an existing and well-supported frame through which climate change impacts can be addressed without descending into partisan politics. Australia has been repeatedly described as a laggard in relation to climate change mitigation and adaptation (Garnaut, 2019; Tangney, 2019) with binary ideologically driven framing amplifying this situation in policy and public discourse.

So, walking into this array of debate, information and ideology, we have found it useful to focus our thinking on questions that link why, when, what and how. As researchers, we embrace the collecting, analysis and sharing of information, and we encourage you as a reader and actor in the world to draw on existing and emerging knowledge about climate change and its impacts on our work and life more generally. We are, however, mindful of the importance of understanding how we can and do make sense of this information and shape action from it. We have been asking whether there are more effective ways to support action on climate change that includes social justice if we move from an either/or frame to alternatives. These alternatives may open possibilities for more diverse and inclusive connection with the motivations for why people act on anything important to them, what they can and are most likely to do and how this action can most effectively be supported. Such an approach does not minimise the dire impacts of climate change, nor the urgency for action at all levels. Rather, it may make the unhelpful but often invisible frames within which we understand climate change less tacit and more visible. In doing this, we can start constructing more effective frameworks for action.

In both the diverse range of published research we discuss through the book and from our own research across the areas of disasters, community development, health, disability, decolonisation and social change, we have looked for and include themes, ideas and perspectives which support our understanding of issues and our desire for action. Questions about how we go about acting on climate change and the consequences of acting in particular ways have emerged as major themes as we have written the book. Locating justice for Earth and all residing here at the centre of our thinking has been particularly helpful in clarifying how we might shape and analyse policy and action (more on this in later chapters). If we look now at some of the key ideas which set the parameters for widely held perspectives or frames, we can start to see this process in action.

Responsibility

The question of how notions of responsibility are framed in relation to climate change and social justice is critically important in guiding policy and practice settings now and into the future. How do we make sense of public, policy and media narratives about responsibility and risk in relation to climate change? Are these ideas useful in supporting action? What are the directions which open up and close down when we frame climate change as predominantly an individual responsibility or a risk to be managed?

Roussin and colleagues (2018) are helpful here, arguing that the scale and complexity of climate change create a context where responsibility is both dispersed, or difficult to pin down at a global level, and at the same time very sharply focused within a risk management framework where individuals are seen as wholly responsible for specific disasters and events. As we write this book, communities along the east coast of Australia are experiencing devastating floods where the consequences of this contradictory set of parameters are being played out as politicians resoundingly locate responsibility for the impacts of floods on households who 'choose' to live in the floodplain and should know about the consequences (Cormack, 2022) while responsibilities regarding climate change-related policy decisions are not linked directly to flood impacts (Hurst, 2022; Purtill, 2022). Alongside this, the role of government in opening up land for more affordable housing on the floodplain, of developers in keeping flood risk information vague and opaque in their communications with buyers and of housing companies for designing and selling houses not built with flood mitigation or adaptation in mind is obscured in the public and policy narratives. While the decisions of individuals and families to buy the housing they can afford certainly contribute to flood impacts, the burden of these impacts falls disproportionately on their shoulders and not on those of arguably more powerful decision-makers whose contribution is great but whose responsibility is much harder to pin down.

In a similar way, notions of *shared responsibility*, which have become pervasive in disaster risk reduction policy and planning (Lukasiewicz et al., 2017; Atkinson & Curnin, 2020), have been increasingly critiqued by researchers and practitioners as a process for governments and Emergency Management (EM) agencies to shift rather than share responsibilities for disaster preparedness, response and recovery onto individuals while decision-making power and even participation in planning is very clearly not included in the process of sharing (McLennan & Eburn, 2015). Here, responsibility is framed as a moral and survival imperative for individuals who are increasingly exhorted to become more responsible or blamed as lacking responsibility while the responsibilities of others in the complexity of disaster cycles are much less clear. It is quite an old-fashioned idea of responsibility attempting to simplify who needs to be responsible so that the issue can be easily resolved. It would be a mistake, however, to view this process as a conspiracy or a straightforward and intentional blame allocation exercise. The temptation to take this line with governments fulfilling the role of the blameworthy makes the same mistake in the other direction. In spite of the best efforts of many, understanding what responsibility means in this context is far from simple.

Roussin, Gould and Larrere, drawing on the work of Dale Jamieson (1992, 2014) and Hans Jonas (1984), argue that climate change fundamentally challenges existing paradigms of responsibility as it creates a paradox where we are both responsible for the creation and consequences, but the complexity and parameters of climate change are such that it is impossible to attribute responsibility within existing approaches to moral responsibility. Climate change is the result of multiple decisions and acts over time, many of which were not designed or implemented to do harm but as a result have created a situation of cascading harm and threat to earth and all who live here. Reducing this array of decisions and actions over time and space to particular events of responsibility allocation fails to understand the complexity of the processes for which we are trying to allocate responsibility. They highlight the limitations of individual responsibility and the 'mechanical world view' (p.429) upon which this approach to responsibility is based. They argue for a collectivisation of responsibility as a way forward with national governments providing a collective policy and organisational structure to act as conduits between global frameworks and actions and community level and individual behaviour. This is then taken a step further utilising Iris Marion Young's (2006) model of collective responsibility through social connection. Here responsibility is understood as linked to structural justice and injustice with individuals being seen within the context of social processes and structures, contributing to climate change. Individual responsibility or blame is not the important question, but rather, how I am connected to social structures and processes which bring about injustice. I am essential to change, but it is my connection to and collective action with others in the context of social structures which frames responsibility and agency. This shift in thinking seems to offer a potential path for understanding and action in relation to responsibility which takes account of the context in which we live and supports a much more shared embracing of our collective and dispersed responsibilities to act justly on climate change. So, our process of thinking through, making sense of and moving outside existing frames regarding responsibility has set up some new possibilities, which we hope you will take with you as you read the book.

Risk

The second idea worth working through is that of risk. Both climate change and disaster policy, practice and research have become increasingly dominated by a risk management paradigm (Crosweller & Tschakert, 2021). We have seen this being driven by both the very real concerns across the globe about the life-threatening and life taking impacts of disasters on communities which are being linked more explicitly with climate change (Howes et al., 2015), and also by increasing economic costs associated with such disasters (Linnerooth-Bayer & Hochrainer-Stigler, 2014). It seems obvious that faced with the kinds of impacts which climate change-induced disasters are already having across the world and the likelihood of more and more intense disaster events looming in the immediate future, that risk management is a very sensible frame of reference. If we take a closer look at this frame, however, we start to see very clear lines within which legitimate action is shaped and a particular worldview is rendered as truth. Climate change and disaster risk management, in many ways, reflect historical understandings of the natural world as hostile and needing to be controlled by humans to make it manageable. This frame does not engage with broader questions about how humanity might live as part of the natural world and respond to patterns of weather, the movement of tectonic plates in the Earth's crust or ecological events as part of Earth systems. Rather, this paradigm is shaped by an understanding of humanity as separate from broader ecological and natural systems. Non-human life on earth – plants and animals – is rarely factored into risk assessments. Understanding risk as something to be stopped or at the very least reduced makes absolute sense as a survival strategy, as our dominant imperative for planning and action tends to shut down or exclude other ways in which we might think and act in relation to climate, environment and the shocks we experience through weather and other events. Managing and reducing risk forms a powerful narrative which is hard to counter. Why would anyone argue against keeping people safe and alive? This binary shaping of arguments about living safely in a world increasingly impacted by climate change feeds very effectively into fears (both real and imagined) which often precipitate simple, certain answers and actions. Examples here include imperatives to raise dam walls further to protect those living in the floodplain or increasing resources for crisis response including deploying more defence force personnel in response to disaster events. This increases a crisis orientation to our action and planning which inadvertently restricts or excludes a broader approach.

In social work and human services, we are very familiar with the capacity of crises to overtake planning and for a crisis management approach to eat up time, energy and resources to the exclusion of all else. It appears to be a commonsense idea that reflects the truth of the way things are, with pathways for action also appearing as clear and straightforward. And yet risk management only began as an area of knowledge and interest after the Second World War developing as an insurance strategy and in engineering (Dionne, 2013). We invite you, as we have done, to ask about what sits inside a frame where the focus is only on risk management (an example here is the rapidly expanding area of disaster risk reduction shaping policy and practice in disaster preparedness, response and recovery globally, following the endorsement of the Sendai Framework (United Nations Office for Disaster Risk Reduction, 2022). What are some of the other possible frames which might be helpful in addressing climate change and social justice?

O'Hare and White (2018) draw our attention to the narrow focus of mainstream risk management approaches in floods where communities are treated as homogenous. These researchers found this approach fails to engage with the range of more complex contours of disadvantage experienced by community members, which means planning and responding to flood impacts within a risk framework is not possible for many. This research invites us to think about risk as much more layered and uneven frame. Here we need to observe and learn from contextual contours which map both experiences and understandings of risk related to climate change.

Research by Elijido-Ten and Clarkson (2017) which focused on evaluating sustainability strategies among the largest 500 corporate firms globally found that superior sustainability performers consistently adopted a proactive capability- and opportunity-focused approach to climate change and did not engage in a risk management framework at all. These researchers highlight the limiting aspects of risk management frameworks and draw our attention to more generative ways of working in relation to climate change and sustainability.

In our research with communities in relation to disasters, we found communities understand and engage with risk in practical and creative ways, weighing up a range of risks present during extreme weather and other disaster events and making decisions about taking and avoiding risks based on a complex array of values, knowledge, connections and care (Howard & Rawsthorne, 2019).

Resilience

Along with responsibility and risk, another very powerful idea which has come to prominence in discussions about climate change is that of resilience. Like responsibility, resilience is commonly understood and spoken about in policy, media and practice narratives as something individuals and communities need more of. This idea is one we also want to flag and invite you to think critically about.

Resilience has become a ubiquitous concept in policy, research and practice focused on climate change and disasters (Cutter & Derekhshan, 2019: Adekola et al., 2020). Its utility and capacity to describe those things which make us more likely to withstand shocks and disruptions have made it a powerful, though contested, idea worldwide (Jolly, 2020; Nguyen and Akerkar, 2020; Beilin & Paschen, 2021). As with many ideas which become so universally utilised, resilience is one which bares close analysis particularly if we are interested in understanding climate change and social justice as complex interconnected systems.

Resilience and resilience thinking in relation to climate change have found their way from ecology and the study of ecological systems through environmental resource management (Walker et al., 2006) and into the realms of social policy and practice over the past 15 years.

As part of this process, the idea has been framed in very particular ways and applied often simplistically to individuals and communities. Common framing in relation to resilience locates a lack of resilience and the responsibility to become more resilient squarely on the shoulders of communities who are exhorted to ensure their own resilience in the face of both disaster and climate change impacts. Beilin and Paschen (2021) describe this frame as shaping 'reactive life' (p.516) where order is maintained in the face of disaster through clear hierarchies and communities become resilient through compliance with policy directives and taking responsibility for their own safety. They contrast this framing with another they describe as 'relational life' (p.516) where community relationships, dispersed and networked decision-making and multiple emerging perspectives shape a practice of resilience grounded in a recognition of uncertainty and messiness as normal in responding to disruptions. This second framing of resilience lends support to the growing critiques of resilience as simplified into slogans such as bouncing back, bouncing forward and building back better (Mannakkara et al., 2018; Adekola et al., 2020; Mika & Kelman, 2020).

Another very powerful frame which is shaping understandings of resilience is that of measurement (Mayer, 2019). Again, this frame conveys a simplistic idea of resilience as something which communities can fill up on and, once measured as fully resilient, are able to adapt and survive in the face of disaster and climate change (Hong et al., 2021). Alongside the measurement movement which has been growing in the area of resilience, more nuanced analysis and discussion of this idea questions reductive approaches to resilience, highlighting the inequities which are hidden when we understand resilience building as apolitical. For example, Jolly (2020) argues that resilience has become weaponised in Australian disaster resilience policy and practice. For Jolly, resilience discourse utilises neutral language and scientific narratives to disguise the way those most impacted by disasters are blamed for a lack of resilience. While measures of resilience are utilised widely, little attention is given to utilising existing measures of inequality which are amplified during and after disasters.

For us, resilience remains a useful idea but one which, like responsibility and risk, requires thoughtful consideration and questioning in the range of contexts it is being used. In our research, we have seen extraordinary resilience among individuals and communities impacted by climate change and disaster. We worry that this resilience continues to be drawn down by governments who rely on it but largely fail to invest in long-term social and community infrastructure, knowledge and relationships. Resilience then also emerges as an idea and practice requiring close and contextual attention and ongoing clarification.

Making sense of action: mitigation and adaptation?

Before leaving our set of ideas for closer examination, we want to briefly discuss two approaches to action which are considered central to climate change. Much of the argument about the ways in which climate change should be 'tackled' has centred on notions of adaptation and mitigation (Gates, 2021; Khan & Munira, 2021). What do these two, commonly accepted, approaches to climate change entail and how might we make sense of them in the context of social justice. In looking more closely at the way mitigation is framed, the political contours of climate change become very visible, and inequities at a global level are quite visible. As does the peripheral attention paid to non-human life.

A mitigation approach seeks to change the problem, to reduce and stop the emission of greenhouse gases, for example. Globally, this has become a point of debate regarding the equity of the goal, across nations with very different levels of wealth. One perspective argues that the richest countries need to reach zero emissions by 2050, with countries having more limited resources following in sequence. Adding to this complexity, while some measures suggest the US and Europe are reducing emissions and developing countries are producing more, questions regarding trade and industrial relationships between countries with very different wealth can be obscured when such direct measures are used. For example, countries such as India, China and Nigeria are increasing emissions, in part, because the richer countries have outsourced manufacturing to other locations (Gates, 2021).

At a more local level, mitigation policies have been increasingly criticised for their regressive outcomes placing disproportional burden on the poorest house-holds. Büchs and colleagues (2011) analysed a range of mitigation policies in-cluding regulation, taxes (such as carbon on environment taxes), subsidies and trading schemes. They found that apart from in the case of transport (where taxes on personal transport and air travel can act as progressive measures), these miti-gation policies are all regressive. That is, they work against the fair distribution of resources, so poor people end up paying more although their emissions are less, while the rich people generate more emissions and either continue with a high-carbon lifestyle as they can afford it or reduce their carbon footprint with less personal burden than those with less resources.

Globally, this inequity plays out in arguments for countries which have traditionally been low emitters to be given 'grace' to play catch-up, arguing, particularly in agrarian societies, the manufacturing of machinery will increase their overall wealth and, therefore, improve the living standards for poorer people. In essence, this is an argument that gives each country a quota of carbon emissions (Jakob & Steckel, 2014; Gates, 2021).

Adaptation, as a concurrent and alternative strategy for addressing climate change, has, like mitigation, come under an increasingly critical gaze in relation to social justice. Morchain, in Klepp & Chavez-Rodriguez (2018), argues that without proactive analysis of and attention to social justice concerns, adaptation strategies are and will continue to be designed and implemented in the Global South by those in the Global North who have contributed most to climate change impacts but are least impacted. Morchain's analysis found the significant power imbalance between those making decisions about and designing adaptation strategies (those in the Global North) and those cast as recipients of adaptation programmes with least decision-making power (those in the Global South) creates a frame of accelerating injustice for those who must adapt most but are least implicated in the reasons adaptation is necessary.

In making sense of adaptation, Morchain invites us to consider the layered and complex political landscapes in which adaptation frames are shaped and to recognise the importance of understanding local power dynamics as well as those enacted globally in any climate adaptation initiative.

Earlier research by Bassett and Fogelman (2013) also invites us to question and investigate the framing of climate adaptation. Their analysis of key climate change documents including IPCC reports revealed a spectrum of approaches to adaptation ranging from adjustment (where climate impacts as events in the natural world create vulnerability) to reformist (where socioeconomic vulnerabilities are acknowledged but change occurs within existing systems) through to transformative (where fundamental questions regarding structural inequity and the need for system change are core). For these researchers, there is promise in utilising a combination of reformist and transformative approaches which link climate change adaptation and social justice outcomes.

The themes drawn out by Morchain and Bassett and Fogelman are becoming increasingly important for researchers focused on adaptation and mitigation (Bravo, 2009; Cameron, 2012; Taylor, 2015; Klepp & Chavez-Rodriguez, 2018). We can see here that even from a brief process of critical analysis in relation to mitigation and adaptation, as with the other ideas we have discussed here, a more complex picture emerges. Ideas which seem, and are often used as if they are straightforward, neutral and even procedural when applied to climate change, reveal themselves are complex, political and social in the ways they are operationalised on the ground.

Locating social work and human services – ethics, care and social justice

Before we leave this discussion of how ideas and actions are framed, we want to briefly spend some time locating social work and human services in the debates focused on climate change, which are increasingly permeating most areas of work and life. We start broadly in the world of activism and then look at how ethics at play here apply to the work we do in the everyday.

Emilsson et al. (2020), in their research on climate strike protesters, were interested in whether strikers framed their activism primarily via environmental, economic or welfare concerns. While environmental concerns were consistently identified as more important than economic concerns among the 900 participants in their survey, the relationship between environment and welfare was much more complex and interconnected. The questions raised through this research invite the possibility, for us, of asking some fundamental questions about the ways in which complex, comprehensive system shifts, such as those precipitated by and accompanying climate change, might change the systems in which social work and broader human services operate. If the impacts of climate change mean that business as usual in the industrialised world is no longer an option, surely welfare, health, income support, child protection and other social support systems will be impacted comprehensively as well. Rather than seeing the relationship between social work/human services and climate change as one where it will be business as usual, only more so (which is one option) as impacts begin to bite, what might happen if we view that relationship as inescapably entangled? What if the change required brings an opportunity for us to examine the parameters of what we do and the systems we work in and imagine some different scenarios shaped by different relationships and ethics when it comes to earth and all who live here. In Chapter 10, we imagine what a different paradigm for social work and human services might look like across key areas of practice. Here, we want to ask about the ethics, values and knowledges which shape the relationship between social work and human services and climate change right here and right now.

Care, ethics and intersections

We suggest that two starting points may be helpful in placing ourselves and our work in social work and human services inside climate change action. The first of these is an ethics of care from which we largely build our practice with people. This attention to care and the ethics of care for people in systems provides an important foundation from which social work and human services might expand to include care for all (human and non-human) who live on Earth and Earth. So, what do we understand care, care ethics and care work to include? Unsurprisingly, social work and human services literature examines care as a political idea and practice as well as one grounded in relational and moral connections (Gilligan, 1995; Banks, 2014; Pease et al., 2017). Questions about who does caring work, who is cared for and who is often excluded from individual and collective care and how caring is practised are all core areas of interest for social and human services workers and researchers. Widening this examination of care and ethics to include the more than human as well as locating our work as part of broader than human ecosystems may not be a dramatic departure for social work and human services workers, but it is one we have only begun to take. Boddy, in Pease et al.'s (2017) discussion of critical ethics of care in social work, argues that social workers urgently need to reassess their work as enacting compassionate social justice as part of the natural world. She encourages us to shift from a focus on a compartmentalised and separate humanity and reframe our ethics and practice within much more complex earth-centred ecosystems. In a similar vein but from an animal justice perspective, Fraser and MacRea call for greater recognition of the 'commonalities between animal welfare, conservation and human well-being' (2011, p.581). In this context, we bring an acute understanding of the ways power and inequity manifest themselves in social contexts and broaden this to learn what our contribution might be as part of broader and deeper systems where convergent interrelationship and interdependencies are central. In the next chapter, we explore this further, grounding our learning in First Nations Worldviews in this learning process.

Globally, care grounded in social and environmental justice makes visible the contours of inequity for people as we saw earlier in our discussion of mitigation and adaptation. At a local level, often invisible and unrecognised care practices are utilised by workers and people we work with as a form of everyday or quiet activism (Horton & Kraftl, 2009; Hackney, 2013; Pottinger, 2017). They are forms of decision making, not always recognised as such where the personal and relational intersect. These relational forms of care activism can often go unnoticed. Both Pottinger (2017) and Warner and Inthorn (2022) draw our attention to the creative and embodied forms of activism which link work with communities with making and doing as political acts of care. We discuss this in more detail later in the book in relation to craftivism.

So, care ethics and politics of care as core to social work and human services are important starting points as we recalibrate our work to encompass a broader and deeper relationship with earth and the natural world. The second starting point which we have found helpful in locating our work in the context of climate change is the recognition that inequities are intersecting and amplifying. Intersectional analysis (Collins et al., 2021; Hartsock, 1985; Harding, 2004; Moreton-Robinson, 2014; Stoetzler & Yuval-Davis, 2002) of the social world underpins much of social work and human services practice highlighting the amplifying impacts of disadvantage for individuals and communities where, for example, poverty, racism, gendered discrimination and violence are all part of day-to-day life, shaping both workers understanding and approach. We have seen already in our discussion that intersecting contours of disadvantage play out in climate change impacts at all levels, and also the critical role social justice perspectives can contribute in making sense of and designing action on climate change that is fair and equitable. Social and political issues in response to climate change have gained ground in research literature and public discourse; however, intersectionality and equity have been slower to emerge as being central to the debate (Kaijser & Kronsell, 2014). Communities where we have undertaken disaster research have experienced the full weight of intersectional disadvantage (disorder) due to race, gender, sexuality, poverty and disability through exclusion from decision making and planning before disasters, poor or non-existent recognition during and after a disaster and an expectation that one size fits all when it comes to practical support to recover from disasters. The operation of power that intensifies intersectional exclusion through hierarchical decision making and organisational structures has been very evident in our research across many settings. However, critical theory reminds us to question any framing of experience through binaries (exclusion/inclusion; disorder/order; climate/humans). Taylor (2015) argues the continued separation of climate and human and non-human existence works to continue to de-politicise the climate debate in separating the systems and positing climate change as something external, impacting an otherwise functional system.

Intersectional analysis can be used in ways that inadvertently pigeonhole experiences and accordingly is a starting point for analysis and action rather than a complete explanation. In Chapter 4, we examine complexity thinking and complex systems theory, which we have found provides possibilities for social work and human services in making sense of some of the entangled enactment of power we have seen. Where intersectional analysis remains vital for us as a launch point and critically important in understanding the social justice dimensions in climate change, complexity thinking has enabled us to think through possible futures, emergent ideas and scenarios beyond an analysis of current frames. Having said this, we argue that along with care, intersectional thinking and practice provide important foundations for social and human service workers in thinking through and acting ethically and with positive impact in the entangled context of climate change and social justice.

Ideas to action

So finally, how are we hoping that you will engage with ideas, action and the translation of ideas to action and action back into ideas? In this chapter, we have worked through a number of key concepts in climate change debates, seeking to unpack how these are *framed*. We have argued that this framing enables specific action (and makes impossible others) and gives rise to particularly discourses through which we make sense of the world. We offer this concept of *frame* as a tool to support your thinking and practice in relation to climate change. We hope that you will engage with ideas and actions (both intended and unintended) with a curiosity, a willingness to look deeper, to question assumptions (including ours) and to keep clarifying the ways you and others are making sense of what is an immersive and lifelong process of learning. We hope the discussion here has provided some guidance and some practical support for your reading through the book and for your work in climate change and social justice once you have finished reading. Now, onto the really big concepts shaping the book.

As we have noted, this book is guided by First Nations Worldviews: ways of knowing, ways of being and ways of doing. The next chapter will focus our attention to First Nations ways of thinking about social and climate justice and explore examples of First Nations responses to climate change and disaster.

References

Adekola, J., Fischbacher-Smith, D., & Fischbacher-Smith, M. (2020). Inherent complexities of a multi-stakeholder approach to building community resilience. *International Journal of Disaster Risk Science, 11*(1), 32–45. https://doi.org/10.1007/s13753-020-00246-1

Ahamer, G. (2013). Game, not fight: Change climate change! *Simulation & Gaming, 44*(2–3), 272–301. https://doi.org/10.1177/1046878112470541

Atkinson, C., & Curnin, S. (2020). Sharing responsibility in disaster management policy. *Progress in Disaster Science, 7*, 1–9. https://doi.org/10.1016/j.pdisas.2020.100122

Bain, P. G., Hornsey, M. J., Bongiorno, R., Kashima, Y., & Crimston, D. (2013). Collective futures: How projections about the future of society are related to actions and attitudes supporting social change. *Personality & Social Psychology Bulletin, 39*(4), 523–539. https://doi.org/10.1177/0146167213478200

Banks, S. (2014). *Critical and radical debates in social work*. The Policy Press.

Bassett, T. J., & Fogelman, C. (2013). Déjà vu or something new? The adaptation concept in the climate change literature. *Geoforum, 48*, 42–53. https://doi.org/10.1016/j.geoforum.2013.04.010

Beilin, R., & Paschen, J.-A. (2021). Risk, resilience and response-able practice in Australia's changing bushfire landscapes. *Environment and Planning D, Society & Space, 39*(3), 514–533. https://doi.org/10.1177/0263775820976570

Bravo, M. T. (2009). Voices from the sea ice: The reception of climate impact narratives. *Journal of Historical Geography, 35*(2), 256–278. https://doi.org/10.1016/j.jhg.2008.09.007

Büchs, M., Bardsley, N., & Duwe, S. (2011). Who bears the brunt? Distributional effects of climate change mitigation policies. *Critical Social Policy, 31*(2), 285–307. https://doi.org/10.1177/0261018310396036

Cameron, E. S. (2012). Securing indigenous politics: A critique of the vulnerability and adaptation approach to the human dimensions of climate change in the Canadian arctic. *Global Environmental Change, 22*(1), 103–114.

Collins, P. H., da Silva, E., Ergun, E., Furseth, I., Bond, K. D., & Martínez-Palacios, J. (2021). Intersectionality as critical social theory. *Contemporary Political Theory, 20*(3), 690–725. https://doi.org/10.1057/s41296-021-00490-0

Cormack, L. (2022, March 8). *"Farcical": Minister shoots down flood relocation, says residents know the risks*. Sydney Morning Herald. https://www.smh.com.au/politics/nsw/farcical-minister-shoots-down-flood-relocation-says-residents-know-the-risks-20220308-p5a2qg.html

Crosweller, M., & Tschakert, P. (2021). Disaster management leadership and policy making: A critical examination of communitarian and individualistic understandings of resilience and vulnerability. *Climate Policy, 21*(2), 203–221. https://doi.org/10.1080/14693062.2020.1833825

Cutter, S. L., & Derakhshan, S. (2019). Implementing disaster policy: Exploring scale and measurement schemes for disaster resilience. *Journal of Homeland Security and Emergency Management, 16*(3), 2707. https://doi.org/10.1515/jhsem-2018-0029

Dionne, G. (2013). Risk management: History, definition, and critique. *Risk Management and Insurance Review, 16*(2), 147–166. https://doi.org/10.1111/rmir.12016

Elijido-Ten, E. O., & Clarkson, P. (2017). Going beyond climate change risk management: Insights from the world's largest most sustainable corporations. *Journal of Business Ethics, 157*(4), 1067–1089. https://doi.org/10.1007/s10551-017-3611-6

Emilsson, K., Johansson, H., & Wennerhag, M. (2020). Frame disputes or frame consensus? "Environment" or "Welfare" first amongst climate strike protesters. *Sustainability, 12*(3), 882. https://doi.org/10.3390/su12030882

Fraser, D., & MacRae, A. M. (2011). Four types of activities that affect animals: Implications for animal welfare science and animal ethics philosophy. *Animal Welfare, 20*(4), 581–590.

Garnaut, R. (2019). Australia can be a superpower in a low-carbon world economy. *2019: Weathering the 'Perfect Storm' – Addressing the Agriculture, Energy, Water, Climate Change Nexus, 12–13 August 2019*. Crawford Fund. https://econpapers.repec.org/paper/agscfcp19/301970.htm

Gates, B. (2021). *How to avoid a climate disaster: The solutions we have and the breakthroughs we need*. Random House Large Print.

Gilligan, C. (1995). Hearing the difference: Theorizing connection. *Hypatia, 10*(2), 120–127. https://doi.org/10.1111/j.1527-2001.1995.tb01373.x

Hackney, F. (2013). Quiet activism and the new amateur. *Design and Culture, 5*(2), 169–193. https://doi.org/10.2752/175470813X13638640370733

Harding, S. (2004). *The feminist standpoint theory reader: Intellectual and political controversies* (1st ed.). Routledge

Hartsock, N. C. M. (1983). *Money, sex, and power: Toward a feminist historical materialism*. Northeastern University Press.

Hong, B., Bonczak, B. J., Gupta, A., & Kontokosta, C. E. (2021). Measuring inequality in community resilience to natural disasters using large-scale mobility data. *Nature Communications, 12*(1), 1870–1870. https://doi.org/10.1038/s41467-021-22160-w

Horton, J., & Kraftl, P. (2009). Small acts, kind words and "not too much fuss": Implicit activisms. *Emotion, Space and Society, 2*(1), 14–23. https://doi.org/10.1016/j.emospa.2009.05.003

Howard, A., & Rawsthorne, M. (2019). *Everyday community practice*. Allen & Unwin.

Howes, M., Tangney, P., Reis, K., Grant-Smith, D., Heazle, M., Bosomworth, K., & Burton, P. (2015). Towards networked governance: Improving interagency communication and collaboration for disaster risk management and climate change adaptation in Australia. *Journal of Environmental Planning and Management, 58*(5), 757–776. https://doi.org/10.1080/09640568.2014.891974

Hu, T. Y., Li, J., Jia, H., & Xie, X. (2016). Helping others, warming yourself: Altruistic behaviors increase warmth feelings of the ambient environment. *Frontiers in Psychology, 7*, 1349. https://doi.org/10.3389/fpsyg.2016.01349

Hurst, D. (2022, March 7). Climate council says too many leaders are silent on global heating's role in 'megafloods'. *The Guardian*. https://www.theguardian.com/australia-news/2022/mar/07/its-not-a-footnote-its-the-story-climate-council-says-too-many-australian-leaders-silent-on-cause-of-floods?fr=operanews

Jakob, M., & Steckel, J. C. (2014). How climate change mitigation could harm development in poor countries. *Climate Change, 5*(2), 161–168. https://doi.org/10.1002/wcc.260

Jamieson, D. (1992). Ethics, public policy and global warming. *Science, Technology and Human Values, 17*(2), 139–153. https://doi.org/10.1177/016224399201700201

Jamieson, D. (2014). *Reason in a dark time: Why the struggle against climate change failed – and what it means for our future*. Oxford University Press.

Jolly, M. (2020). Bushfires, supercyclones and "resilience": Is it being weaponised to deflect blame in our climate crisis? *Scottish Geographical Journal*, *136*(1–4), 81–90. https://doi.org/10.1080/14702541.2020.1863607

Jonas, H. (1984). *The imperative of responsibility: In search of an ethics for the technological age.* University of Chicago Press.

Kaijser, A., & Kronsell, A. (2014). Climate change through the lens of intersectionality. *Environmental Politics*, *23*(3), 417–433. https://doi.org/10.1080/09644016.2013.835203

Khan, M. R., & Munira, S. (2021). Climate change adaptation as a global public good: Implications for financing. *Climatic Change*, *167*(3–4), 50. https://doi.org/10.1007/s10584-021-03195-w

Klepp, S., & Chavez-Rodriguez, L. (Eds.). (2018). *A critical approach to climate change adaptation: Discourses, policies and practices.* Routledge.

Lakoff, G., & Johnson, M. (1981). *Metaphors we live by.* University of Chicago Press.

Linnerooth-Bayer, J., & Hochrainer-Stigler, S. (2014). Financial instruments for disaster risk management and climate change adaptation. *Climatic Change*, *133*(1), 85–100. https://doi.org/10.1007/s10584-013-1035-6

Lukasiewicz, A., Dovers, S., & Eburn, M. (2017). Shared responsibility: The who, what and how. *Environmental Hazards*, *16*(4), 291–313. https://doi.org/10.1080/17477891.2017.1298510

Mannakkara, S., Wilkinson, S., & Potangaroa, R. (2018). *Resilient post disaster recovery through building back better* (1st ed.). Routledge.

Markam, A. (2018, October 11). Why people aren't motivated to address climate change. *Harvard Business Review.* https://hbr.org/2018/10/why-people-arent-motivated-to-address-climate-change

Mayer, B. (2019). A review of the literature on community resilience and disaster recovery. *Current Environmental Health Reports*, *6*(3), 167–173. https://doi.org/10.1007/s40572-019-00239-3

McLennan, B., & Eburn, M. (2015). Exposing hidden-value trade-offs: Sharing wildfire management responsibility between government and citizens. *International Journal of Wildland Fire*, *24*(2), 162–169. https://doi.org/10.1071/WF12201

Mika, K., & Kelman, I. (2020). Shealing: Post-disaster slow healing and later recovery. *Area*, *52*(3), 646–653, https://doi.org/10.1111/area.12605

Moreton-Robinson, A. (2014). Subduing power: Indigenous sovereignty matters. In T. Neale, C. McKinnon, & E. Vincent (Eds.), *History, power, text: Cultural studies and Indigenous studies* (pp. 189–197). UTS ePress

Nguyen, H. L., & Akerkar, R. (2020). Emergency information visualisation. In R. Akerkar (Ed.), *Big data in emergency management: Exploitation techniques for social and mobile data* (pp. 149–183). Springer International Publishing. https://doi.org/10.1007/978-3-030-48099-8_8

O'Hare, P., & White, I. (2018). Beyond 'just' flood risk management: the potential for- and limits to-alleviating flood disadvantage. *Region Environmental Change*, 18(2), 385–396. https://doi.org/10.1007/s10113-017-1216-3

Pease, B., Vreugdenhil, A., & Stanford, S. (Eds.). (2017). *Critical ethics of care in social work: Transforming the politics and practices of caring.* Taylor and Francis. https://doi.org/10.4324/9781315399188

Pottinger, L. (2017). Planting the seeds of a quiet activism. *Area*, *49*(2), 215–222. https://doi.org/10.1111/area.12318

Purtill, J. (2022, March 10). Climate Council says too many leaders are silent on global heating's role in 'megafloods' | Australian politics | *The Guardian.*

Rawsthorne, M., & Howard, A. (2011). *Working with communities: Critical perspectives.* Common Ground Publishing. ISBN: 978-1-86335-934-4

Roussin, J., Unger, M., Gould, C., & Larrere, C. (2018). Responsibility in a global context: Climate change, complexity, and the "Social Connection Model of Responsibility." *Journal of Social Philosophy, 49*(3), 426–438. https://doi.org/10.1111/josp.12255

Saleebey, D. (2002). *The strengths perspective in social work practice* (3rd ed.). Allyn and Bacon.

Stoetzler, M., & Yuval-Davis, N. (2002). Standpoint theory, situated knowledge and the situated imagination. *Feminist Theory, 3*(3), 315–333. https://doi.org/10.1177/146470002762492024

Tangney, P. (2019). Between conflation and denial – The politics of climate expertise in Australia. *Australian Journal of Political Science, 54*(1), 131–149. https://doi.org/10.1080/10361146.2018.1551482

Taylor, M. (2015). *The political ecology of climate change adaptation: Livelihoods, agrarian change and the conflicts of development*. Routledge.

United Nations Office for Disaster Risk Reduction. (2022). *What is the Sendai framework?* United Nations. Retrieved from https://www.undrr.org/implementing-sendai-framework/what-sendai-framework

Walker, B. H., Salt, D., & Reid, W. (2006). *Resilience thinking: Sustaining ecosystems and people in a changing world*. Island Press.

Warner, H., & Inthorn, S. (2022). Activism to make and do: The (quiet) politics of textile community groups. *International Journal of Cultural Studies, 25*(1), 86–101. https://doi.org/10.1177/13678779211046015

Xiang, P., Zhang, H., Geng, L., Zhou, K., & Wu, Y. (2019). Individualist-collectivist differences in climate change inaction: The role of perceived intractability. *Frontiers in Psychology, 10*, 187–187. https://doi.org/10.3389/fpsyg.2019.00187

Young. I. M. (2006). Responsibility and global justice: A social connection model. *Social Philosophy & Policy, 23*(1), 102–130. https://doi.org/10.1017/S0265052506060043

3

FIRST NATIONS WORLDVIEWS – THE FIRST SUNRISE

This chapter focuses our attention to ways of knowing about climate change (epistemology); beliefs during these often-tumultuous times where, internationally, natural disasters are common events (ontology); and finally ways of going forward, what action do we need to undertake to support better understanding and respect for the environment (axiology).

Author standpoint

In the interest of my tribal epistemological responsibilities, I will introduce myself so that you can note my connections and relatedness responsibility. My name is Mareese Terare, I am a Bundjalung Goenpul woman from Tweed Heads – Goenpul Country including Minjungbal Bundjalung and North Stradbroke Island. I am writing this chapter from my standpoint. That is my Bundjalung Goenpul woman, mother and grandmother standpoint. My standpoint provides me with my worldview, the lore of being, my epistemological, ontological and axiological way in the world. Whilst I am guided by ancestors and Mother Earth, living life in modernity (Moreton-Robinson, 2006) has been impacted by the sociopolitical and historical contexts post-1788 and the legal doctrine of Terra Nullius. This period encompasses major changes to First Nations countries and nations. This period has encountered major disruptions to our worldviews and most importantly to our relatedness with entities (Martin, 2009) and our connectedness, our Kanyini (Randall et al., 2006).

First Nations in this land mass we call Australia has encountered major losses to flora and fauna where many species of fauna and flora are considered endangered and sadly many have become extinct. These provide a completeness to our worldview; when these are not sufficient, then we encounter an imbalance. My Bundjalung and Goenpul epistemes are about maintaining humanity with

DOI: 10.4324/9781003146339-3

all our entities and our ecosystems – therefore, human rights extend to care and protection of, our, Mother Earth (Arabena, 2015).

I am writing this chapter from my Bundjalung Goenpul standpoint of relatedness by honouring my responsibility of reciprocity for our Mother and her entities. This chapter is my invitation to you to join us in this ongoing challenge.

The first sunrise – time immemorial

First Nations people have lived on the continent now called Australia for over 50,000 years, some may say since time immemorial, creating the longest continuous culture in human history. This span of time has included many human and non-human changes. Over the past 8,000 years (Ruddiman, 2005), the dominant influence on the climate and the environment has been human activity, referred to as the current geological age of the Anthropocene. In this chapter, we seek to learn from the ancient knowledges of First Nations people about custodianship of Country as well as exploring the possibilities that flow from an Aboriginal Worldview. We discuss the importance of caring for earth and for changing the relationship between people and where we live from one of exploitation to one of relational stewardship, custodianship and respect. We outline here how this change might then shape the way we practise social and environmental justice (EJ).

At the time of the invasion, 1788, life for the Eora people was balanced, and there was rightness to the world. The cyclic nature of the seasons where food was plentiful gave them opportunities to trust the future. This brought knowledge of the environment and the reciprocal nature of renewal and regrowth (Elder, 1988). Imagine what life would have been like had there been a meaningful and respectful introductory meeting in 1778 – where the English were guests who were welcomed onto country – where Terra Nullius was a mere legal doctrine and not a premise to murder, control, rape, pillage and oppress? Where the visitors behaved respectfully and the exchange of meaningful dialogue with the Eora people about respecting Worldviews; respecting ways of being doing and knowing? This however was not the case; the British invaded and colonised every aspect of Eora nation. Through the invasion of unceded Eora country where First Nations Worldviews were ignored, and Western Worldviews became the reality, the process of genocide and colonisation began.

This chapter examines historical context of colonial control and explores several theoretical perspectives that we may need to consider to support our worldviews to protect and nurture our Mother – Mother Earth, these include our epistemological ways of knowing about climate change; ontological beliefs during these often-tumultuous times where, internationally, natural disasters are common events; and finally our axiological ways of going forward, what action do we need to undertake to support better understanding and respect for the environment through the ontological ways of knowing – our relational reciprocity responsibilities. We understand these as rooted in ancient knowledges but adapting and changing allows new knowledges to emerge.

First Nations Worldviews

Worldviews provide 'frameworks for interpreting and exploring the world, supporting the way we act and relate to our world' (Sherwood, 2010, p.57). Although similar to a theoretical framework, Worldview is much more than a theoretical framework: it informs who I/we am/are and how I/we understand and relate in the world. Much of the wisdom of Elders and Indigenous knowledges in relation to Worldview sits outside of Western academic texts. It is worthy of note that First Nations Worldview was rendered invisible through colonial processes and therefore not considered a framework to measure one's life against. Settler colonialism by contrast supports 'white/western' way of being and thinking and doing, becoming the rule of all social measurements. Formal education and other hegemonic institutions like the media have played a powerful role in presenting and normalising Western ways of being into Australian culture (Fogarty & White, 1994). In education, media and political discourse Aboriginal Worldviews have often been positioned (ironically) as alien and uncivilised. Settler colonialism supports and enables exploitative capitalism, silencing First Nations Worldviews which centre on connection to country, belief systems, spirituality, land and kinships. Whilst Weir and colleagues (2011) argue that 'Indigenous people inherit holistic, place-based knowledge frameworks that are distinctly different from Western knowledge traditions, which focus on universal values and methodologies', they also hold out the possibility of dialogue between these different cultural traditions (2011, p.4).

First Nations Worldview encompasses a unique set of values and beliefs system, creating a spiritual location for First Nations people and culture. Creation stories and belief systems were well established in Australian First Nations lives before 1788 (Williamson et al., 2010).

> For Aboriginal peoples, story and storytelling commenced at the beginning. Stories are embodied acts of intertextualised, transgenerational law and life spoken across and through time and place. In and of the everyday and every time, stories – whether those that told of our origin or of our being now – all carry meaning: a theorised understanding that communicates the world.
>
> *(Phillips et al., 2018, p.8)*

First Nations Worldviews treasure and revere the wisdoms of Elders, passed down through story and ceremony. This Worldview provides the essence with which one sees them self within the world. One's purpose and success within life are measured by their worldview (Sherwood, 2010). The axiology of Aboriginal Worldviews is being accountable and responsible to your connections and relationalities. It demands you are accountable to your knowledge and beliefs. It asks: what do you do? How do you do it? What are your intentions? (Wilson, 2008). Ontologically, First Nations Worldview centres on the individual's relational responsibilities within the tribe and to Country. A key departure from Western scientific knowledge, epistemologically First Nations Worldview derives from Country, from tribal responsibilities of reciprocity and relationships. In this way, we cannot speak of social justice and environmental justice as if these are two separate entities: they are one.

The core of First Nations Worldviews is Kanyini – connections to Mother Earth (Randall, 2006). The nature of this connection is often described as unconditional love. This essence of unconditional love has evolved into a belief system which inclusively underpins relational values and ensures the responsibility of reciprocity as lore. These values and beliefs underpin First Nations nationally and internationally over thousands of years (Randall, 2006). The deep understanding has evolved over 65,000 years or as commonly known among First Nations peoples, since the first sunrise. It is the way it is and has provided purpose and meaning to the lives of First Nations people through their worldview. First Nations Worldviews guide how communities and societies interact and live with each other and our entities (Martin, 2009). Uncle Bob Randall (a tjilpi (Elder) Anangu man from the Yankunytjatjara and Pitjantjatjara Nations) explains his worldview through Kanyini, connectedness to four concepts:

- Nguru – Country/land, flora and fauna
- Tjuukurpa – Belief system
- Walytja– Family/kinships
- Kurunpa – Culture

Uncle Bob refers to the underlying principles of unconditional love towards his connections to country land, flora and fauna. This centres him as being responsible for country land, flora and fauna. The commitment extends to reciprocal responsibilities. This is the profound and significant process of a First Nations Worldview – this deep connection is the essence of reciprocity, an opportunity to demonstrate love to/for those aspects that give and enhance one's life. The connections are collective rather than individual. The whole tribe held these beliefs. It was a togetherness and united approach. This love for country is evident in contemporary First Nations communities with their ongoing movement for sovereignty of land. This also demonstrates resistance for the rape – ongoing development – and pillage of our Mother.

Dulumunmun Harrison (2012) explains First Nations Worldviews, 'way of being' looking at what the earth has to offer with 'ancient eyes', not his eyes, the eyes of his ancestors. This is a connection so profound that it is beyond the human capacity and transcends into the metaphysical world. This is a significant component of a First Nations Worldview and connection to spirit world – the dreamtime and individual tribe's and clan's creation stories. More significantly Harrison's (2012) wisdom reflects the importance of connection to Country, which is beyond and deeper than his current life; it is beyond his time and place.

This belief and understanding goes back thousands and thousands of years and is learned from a lifetime of inner deep listening.

Tribal connections to country are deep and intricate. Tribes knew from their ancestral teachings changes to seasons would bring certain bush food and medicines, where time was measured by the moons and by the changing of the weather. The cycle of life also extends beyond the individual. Tribes knew when flora changed, it indicated other things, e.g. in the Bundjalung tribes, would watch and wait for the wattles to blossom in their yellow to know the mullet would be plentiful in the ocean, inlets and estuaries. A flock of black cockatoos screeching loudly as they fly over is a warning of heavy rainfall and potential flooding. In this way, First Nations people were deeply rooted with country creating a natural process of being as one with the environment. Dulumunmun Harrison (2012), a Yuin Elder, argues this interconnectedness is beyond a Western scientific paradigms and discourse. Knowledge has been passed on from one generation to the next, and this occurred since time immemorial. The scenario of absolute sense of trust for the environment is created and adhered to. Within this trust is a deep understanding of love and respect. Harrison explains more of Yuin tribal and ancient belief systems to include earth, sky, sun and moon, which he endearingly relates to as mother earth, father sky, grandfather sun and grandmother moon (Terare, 2020). This is about being part of the environment – being whole within their worlds. As noted by Sharifian in Smith (2020):

> within Indigenous Australian cosmos, power flows from inherently powerful ancestral beings to the land, which is imbued with a potency given to it by the actions of people and ancestors in the past. In this way, every facet of the landscape becomes imbued with ancestral associations A cultural-conceptual approach and world and ascribed with social identity. This power flows through to living people, some of whom have the ability to call upon the force and authority inherent in both the land and the ancestral beings.
>
> *(Smith 2020, p.18)*

This deep spiritual connection to land is not unique to Australian First Nations peoples. Poonwassie and Charter argue in relation to Canadian First Nations peoples that at a

> fundamental cultural level, the difference between traditional First Nations and Western thought is the difference in the perception of one's relationship with the universe and the Creator.
>
> *(2001, p.64)*

This way of being reflects ancient wisdoms. Davis (2009) in his Massey Lecture tells us about the wayfinders: Polynesians who are using the wisdoms of their Elders to map their way across the Pacific Ocean from island to island. He tells how the warriors become as one with the teachings of the sea: whilst at sea, they are guided by nature and the environment and more specifically birdlife. Specific birdlife indicates how far land is; the frigate bird heading out to sea indicates calms, white terns indicate land is within 200 kilometres and the brown tern reaches out as far as 65 kilometres. The nature of the tides provides them with sufficient evidence to forecast the weather, where certain clouds provide guidance regarding the weather, e.g., brown clouds bring strong winds and high clouds bring lots of rain and no wind. This is information passed down over the years; the learning of ancient wisdoms – the way to learn is to listen. Elders teach the warriors to become familiar with the sea at a very young age (Davis, 2009).

Some use the English word 'dreamtime' to describe the role of stories in Aboriginal culture, but this is inadequate (Korff, 2020). 'Dreaming' is preferred, capturing the ongoing acts of creation through stories. The dreaming arises from connection to Country and reflects a relationship of reciprocity and responsibility. Davies (cited in Korff, 2020) notes

> The Dreaming is, however, more than just an explanation of cultural norms, and where we came from. The Dreaming is a complete guide to life and living – it is an encyclopaedia of the world. It is not just stories – it is art, songs, dance; it is written into the land itself. Through the Dreaming we are taught knowledge of plants and animals, to us many of the flowering plants are treated as signs of animals available to hunt, fish about to appear, fruits about to ripen; the movement of the stars foretells the changing of weather, the birth of animals, the time for ceremony and gatherings.
>
> Songlines are likewise important cultural and spiritual practices founded in relationship to Country. Songlines are ancient stories tracing astronomy and geographical elements of Country, describing how these things have helped shape the landscape as it is now (Glynn–McDonald, 2022). Knowledge of the dreaming and songlines are held by Elders. Accordingly, connection to the wisdoms of Elders is an essential part of First Nation epistemology.

The Elder status and title are not a given; you don't become an Elder because you reach a certain age (Poonwassie & Charter, 2001, p.65). The bestowment of this status relies on one's capacity to live within humanity and not within self – it relies on collective approaches. To be bestowed with this title, one needs to be guided by integrity and humility. Elders are not required to behave in a certain way; rather their behaviour is part of who they are and is a given process that is beyond entitlement and ingrained in one's responsibility for the whole tribe. It is bigger than one person and one family; it is the human strength of the tribe. The tribe is the core, the hub of life, and each individual are required to maintain their responsibilities and ensure protocols are followed. The term 'Elder' is used to describe someone who has knowledge and understanding of the traditional ways of his or her people, both the physical culture of the people and their spiritual tradition (Mindell, 2001).

For those working towards climate justice in Australia, understanding the position of Elders among First Nations peoples is vital. Elders are likely to be the holders of knowledge about Country that can guide our work. In one example, a respectful relationship with Elders was found to be vital to the successful opposition to the expansion of uranium mining in Jabiluka. The Jabiluka Action Group (based in southern cities) was *invited* to work alongside and learn from the Mirrar people, the Traditional Owners of the land and Gundjehmi Aboriginal Corporation (Hintjens, 2000). Thousands of Australians joined the peaceful resistance to corporate and political power. The Mirrar Elders were concerned not only about the damage to their lands but also believed they bore responsibility for the impacts that activity on their land has on others (Gundjeihmi Aboriginal Corporation, 2022). When Fukushima in Japan was impacted by earthquake, tsunami and subsequent nuclear disaster, the Mirrar Elders expressed their sorrow as

> it is likely that the radiation problems at Fukushima are, at least in part, fuelled by uranium derived from our traditional lands. This makes us feel very sad.
>
> *(Yvonne Margarula, Gundjeihmi Aboriginal Corporation, 2022)*

Since invasion, there has been profound damage to Country, to the dreaming and songlines. Again, we turn to Elders for guidance; how do we heal this damage? Confronting our colonial history, truth telling and returning balance to the land must be part of our response to climate change. We can learn from Elders who sit still and wait, examine the moment, acknowledge ghosts (problems that are entrenched and unspoken) and unresolved issues, learn from others and try to find the truth in everyone (Mindell, 2001). The Elder shows deep consideration, humility and respect, demonstrating wisdom by actions and telling stories – wisdoms of creation stories. For First Nations peoples 'healing through stories is but one aspect of synthesizing our relationship with ourselves and with the entire universe' (Buffalo cited in Poonwassie & Charter, 2001, p.67). As we work towards climate justice, we will need to acknowledge past hurts and negotiate conflicts. The Prun, a ceremony embedded in First Nations ways of being, provides guidance on dealing with conflict. It enables a cleansing of past hurts allowing relational responsibilities to be maintained (Kelly & Behrendt, 2006). First Nations activist Bobby McLeod (nd) reminds

> When the earth is sick and polluted, human health is impossible. To heal ourselves we must heal our planet, and to heal our planet we must heal ourselves.

Climate action and Aboriginal Worldviews

We are in the position now to critique and challenge the oppressive nature of colonialism and its silencing of Aboriginal knowledges. We are witnessing a reclaiming of these knowledges and the possibility to embrace a more humane worldview that honours Mother Earth and her entities, our ecosystems. This reminds us that knowledge is socially produced and hence changing. In this section, we explore a number of examples of action on climate change that embed Aboriginal ways of knowing, being and doing but in new ways, in ways that share knowledge and are built on reciprocal responsibilities. These show we are learning through dialogue and respect, imagining a different future. This does not come easily and requires a shift in the way we critically reflect about the world we live in, our role and purpose.

Country that is not cared for is sick or unhealthy, in the view of many Aboriginal people. Since colonisation, First Nations people have witnessed the impact of habitat destruction, weeds, feral animals, the over-allocation of water and climate change on their country (Weir et al., 2011).

> People talk about country in the same way that they would talk about a person: they speak to country, sing to country, visit country, worry about country, feel sorry for country, and long for country. People say that country knows, hears, smells, takes notice, takes care, is sorry or happy … country is a living entity with a yesterday, today and tomorrow, with a consciousness, and a will toward life.
>
> *(Rose, cited in Weir et al., 2011, p.3)*

Reciprocity informs these practices and is foundational to First Nations epistemes and ontology. This reciprocity extends beyond human relationships with each other to an interrelatedness with our greater surroundings (Martin, 2009). Noonuccal and Bidjara woman, Karen Martin, outlines seven entities that define Quandamooopah relational responsibilities, 'People, Land, Animals, Plants, Skies, Waterways and Climate' (Martin, 2009). Mother Earth and her entities are regarded as our equal, and it is our responsibility to nurture, care and protect them. It asks us to take what you need, not what you want, ensuring equilibrium and balance. This is starkly different to exploitative ways of thinking about the world.

Thinking about Country in this way offers hope and the possibility of renewed connections with Mother Earth. This way of knowing, being and doing in reciprocal relationship with Mother Earth is relevant to both First Nations and non-Indigenous people. We are seeing evidence of a much greater willingness by 'white' Australians to draw on ancient knowledges in caring for country (Gillies, 2022). Burgess and Morrison (cited in Weir et al., 2011) identify a range of cultural practices that derive from caring for country, including

> Burning (which will be discussed in more detail later in this chapter)
>> Letting the country know we are there – using resources, hunting and fishing
>>> Protecting the integrity of the country through respect
>>> Protecting and enhancing species diversity

Protecting sacred areas
Providing a new generation and teaching them on country
Learning and performing ceremonies.

Many First Nations young people are acting on climate change creating social movements that captured the energy and passion of thousands of people, young and old, nationally and internationally. These social movements seek to educate and inform the general public as well as influence political decisions through campaigns and advocacy. Social movement organisations such as SEED, Australia's first Indigenous youth climate network, advocate for a just and sustainable future with strong cultures and communities, powered by renewable energy (SEED, 2021). SEED is based on participation, through volunteering, storytelling and political petitions. For Aboriginal and Torres Strait young people, it provides a new form of connection to and caring for Country. Social movements are sophisticated users of newer forms of media, powerfully communicating with thousands. Increasingly social movements are using consumer boycotts as a form of asserting power and influence. Whilst these individual organisations often have specific targets (such as stopping fracking in the NT), they often work in reciprocal relations with others. SEED, for example, partners with the Australian Youth Climate Coalition which is an independent non-profit organisation with 120,000 members and over 1,000 active volunteers nationally (SEED, 2021).

Cultural burning, a renewed interest

The summer of 2019/2020 will be remembered as one of horrific bushfires that burned more than 10 million hectares of land in Southern Australia. These fires encompassed an area greater than the Ash Wednesday Fires of 1983 and Black Saturday Fires of 2009 combined (Commonwealth Scientific and Industrial Research Organisation [CSIRO], 2020). Much of the subsequent discourse has centred around the cause of this extreme fire season. The CSIRO addresses this, stating the risk of bushfires starting or becoming out of control is highest in 'fire weather'. This is defined as a combination of strong winds, low humidity and high temperatures. Weather and vegetation, and its dryness, also impact this. These factors, including record low rainfall (2019 was Australia's driest year since 1900, when records began), contributed to an increase in 'fire-days' and created a perfect storm for bushfires (CSIRO, 2020).

The CSIRO, in its report *The 2019–2020 bushfires: A CSIRO explainer* clearly notes a third factor in contributing to this extreme fire season, climate change. While noting climate change doesn't directly cause fire, the report articulates that 'it has caused an increase in the occurrence of extreme fire weather and in the length of the fire season across large parts of Australia since the 1950s' (p.1). The fact that in addition to 2019 being the driest year on record, it was also Australia's warmest year is noted in the conclusion. It is clear that the impact of climate change has led to longer, more intense fire seasons (CSIRO, 2020).

During the media coverage of Australia's 2019–2020 bushfires, two key themes emerged: the need for better strategies for bushfire management and, by extension, greater attention and interest in Aboriginal cultural burning practices (Plange, 2021; Stevens & Sales, 2020). This interest extended to the inclusion in the terms of reference for the Bushfire Royal Commission to look at ways in which traditional land and fire management practices of Indigenous Australians could improve Australia's resilience to natural disasters (Romensky et al., 2020).

This is somewhat ironic, given the ongoing suppression and devaluing of the art and science of First Nations land development and management to support the preferred invader/coloniser narrative of Terra Nullis or 'empty land'.

Trent Nelson, Chair of Forest Fire Management Victoria and Dja Dja Wurrung Clans Aboriginal Corporation (DDWCAC), describes how historically Indigenous communities had been excluded from conversations about land management stating: 'Our voice was really extinguished for a long period of time' (Romensky, et al., 2020).

What is cultural burning?

Cultural burning has been part of First Nations cultural land practices for at least 65,000 years (Palmer, 2020). There are many interconnected objectives, which include protecting cultural or natural assets by maintaining the health of surrounding country, ceremony, habitat protection and fuel reduction (Eriksen & Hankins, 2014; Pasco, 2018). But fuel reduction – targeted burning to reduce the amount or density of foliage – is often not the primary objective. Pasco (citing Kohen, 2018, p.165) provides this illuminating quote.

> While Aboriginal people used fire as a tool for increasing the productivity of their environment, Europeans saw fire as a threat. Without regular low intensity burning, leaf litter accumulates and crown fires can result destroying everything in their houses ... Yet the environment so attractive to them was created by fire.

Plange (2021) highlights this in reminding us that,

> Despite the ecological and scientific value of Aboriginal place-specific knowledge that has developed alongside the changes of this continent's vast ecosystems, the establishment of the settler-colonial system has deemed this knowledge invalid and unscientific (p.3).

Environmental justice

While analysing the disruption of Indigenous land management as an ongoing impact of invasion/colonisation, it is also useful to take an environmental justice (EJ) view. Environmental justice originated in protests in the 1980s by community groups in the USA against the repeated siting of polluting factories and waste sites in predominantly black neighbourhoods and Indigenous peoples' reservations (Stephens & Church, 2017).

In Australia, the literature on environmental justice is relatively sparse by comparison and has tended to also focus upon certain disadvantaged communities battling against environmental decisions that adversely impacted upon them to a disproportionate level (Katrak & Harris, 2019). However, we can also analyse the suppression and disruption of Indigenous land practices as environmental justice concerns. Parsons and colleagues (2021) highlight that the environmental justice framework at present provides limited focus on the impact of invasion/colonisation on First Nations peoples and note that the 'colonised rule' increases and/or worsens environmental injustices experienced by First Nations peoples. By focusing on an Indigenous Environmental Justice framework, they invite us to consider moving beyond the current scholarship focusing on human-to-human interactions and move to an understanding 'of interactions between humans and more-than-humans (nonhumans) on a spiritual, cultural, and temporal level' (p.62).

Plange (2021), in *Decolonising fire: Recognition justice and Aboriginal fire knowledge in the 2019–2020 Australian bushfire news narrative*, makes the observation that the environmental justice framework emphasises the importance of recognising distributive, recognition and participative injustices that are worsened by climate change. Noting that while climate change has magnified the intersections of environmentalism and recognition, it has also, somewhat incongruously, as noted, 'sparked global interest in Indigenous knowledge' (p.25).

The Victorian Traditional Owner Cultural Fire Strategy

It is interesting to explore how cultural burning has and continues to gain acceptance in the closely regulated and previously risk management landscape of government policy and implementation. The mainstream acceptance and integration of cultural burning is clearly crisis driven; it is an acknowledgement of the failure of the Western way of fuel reduction/fire as a threat model. However, it is also a return to First Nations ways of land management, including the understanding that cultural burning is no quick fix and actually requires a long-term approach. This requires a significant philosophical shift in Western thinking and an embracing of Aboriginal epistemologies.

The positive impact of this reintegrating of traditional practices is evident, as articulated by local Aboriginal community members whether employed in land management or not:

> Not only are there environmental and community safety benefits, it also gives community a stronger connection to Country continuing ancient practices …
>
> *Interviewee 1*

The development of the Victorian Traditional Owner Cultural Fire Strategy was funded by the Department of Environment, Land, Water and Planning (DELWP) to support Traditional Owner rights and interests in reintroducing Cultural Fire to the landscape (Victorian Traditional Owner Cultural Fire Knowledge Group, 2018), following a reclamation and resurgence in promoting the practice, largely from within First Nations communities. This has been a long time coming:

> it saddens us when existing regulatory frameworks exclude us from positively effecting sensible land management practice to reduce fire risk.
> *(Victorian Traditional Owner Cultural Fire Knowledge Group, 2018 p.4)*

The Victorian Traditional Owner Cultural Fire Strategy was launched in 2018 with the aim to reinvigorate cultural fire through Traditional Owner-led practices across all types of Country and land tenure, enabling Traditional Owners to heal Country and fulfil their rights and obligations to care for Country. It is apparent that the commitment to the holistic caring for Country are paramount, as articulated here:

> It's about getting Mob back on Country to reconnect and regain and share knowledge. It allows us to work collaboratively to reach our intended objectives. It also allows us to build Traditional Owners capacity within the Community which enables them to be able to employ more of the Mob to undertake these land management /bushfire management roles. It also shows that we knew what we were doing back then so cultural burning practices should be more widely used.
> *Interviewee 3*

Given the displacement of Aboriginal people and disruption of traditional land care practices for close to 200 years, this is clearly no small task.

In examining the vision, framework and strategy, what is evident is the deep commitment and understanding of the healing of the land that is required, before traditional cultural burning can take place, and the reality that this is no short-term measure but rather a long-term integration into existing practices.

> We're gonna need to do some small burns to clean up the years of litter and weeds first, before we can get back to doing proper cultural burning. This is a process of decolonising the land.
> *Traditional Owner Cultural Fire Knowledge Holder Group, February 2018*

As articulated below, the recognition of Aboriginal peoples' ways of knowing, being and doing is considered long overdue.

> It is the acknowledgement of those that have come before us in the management of our land. The fact that we weren't just here doing nothing, everything that was there and the way it all existed harmoniously was a thought-out process ... and it's about time!
> *Interviewee 2*

Human rights and social work

Like Calma and Priday, we argue that

> social workers are by definition human rights workers, who have the power to help Indigenous people realise their individual as well as collective rights.
>
> *(2011, p.148)*

The United Nations Declaration of the Rights of Indigenous Peoples enshrines the right of Indigenous people to be acknowledged and respected. On 13 September 2007, the Declaration on the Rights of Indigenous Peoples was passed, despite Australia voting against the Declaration. In a reversal of the Howard Government's stance, the Rudd Government gave formal support to the Declaration in April 2009. The preamble and 46 Articles clearly define the rights of First Nations people. The broad definition of Article 31 not only demonstrates First Nations rights to ongoing connection to country and the importance and rights to custodianship but also provides others with key information about the significance of connection to entities (United Nations, 2008). This framework is an opportunity for us to collectively join together with mutual purpose and vision.

Article 31

> Indigenous peoples have the right to maintain, control, protect and develop their cultural heritage, traditional knowledge and traditional cultural expressions as well as the manifestations of their science, technologies and cultures, including human and genetic resources, seeds, medicines, knowledge of the properties of fauna and flora, oral traditions, literatures, designs, sports and traditional games and visual and performing arts. They also have the right to maintain, control, protect and develop their intellectual property over such cultural heritage, traditional knowledge, and traditional cultural expressions.
>
> *(United Nations, 2008, p.22)*

The Australian Association Social Workers (AASW) has likewise declared a commitment to supporting and working with First Nations people and their connections to Country/land. The AASW Innovate Reconciliation Action Plan 2020–2022 defines their memberships' commitment and responsibilities, through four key focus areas. Focus area two relates directly with connection to Country and First Nations Worldviews:

> demonstrating appreciation and respect for Aboriginal and/or Torres Strait Islander ways of doing, being and believing as embodied in First Nations' cultures, beliefs and relationships with the land.
>
> *(AASW, 2020)*

The United Nations Declaration and AASW Reconciliation Action Plan make commitments to paying specific attention to the importance and integral role of Country. They challenge us to acknowledge the difference and diversity within Australian First Nations groups, although with a common episteme and ontological connections and relatedness to Mother Earth. First Nations peoples are not a homogenous group as implied in the singular 'Aboriginal' and thus broadens our understanding of the diversity within First Nations groups. These international and national documents support a shift in our day-to-day practice, thinking beyond human support to a more holistic approach to well-being for all entities.

Adopting a human rights framework in our practice means paying attention to different 'generations' of rights (Calma & Priday, 2011). First-generation rights consist of civil and political rights: the right to vote and right to be counted in census. Second-generation rights consist of economic and social and cultural rights: access to employment and social services. Third-generation rights relate to collective, tribal and community development rights: placing decision-making power with communities, working alongside people. However, it is the fourth-generation section that is most pertinent to those interested in climate justice. Fourth-generational rights are holistic and extend to care of ecosystems. This approach extends human rights practice to embrace our biodiversity and ecosystems, locating practice within First Nations Worldview (Arabena, 2015). The invitation is there: to broaden knowledge and change practice to include understandings of worldviews and to include care for country as an extension of your life's work. In doing so, we need to attend to underlying Western beliefs that maintain the problems (Crampton, 2015). This means critiquing and challenging the complex systems that embed oppressive, colonial and extractive practices that do not consider our ecosystem. Moreton-Robinson (2006) describes these practices as derived from 'narcissistic' ontologies, privileging humans above all other entities. First Nations Worldviews remind us that we are not bigger or better than the environment, we are as one. Arabena (2015, p.179) importantly brings attention to the element of accountability in this shift, arguing for a human rights approach that

> is a broader framework that builds on cultural strengths and elements of professional practice that sees us accountable to our communities and our country.
>
> *(2015, p.179)*

Practical tools

What does this practically mean for those interested in climate justice and learning from First Nations Worldviews? How might we use these ideas in our everyday practices? In this section, we explore some tools that might help us in our work.

Cultural humility

Adopting a position of cultural humility disrupts assumptions and opens possibilities for new understandings to emerge. It is supported by a commitment to ongoing professional development and lifelong learning (Tervalon & Murray-Garcia, 1998). Herring et al. (2013) propose a three-pronged approach for non-Indigenous workers: educate yourself, take a stance and reach out. Learning about, reflecting on and understanding our own histories on this land builds cultural humility. This will also challenge the 'whitewash' of Australian history. This disruption includes questioning not only solutions but also how problems are understood (or represented) in our practice. In this way, cultural humility provides the foundation for beginning a process of decolonising our work, of learning from and embracing First Nations Worldviews.

Decolonisation

A commitment to decolonising our practice includes identifying destructive beliefs and practices, reclaiming Indigenous beliefs and practices and learning from and with First Nations communities about the environment. According to Anderson et al. (2007), colonisation encompasses three distinct phases: invasion and frontier violence, intervention by well-meaning paternalistic religious and philanthropic groups and the reassessment of government responsibility to Indigenous needs. Many First Nations activists believed the final phase is the one that does the most damage. This is due to the subtle nature and more specifically the application of Western Worldviews and their maintenance of colonial thinking and structures (Anderson et al., 2007). Decolonising our practice requires sensitivity to the social, historical and political construction of knowledge in place and time. A core element of colonial power is how it has silenced any other way of knowing, being or doing. It is often seen as a permanent and rigid worldview. The idea of impermanence must be part of our new order of thinking (Crampton, 2015). This consciousness is ever evolving and requires ongoing effort and reflection. Decolonisation requires a commitment to repair the damage of colonialism generally and more specifically about reconnecting to Mother Earth, ensuring First Nations people's roles of custodianship are defined and respected.

Listening deeply

Listening is not merely using our ears. It is about using our eyes and our hearts. It is about stillness of mind and body. We explore and create new understandings through listening. Dadirri is a form of deep inner listening based on mutual respect and willingness to learn (Baumann & Wells, 2007). The term 'Dadirri' is from the Ngan'gikurunggurr and Ngen'giwumirri languages of the First Nations people of the Daly River region. Ensuring open dialogue and active exchange allows for positive transformation of ideas and actions (Crampton, 2015). Deep listening supports interventions or work that is responsive and relational, rather than self-contained and instrumental. Atkinson (2002) argues that dadirri – listening deeply to ourselves, Mother Earth and those who are in relationship with – is essential to healing.

Acknowledgement

Whilst Acknowledgement of Country has become commonplace in Australian society, it is important this does not become token. When we Acknowledge Country, we are acknowledging custodianship and relationship to all other entities. We are not just acknowledging people. In this act, we are also (re)committing ourselves to how we will be on Country, what we value and expressing cultural humility. As such, we can personalise our acknowledgement and use it as an opportunity to raise awareness of the need for change.

Critical reflection

Social workers will be very familiar with the practice of critical reflection. It provides the tools to constantly critique personal power and privilege, recognising and challenging power imbalances and mapping institutional and structural power (Beres & Fook, 2019). In the context of this book, we extend the idea to include the notion of reciprocity. This means in critically reflecting on our practice, we ask ourselves: how have I met my responsibility to nurture, care and protect? In what ways has my practice reciprocated the respect, welcome and goodwill that I have received from Country?

Having considered how this book is guided by First Nations Worldviews, the following chapter explores complexity theory and how we can draw from First Nations and other traditions for meaning making around complex issues of climate change.

References

Anderson, I., Baum, F., & Bentley, M. (2007). *Beyond bandaids: Exploring the underlying social determinants of Aboriginal health. Papers from the social determinants of Aboriginal health workshop.* Cooperative Research Centre for Aboriginal Health.

Atkinson. (2002). *Trauma trails, recreating song lines the transgenerational effects of trauma in indigenous Australia* (1st ed.). Spinifex Press.

Arabena, K. (2015). Social work and public health: Intersections and opportunities. In C. Fejo-King & J. Poona (Eds.), *Emerging from the margins – First Australians' perspectives of social work* (pp. 165–179). Magpie Goose Publishing.

Australian Association of Social Workers [AASW]. (2020). Innovate Reconciliation Action Plan 2020–2022. https://www.aasw.asn.au/document/item/13033

Baumann, M.-R. U., & Wells, J. T. (2007). Education is for living and for life. In P. Duignan & D. Gurr (Eds.), *Leading Australia's schools.* Australian Council for Educational Leaders.

Béres, L., & Fook, J. (Eds.). (2019). *Learning critical reflection: Experiences of the transformative learning process*. Routledge.

Calma, T., & Priday, E. (2011). Putting indigenous human rights into social work practice. *Australian Social Work, 64*(2), 147–155. https://doi.org/10.1080/0312407X.2011.575920

Commonwealth Scientific and Industrial Research Organisation [CSIRO]. (2020). *The 2019–2020 bushfires: An explainer*. Retrieved April 9, 2022, from https://www.csiro. au/en/research/natural-disasters/bushfires/2019-20-bushfires-explainer

Crampton, A. (2015). Decolonising social work "Best Practices" through a philosophy of impermanence. *Indigenous Social Development, 4*(1), 1–11. https://scholarspace.manoa. hawaii.edu/bitstream/10125/37624/v4i1-03crampton.pdf

Davis, W. (2009, November). The Wayfinders: Why ancient wisdom matters in the modern world (Part 2). *CBC Massey Lectures*. House of Anansi Press. https://curio. ca/en/collection/massey-lectures-2009-the-wayfinders-1888/

Elder, B. (1988). *Blood on the wattle – Massacres and maltreatment of Aboriginal Australians since 1788* (3rd ed.). New Holland.

Eriksen, C., & Hankins, D. (2014). The retention, revival, and subjugation of Indigenous fire knowledge through agency fire fighting in Eastern Australia and California. *Society & Natural Resources, 27*(12), 1288–1303.

Fogarty, G. J., & White, C. (1994). Differences between values of Australian aboriginal and non-aboriginal students. *Journal of Cross-Cultural Psychology, 25*(3), 394–408. https://doi.org/10.1177/0022022194253006

Gillies, C. (2022). *Traditional aboriginal burning in modern day land management*. Landcare Australia. Retrieved April 9, 2022, from https://landcareaustralia.org. au/project/traditional-aboriginal-burning-modern-day-land-management/

Glynn-McDonald, R. (2022) *Songlines. Common ground first nations*. Retrieved April 13, 2022 from https://www.commonground.org.au/learn/songlines

Gundjeihmi Aboriginal Corporation. (2022). *Uranium mining*. Retrieved April 9, 2022, from https://www.mirarr.net/uranium-mining

Harrison, M. D., & McConchie, P. (2012). *My people's dreaming: An aboriginal elder speaks on life, land, spirit and forgiveness*. Finch Publishing.

Herring, S., Spangaro, J., Lauw, M., & McNamara, L. (2013) The intersection of trauma, racism, and cultural competence in effective work with aboriginal people: Waiting for trust. *Australian Social Work, 66*(1), 104–117. https://doi.org/10.1080/0312407X. 2012.697566

Hintjens, H. M. (2000). Environmental direct action in Australia: The case of Jabiluka Mine. *Community Development Journal, 35*(4), 377–390. https://doi.org/10.1093/cdj/35.4.377

Katrak, M., & Harris, M. (2019). Native title and community: A social and environmental justice perspective. *Social Work and Policy Studies: Social Justice Practice and Theory, 2*(1), 1–16. https://openjournals.library.sydney.edu.au/index.php/SWPS/article/view/ 13258

Kelly, L., & Behrendt, L. (2006). *Resolving indigenous disputes*. The Federation Press.

Korff, J. (2020). *What is the 'dreamtime' or the 'dreaming'?* Retrieved April 13, 2022, from https://www.creativespirits.info/aboriginalculture/spirituality/what-is-the-dreamtime-or-the-dreaming

Martin, K. L. (2009). *Please knock before you enter: Aboriginal regulation of outsiders and the implications for researchers* [Doctoral thesis, James Cook University]. https://researchonline. jcu.edu.au/4745

Mindell, A. (2001). *Sitting in the fire: Large group transformation using conflict and diversity*. Deep Democracy Exchange.

Moreton-Robinson, A. (2006). Towards a new research agenda? Foucault, whiteness and indigenous sovereignty. *Journal of Sociology, 42*(4), 383–395. https://doi.org/10.1177/1440783306069995

Palmer, B. (2020). Aboriginal burning practices: A solution to Australia's wildfires? *New Horizons Newsroom*. Retrieved February 10, 2022, from https://casw.org/news/aboriginal-burning-practices-a-solution-to-australias-wildfires

Parsons, M., Fisher, K., & Crease, R. P. (2021). *Decolonising blue spaces in the Anthropocene: Freshwater management in Aotearoa New Zealand*. Springer International Publishing. https://doi.org/10.1007/978-3-030-61071-5_2

Pascoe. B. (2018). *Dark emu: Aboriginal Australia and the birth of agriculture*. Scribe Publications

Phillips, L., Bunda, T., & Quintero, E. (2018). *Research through, with and as storying*. Routledge.

Plange, N. (2021). *Decolonising fire: Recognition justice and Aboriginal fire knowledge in the 2019–2020 Australian bushfire news narrative* [Hons thesis]. Department of Government and International Relations. https://hdl.handle.net/2123/25697

Poonwassie, A., & Charter, A. (2001). An aboriginal worldview of helping: Empowering approaches. *Canadian Journal of Counselling, 35*(1), 63–73.

Randall, B. (Creator), Lee, M. (Writer), Hogan, M., (Director), & House, L. (Executive Producer). (2006, August 31). *Kanyini* [Film]. Hopscotch Entertainment.

Romensky, A., Middlemast, A., & Parker, F. (2020, May 30), Destined for failure, unless indigenous cultural burns done in collaboration. *ABC News*. ABC Central Victoria. https://www.abc.net.au/news/2020-05-30/destined-for-failure-unless-indigenous-cultural-burns-done/12302412

Ruddiman, W. (2005). The early anthropogenic hypothesis a year later: An editorial reply. *Climatic Change, 69*(2–3), 427–434. https://doi.org/10.1007/s10584-005-7272-6

SEED (2022) *Young, black and powerful*. Retrieved from https://www.seedmob.org.au/

Sherwood, J. (2010). *Do no harm: Decolonising aboriginal health research* [PhD thesis, University of New South Wales]. https://doi.org/10.26190/unsworks/23129

Smith, C. (2020), *Country, kin and culture: Survival of an Australian aboriginal community*. Wakefield Press. https://tracesmagazine.com.au/2020/11/sneak-peek-country-kin-and-culture/

Stephens, C., & Church, C. (2016). Environmental justice and health. In William C. Cockerham (Ed.), *International Encyclopedia of Public Health* (pp. 499–506, Vol 2). Elsevier Science & Technology. ProQuest Ebook Central. https://ebookcentral-proquest-com.ezproxy.library.sydney.edu.au/lib/usyd/detail.action?docID=4718648

Stevens, J. (Executive Producer), & Sales, L. (Presenter). (2020, August 5). Bushfires lead to surge of interest in cultural burning. *7.30 [TV series]*. Australian Broadcasting Corporation [ABC]. https://www.abc.net.au/7.30/bushfires-lead-to-surge-of-interest-in-cultural/12528286

Terare, M. (2020). *It hasn't worked so we have to change what we are doing: First nations worldview in human service practice* [PhD doctoral thesis, University of Sydney]. University of Sydney repository. https://hdl.handle.net/2123/23499

Tervalon, M., & Murray-Garcia, J. (1998). Cultural humility versus cultural competence: A critical distinction in defining physician training outcomes in multicultural education. *Journal of Health Care for the Poor and Underserved, 9*(2), 8. https://doi.org/10.1353/hpu.2010.0233

United Nations. (2008). United Nations declaration on the rights of indigenous peoples (07–58681). United Nations. https://www.un.org/esa/socdev/unpfii/documents/DRIPS_en.pdf

Victorian Traditional Owner Cultural Fire Knowledge Group. (2018). Victorian Traditional Owner Cultural Fire Strategy. Victorian Government. Retrieved 27 July 2022, from https://www.ffm.vic.gov.au/__data/assets/pdf_file/0024/535209/The-Victorian-Traditional-Owner-Cultural-Fire-Strategy.pdf

Weir, J., Stacey, C., & Youngetob, K. (2011). *The benefits of caring for country: Literature review.* Department of Sustainability, Environment, Water, Population and Communities; Australian Institute of Aboriginal and Torres Strait Islander Studies [AIATSI]). https://aiatsis.gov.au/sites/default/files/research_pub/benefits-cfc_0_2.pdf

Williamson, A., Redman, S., Dadds, M., Daniels, J., D'Este, C., Raphael, B., Eades, S., & Skinner, T. (2010). Acceptability of an emotional and behavioural screening tool for children in Aboriginal Community controlled health services in urban NSW. *Australian and New Zealand Journal of Psychiatry, 44*(10), 894–900. https://doi.org/10.3109/00048674.2010.489505

Wilson, S. (2008). *Research is ceremony – indigenous research methods.* Fernwood.

4

COMPLEXITY

Introduction

In Chapter 3, we considered the importance of learning from Indigenous World-views and argued that such learning is crucial if we are to engage effectively with the wicked problems of climate change and social justice that now confront us. As we noted there, Worldview extends beyond allegiance to a given theoretical framework and requires a deep knowledge about ourselves and our relationships with land, air, water, with the more-than-human beings who share these spaces and with each other. Chapter 4 explores complexity theory as a framework that, while having roots in Western scientific traditions, offers a way for us to draw on Indigenous, Western and other traditions of knowledge and meaning-making and, in doing so, to grapple with wicked problems – those problems that resist simplified, superficial and de-contextualised solutions.

Throughout this book, we refer in different ways to holistic understandings of the worlds we live in, examining physical, emotional, spiritual, social and ecological dimensions. We find that complexity theory provides us with a framework to make sense of the interactions of these dimensions over time and, most importantly, the ways that systems interact with each other. Social workers and others in human service fields are familiar with Bronfenbrenner's (1996) ecological systems theory, and the subsequent development of various forms of ecomaps as tools to represent service users' micro-, meso-, macro- and chrono-level systems. Looking through this theoretical lens, we see micro-level systems, such as a single person, located within a series of wider environmental layers. This might include meso-systems of family and community and beyond these a macro layer of political, legal and wider social systems. In addition to these ever-widening systems which, at least in principle, can be mapped at any point in time (Hartman, 1995), the chronosystem reflects changes to these systems over time.

DOI: 10.4324/9781003146339-4

Ecological systems theory and ecomaps (Harman, 1995) are pervasive in contemporary social work practice. This can be explicit or unstated but evident in
the underlying principles of work with people in their environment. Person-
centred approaches, for example, clearly locate an individual within a family,
community, social and political context and enable us to acknowledge and describe the many environmental layers that influence, and are influenced by, an
individual's experience.

Complexity theory, or complex systems theory, as its name implies, extends
our understanding of systems. While an ecomap allows us to map a system in
two dimensions, complexity theory is more challenging to represent diagram-
matically. Through a lens of complexity, we see interactions within and between
systems occurring in unpredictable and non-linear relationships over time. In
this chapter, we propose that the emphasis on context, diversity and fluidity
that we find in complexity theory provides a useful framework with which to
integrate Indigenous and Western knowledges. We approach these ideas with
what we might term 'respectful curiosity' but also from a critical perspective.
We are committed not only to a description of the responses of complex systems
(human, more-than-human and environmental) to climate change and disaster
but also to an exploration of the role of power, authority and control in shaping
these responses. By developing insights into historic and contemporary events,
we are in a better position to find a vision for new ways of knowing, of being and
of doing social and environmental justice.

Complexity theory's capacity to engage with the shifting, only partially
known elements of the human and wider world, also positions it as an ideal
choice for an exploration of what are often termed *wicked problems*. Wicked problems are, by definition, complex and difficult. They are resistant to simplified
understandings and even more resistant to attempts to implement simplistic solutions. They present us with a daunting array of 'moving parts': diverse and often
conflicting perspectives and priorities, overt and covert relationships between
stakeholders, complex policy and practice implications. These components exist
in an ongoing state of flux. Wicked problems have histories, which must be explored if we are to engage meaningfully with current and future challenges, and
as we engage with these, we become aware that histories are being created and
revised even as we work.

How then can we act effectively and ethically as social and human service
practitioners, when we find ourselves continually off-balance in a dynamic, complex world? It is easy to feel overwhelmed, even paralysed, by our attempts to understand and respond. Perhaps it is natural that we fall back on frameworks that
reduce the complex whole to a simpler, more manageable focus. In this chapter,
we will seek an alternative path, one that avoids both the paralysis of overwhelm
and the seduction of models that are focused and linear but ultimately (in our
experience) ineffective. We will draw on our own research activities, including
work with a community we will refer to by the pseudonym *Ashwater*, to illustrate
the concepts we discuss. The chapter commences with a review of complexity

theory, paying particular attention to concepts of convergence, emergence, self-organisation, feedback loops and adaptation. It moves on to frame the relationship between climate action and social justice as a wicked problem and builds from this conceptual foundation to reflect on the practical opportunities for effective work in social and human services.

The development of complexity theory

The heritage of complexity theory lies in disciplines such as mathematics and biology, drawing on both chaos theory (mathematics) and earlier iterations of systems theory (general and ecological frameworks). The metaphor of a hurricane being caused by the beating of a butterfly's wings, used initially in Edward Lorenz's (1993) seminal work on chaos theory, is familiar far beyond its original use. It has entered the vernacular to such an extent that a rich body of memes has evolved to apply this concept to everything from global COVID (a suggestion that the global pandemic originated in human consumption of a single meal) to the possibility of death as the end result of losing a pen. However inaccurate (and, arguably, sometimes offensive) these memes might be, they reflect an awareness of the unpredictable and disproportionate effects of apparently small life experiences. The familiarity of the butterfly metaphor and its reapplication indicates that complexity theory is not merely a theoretical abstraction of little interest beyond the academic ivory tower but instead offers a way of finding meaning in our complex and uncertain world. We will discuss the implications for social work and human services in more detail later in this chapter.

In the later 20th century, interest began to grow in how the principles of complexity theory might apply to social issues. Much of the literature that came out of this period attends to the education sector and business/organisational management (see, for example, Anderson, 1999; Byrne, 1998; Kauffman, 1995), although some interest in the application of complexity concepts to social work began to emerge at the turn of the century (Warren et al., 1998). In contrast to other established theoretical frames, however, relatively little has been written about complexity theory and social work. This is curious, because complexity, uncertainty and fluctuating social situations are arguably the 'bread and butter' of social work practice, from micro-level casework practice, work with communities, through to systemic advocacy, policy work, education and research. Healy (2014) and Fish and Hardy (2015) suggest that this may in part reflect the difficulties of grappling with the very abstract nature of discussion found in much of the literature on complexity, constraining the translation of concepts with origins in mathematics and sciences into the social world. In this chapter, we aim to strengthen the links between abstract theoretical concepts and practice approaches, to open new debates about climate change and advocacy that might lead to responses that are both hopeful and effective.

While we draw clearly on concepts of complexity *theory*, it is perhaps more accurate to frame our approach as complexity *thinking* (Hager & Beckett, 2019), shifting the focus away from an overemphasis on conceptual structure and towards questions of attitude, process and action. This framing also harks back to Edgar Morin's (1996) description of complex thought as a stance that avoids simplifying or universalising problems, but rather that uses reflexivity to continually question, explore, relate and importantly acknowledge the partial nature of our knowing. Morin rejects a dichotomy of 'simple-complex', instead accommodating simplicity within a broader, richer paradigm. Combining this position with Indigenous knowledges helps us to make meaning of the social implications of climate change and to inform a social work response that is grounded in theory and relevant to every sphere of social work practice. In particular, we argue here that bringing together complexity theory and Indigenous ways of knowing, being and doing offers an approach to understanding and responding to wicked problems that is particularly well aligned, in contrast to attempts to simplify complex problems down to a limited range of components or to use a linear cause-and-effect model to respond to situations that exist in a state of flux.

Complexity theory and social systems

As already noted, complexity theory originated in sciences and mathematics. When we translate such concepts to complex social systems, then, what do we see? Pycroft (2014) provides a detailed discussion of complex systems as they apply to social work and identifies the following key ideas:

- The system has many interconnected elements which interact with each other in changing or adaptive ways.
- Changes in one part of the system can have disproportionate or surprising impacts on other parts of the system, often in a non-linear way.
- Rather than understanding the individual components of the system, as positivist science stipulates, it is the whole system which is the focus of understanding.
- New processes, interactions, connections and results emerge from the system in operation (adaptation).
- System change is driven through positive and negative feedback loops.
- Complex systems intersect with other systems; the boundaries can be hard to detect.
- Complex systems are self-organising, creating opportunities for adaptation.

These ideas offer a framework for grappling with messy, uncertain and constantly shifting issues, directing our attention towards relationships and processes (Hager & Beckett, 2019) over place and time. While there is concern for the elements or components within a complex system, complexity thinking is interested in the dynamic relationships that occur between them. It is these relationships that give the complex system its structure, rather than a notion of the individual elements in some form of static alignment.

Focus concepts

Within this broad picture of complex social and environmental systems, the concepts of convergence, emergence, self-organising systems, feedback loops and adaptation are particularly useful. We will reflect on the experiences of a small semi-rural community ('Ashwater') that has experienced multiple disaster events from late 2019, to illustrate these five concepts.

Case study: Ashwater: cascading disasters on the urban fringe

Ashwater is situated on the outer fringe of a state capital city. We were privileged to share in a series of conversations with organisations in Ashwater over the course of several months as they confronted the impacts of cascading and sometimes overlapping crises: bushfire, flood, pandemic and extreme heat events. The stories we heard gave us valuable insights into the impacts not only of single catastrophic events on such communities but of the ways that complexity theory can help us to frame our understanding of the cumulative effects over time and how these can coalesce to shape the community's networks, relationships and identity. In the following paragraphs, we will draw on these conversations to illustrate the conceptual framework that underpins our approach throughout this book. It is important to note that these concepts themselves are interrelated and non-linear. For instance, we commence with a discussion of convergence, but this concept itself both results from, and leads to, emergence of new characteristics of a system, at the same time shaped by the action of feedback loops and system adaptations.

Convergence

Having talked earlier about the size and diversity of elements and networks within a complex system, it is important also to pay attention to the concept of convergence. Here, we are thinking about a process of 'coming together'. Before and during our research conversations, Ashwater experienced a convergence both of disaster events and of service system responses to this situation. Identifying service responses as convergent illustrates a way of working that moves beyond interdisciplinary silos to create new forms of knowledge and action, incorporating ethic ('why'), method ('how') and outcome ('what') (Lakhina et al., 2021, p.309), using a 'pluralistic approach' that draws on disciplinary, institutional, traditional and phenomenological knowledge (p.300). The United States' National Science Foundation (NSF) envisages convergence research as the 'means of solving vexing problems, in particular, complex problems focusing on societal needs' (NSF 2018, cited in Lakhina et al., 2021). In a complex system this can reflect the intersection of a range of structures and processes over time, including ideas and knowledges, behaviours, networks and relationships, and events. In thinking about convergence in relation to the complexities of climate change and social justice, each of these aspects is relevant, but we will focus here on the way that a commitment to challenging existing structures and their relationships can be transformative, opening up new and creative possibilities.

Distinct from multidisciplinary partnerships that retain siloed identities, Lakhina and colleagues (2021) argue that convergence requires a new approach to working together in order to bring often-excluded knowledges into disaster conversations. Competitive advantage and claimed single sources of truth are familiar in contemporary neoliberal frames; in contrast, convergence represents the combined efforts of diverse entities and a phenomenon of joint agency to achieve a shared goal or common concern. While this can feature all the messiness, uncertainty and power-infused tensions found in any complex system, it brings the possibility of collaboration, emergent creativity, disproportionate impact and, ultimately, system adaptation. Roco and Bainbridge (2013) suggest that bringing together diverse knowledges and technologies in new ways 'allows society to answer questions and resolve problems that isolated capabilities cannot, as well as to create new competencies, knowledge, and technologies on this basis' (p.1).

Confronting the prospect of catastrophic infrastructure failure and natural disaster in Portland, Oregon, Lakhina and colleagues (2021) argue for policy action at multiple levels.

> The urgent need of the hour is for a coherent national climate strategy to outline locally enforceable targets for reducing emissions, adopting clean energy fuel, and strengthening public infrastructure, while addressing social inequities through a convergence approach.
>
> *(p.307)*

Convergence can also be seen in the appearance of similar behaviours in otherwise apparently unconnected elements. Mirbabaie and colleagues (2022) illustrate this in their complexity-based analysis of social media behaviours following three very different crisis events. Their social network analysis illustrated a number of similarities and differences in converging patterns of influence, measured by tweeting and re-tweeting behaviours, in response to a bombing at an English entertainment venue, a shooting at a shopping mall in Germany, and Texas' Hurricane Harvey. Against a backdrop of tensions between unpredictability and certainty, disproportionate impacts and rapidly shifting contexts, they drew on their own network analysis and other literature to identify 13 'convergent behaviour archetypes' that featured in information-sharing in the immediate aftermath of an event (Mirbabaie et al., 2022, p.238). While it is beyond the scope of this book, we would be intrigued to see a similar analysis of social media use in the response to local disaster events, including recent widespread flooding events in New South Wales and Queensland.

Mirbabaie et al. (2022) refer to this aspect of convergent behaviour in their recommendation that

> in connection with the power of minorities to influence the majority over the course of a crisis, EMAs [Emergency Management Agencies] may recruit spontaneous helpers on social media to a) gather crisis-related information and b) spread verified information via distinct types of users
>
> *(p.250)*

The convergence of disparate voices is particularly relevant when we consider the role of policy environments in complex systems. The relationship between emergency management agencies (EMAs), community organisations and individual community members, for example, is driven by policy parameters that set out when, where, how and with whom such relationships can occur. Such relationships are also shaped by diverse discourses, processes and hierarchies of power and influence, from the local level to a great distance from the point at which policy decisions may have impact in a crisis.

Whilst these ideas share some similarities with our position that climate action must be founded on diverse forms of knowledges and actions, they require us to do more than simply listen to different perspectives – although that is crucial. We argue instead for the centring of First Nations Worldviews through deep listening, building awareness in response to specific local contexts and specific complex systems. This process, known as dadirri (West et al, 2012), poses a challenge to the rapidity and superficiality that we find in many traditional Western approaches to problem identification and solution.

Ashwater experienced the convergence of multiple environmental and social crises. New threats appeared even while the community was grappling with emergency responses to, and attempts to recover from, other events. Large EMAs and small local organisations, all keen to save and support community members, found themselves faced with complex and often contradictory processes, vocabularies, cultures and resources in their efforts to achieve their purposes. Out of this experience, however, came opportunities to learn and strengthen relationships and the emergence of new possibilities through further dialogue.

Emergence

When we look at the history of a complex system, it soon becomes evident that the system's dynamism leads to the formation of new relationships, the appearance of new system elements and the emergence of new problems and responses. In many of our research journeys with communities, we have observed that converging elements (threats, responses, relationships and histories, for example) coalesce into a dynamic moment from which new elements, relationships – and histories – emerge.

In the section above, we observed that Ashwater experienced converging disaster events. By late 2019, the town was already well into a bushfire season that went on to be catastrophic across a wide swathe of south-eastern Australia. As the immediate bushfire crisis began to ease towards the end of the 2019–2020 Summer, the COVID-19 pandemic developed, directly affecting the community through local cases of the virus. Extreme weather events and flooding followed – at one time, community members were faced with simultaneous directions to isolate at home and to evacuate.

In contrast to a structured implementation of programmes developed outside Ashwater, new and creative solutions emerged from within the community it-self, often in an ad hoc way and in response to unexpected challenges. Impor-tantly, both problems and responses reflected the unique characteristics of the community system. This included both informal (neighbourhood) and formal (organisational) networks and the relationships between them.

Emergence occurs as an integral aspect of dynamic systems, in other words systems that are constantly responding to changes both within and beyond them-selves. Observing a complex system over a period of time, we witness the co-creation of responses to problematic situations. Through multiple and non-linear interactions, elements are able to influence other parts of the system, with the result that the wider system (and its component parts) respond in a way that is difficult to predict in advance, although may be evident retrospectively.

Self-organising systems

The emergence of Ashwater's responses to its cascading crises illustrates the ca-pacity for systems to self-organise. A local support agency began a programme of outreach calls to service users to check that they were safe, well and able to access supports. Where necessary, practical assistance was provided. In usual times, such a programme change might involve a lengthy process of negotiation of funding, guidelines and formal agreements. In this situation, however, a need was identified and a response designed and implemented. It is useful to note also that the people doing so were often located elsewhere in the system as commu-nity members and/or volunteer emergency responders. Self-organising systems are, by their nature, contextual, demonstrating the coalescence of factors that are unique to a moment in time and space.

The emergence of self-organising systems is commonly seen in disaster events, as people draw on local knowledge, relationships and resources to respond effec-tively (and often creatively) to a crisis. In some cases, local responses take place in the absence of formal services. During the 2019–2020 bushfire season, for exam-ple, EMAs were stretched to capacity and beyond, and messaging was clear that a formal emergency response could not be relied upon given the extraordinary demands on these resources.

Having said this, the relationship between locally organised initiatives and formal emergency management responses can also be fraught, as we discuss in more detail in Chapter 9. Emergency management systems are designed to enter crisis situations with authority and a highly structured approach. This can be at odds with the organic and nuanced nature of local self-organisation. While this presents possible tensions in the crisis phase of a disaster, it also has implications for the relationships between these two systems long before and after such events.

Feedback loops

In Ashwater, the proactive outreach of a local support agency and the response of people in the community demonstrate the role of feedback loops in complex social systems. A bolstered telephone outreach programme, in response to pandemic-related lockdowns, had the effect of forming closer individual connections. Feedback was positive – community members reportedly appreciated the efforts made by agency staff to act on their concern. Moreover, the conversations with service users in this out-of-the-ordinary situation increased the agency's detailed knowledge of needs and resources within the community it served. Meanwhile, the support agency was also changing its playgroup delivery to isolated families. The established playgroup had been accessed by approximately 20 local families. During the pandemic, when on-site playgroup activities were not possible, the playgroup staff set up online activities for families to enjoy together. Managing the group size turned out to be a very different experience in the online 'space', with system data reporting an estimated 4,450 people reached, and widespread engagement well beyond the local community. Based on this feedback, the programme was developed further, and aspects were incorporated into the agency's ongoing programming.

These are examples of feedback loops that embedded and sustained the agency's approach. However, the relationships between the agency and community members were also mediated by influences external to these connections, illustrating the limits of a simple, linear, cause-and-effect analysis. For example, while staff adapted their modes of service delivery, managers were busy responding to requests for local information by State-based emergency response agencies and simultaneously monitoring and accounting for the financial resources and programme guidelines of funding bodies.

It is useful to remember that feedback loops indicate the flow of information between elements of a system, and while this may include intentional reflection and response, it may also include less tangible communication. This is particularly important when we think of the interaction between humans and their physical environment, including both the impact of humans on the climate and human responses to the resulting climate effects. An example is the way that cities can act as heat islands, retaining heat through large expanses of concrete and an absence of natural green cover (Santamouris et al., 2015). The use of technologies such as air conditioners to artificially cool human environments, most notably in work spaces (de Vet & Head, 2020) further increases energy usage (Santamouris et al., 2015) and, arguably, contributing to climate change.

Adaptation

Adaptation goes beyond reactive changes, which may be short term and ultimately replaced by the status quo. When a complex system experiences adaptation, this refers to changes that become part of the system's ongoing structure and function. Feedback loops are an important influence on how a system adapts in the longer term; Ashwater's playgroup is a case in point. Having expanded both its mode and impact, the playgroup was presented with a dilemma: to return to 'business as usual' or to incorporate elements of the new approach into its ongoing programme. In building new skills to enable remote support to families, the playgroup staff were equipped to respond to further challenges through subsequent disaster events, as well as having an expanded repertoire of approaches to use in their routine programming.

> It's nice to know that we're reaching more people, and I think I want to continue doing it even when we go back into the centre for people who aren't able to come to playgroup or are out of area, stuff like that. It'd be good to still reach people.

As you read through the case studies elsewhere in this book, we encourage you to seek out examples of system adaptations to a range of challenges in ways that might either reinforce or reshape existing inequities.

Incorporating a critical lens

In response to criticisms that systems theories have historically been primarily descriptive and devoid of a critical edge, there have been attempts to incorporate a critical lens into complexity thinking (Byrne, 2021; Davis & Sumara, 2008; Woermann & Cilliers, 2012). A concern for the function of power is central to every aspect of socially and ecologically just theory and practice.

Flows of power and inequity exist within complex systems, and we need to seek these out if we are to pursue questions of social and environmental justice through a lens of complexity. One of the criticisms of various iterations of systems theories has been their limitations as primarily descriptive at best identifying rather than critiquing inequality and remaining silent on mechanisms to intervene. However, we have found that the capacity of complexity thinking to accommodate diverse and multiple perspectives, and to do so in a contextualised way over a period of time, provides ample scope for building it into an eclectic approach that also comprises a complementary critical frame. McPherson and McGibbon (2014) illustrate this in their use of complexity thinking and critical feminism, to examine intersecting oppressions within the complexity of justice systems.

Using a critical eye to explore dominant perspectives in climate action and complex social systems quickly uncovers multiple levels of inequality. Perhaps the most obvious of these is the differential impacts of climate change and especially of climate-related disaster. Our recent research with several communities affected by flood and other disasters included a focus on the experiences of people in social housing. This group, along with other people reliant on low-cost housing options, is often limited in both voice and choice when it comes to the location in which they live. Intersecting systemic oppressions such as poverty, disability, literacy, culture and ethnicity may be compounded by the effects of disaster. Moreover, the strengths and resourcefulness of social housing tenants is commonly overlooked in efforts to build community resilience. As this book was being written, extensive flooding was occurring across northern New South Wales and Queensland, and information was just emerging that was consistent with our own research findings.

A critical lens is also crucial when considering hegemony in the cultures, knowledges and worldviews that shape the interconnected elements and dynamic relationships of complex systems. Further, it is important to critique flows of power as we try to make sense of unexpected and disproportionate impacts arising from changes elsewhere within the system or its wider environment. Once again, we can look to disaster preparation, response and recovery to see these complexities in action. As scientific, social and economic perspectives vie for influence, the structures, functions and cultures of diverse service systems also emerge as active contributors. In our critique of power in complex systems, it is useful to remember that complexity thinking opens a space for any and all of these voices, and a critical lens allows us to do so in a way that fosters adaptation towards equality.

Wicked problems

We shift our attention now from the concepts of complexity theory and complex thinking, to explore the connections between climate change and social justice which, individually and in combination, are often referred to as 'wicked problems'.

Before we proceed, take a moment to reflect on the following question. What comes to mind for you when you hear the adjective 'wicked'? Perhaps your thoughts go to the supernatural, or to monsters, cruelty, hurt and horror. If so, you are in good company: the Macquarie Dictionary (2017) offers four definitions for formal use (including evil, mischievous, distressingly severe and 'ill-natured, savage or vicious') and points out that the word may stem from the Middle English word *wicca*, which is associated with witches or wizardry. Further colloquial definitions flip this picture to mean 'excellent, exceedingly good'. What, then, do we mean when we speak of 'wicked problems'? Of the options just mentioned, perhaps the closest match is with a sub-definition of the first, found in the Oxford Dictionary of English app (MobiSystems, Inc, 2022): 'intended to or capable of harming someone or something'. That definition offers the example of a 'wicked-looking dagger'. What common ground can we find between a dagger and the interplay of climate change and social justice? Both speak of capacity for harm, but one is very specific and tangible. The other is the antithesis of these characteristics, neither clear-cut nor easy to grasp.

Rather than implying some kind of essential, pervasive evil, the wickedness of a problem refers to its complexity: the number of interacting elements, their diversity, the influence of time (both as historical development and contemporary context) and the scope of potential consequences. Given our deeply ingrained associations, however, labelling a problem as wicked can inadvertently set up a dynamic of conflict, even disempowerment, between ourselves and the problem. In comparison to our day-to-day, 'ordinary' problems, wicked problems seem big, bad and possibly insurmountable. It is understandable that we might respond by trying to reduce the problem to simple, manageable bites and to address its challenges through a familiar linear framework. For example, using a programme logic (Weiss, 1998) to frame the problem can seem helpful, as it structures our understanding in terms of input (resources), throughput (activities), output and outcomes. Such approaches initially acknowledge the broader context and complexity, before narrowing the scope of attention to a defined area, somewhat like viewing a pie and then choosing which slice to eat. No one would suggest that eating a slice of pie is the same as eating a whole pie, and yet too often we see efforts to respond to wicked problems that imply that focusing on an aspect of a wicked problem in some way grapples with the whole.

Complexity theory provides a different logic. It argues that simplifying a problem might give a sense of action but cannot be effective in the long run, because it is incomplete. However, it also states that it is impossible to fully know the whole of a complex system. Complex systems are *other than* the sum of their parts. While each part of a system has its own characteristics, history and interactions, the system as a whole also has an 'identity' that is beyond a simple sum of its components and that is constantly in flux as the parts within it and the environment within which it exists all continue to change over time.

So, what are we to do?

As Pycroft observes, 'in our efforts to survive and flourish, we have a tendency to try and reduce uncertainty to provide us with at least the illusion of control as we try to navigate the multitude of systems in which we live, leading to an innately reductionist approach' (2014, p.15). Behind this perspective appears to be an assumption that in letting go of order, somehow chaos will unavoidably ensue. However, the binary of order/chaos is itself a useful illustration of the limitations of taking a reductionist approach. Wicked problems are by their nature layered, multifaceted and constantly in flux. A third position, grounded in complexity thinking but aiming for a pragmatic, manageable way to proceed, is to pay greater (and clearly expressed) attention to the twists, turns and intersections of the overall landscape, while maintaining a flexible relationship with the work that allows for multiple simultaneous areas of focus and a layered, nuanced approach to action.

Working in diverse contexts and adapting practice accordingly underpins social work. Working with uncertainty and complexity has been driven by practice experiences but had not traditionally led to a unifying theoretical framework (Green &

McDermott, 2010). Over a decade ago, Green and McDermott argued for social work to move from an outdated reliance on general systems theory, to learn from and engage with complex systems theory as providing a more sophisticated explanation of interdependent and adaptive systems already experienced in practice.

Wicked problems (Rittel & Webber, 1973) and superwicked problems (Sun & Yang, 2016) have been described as complex problems where different understandings or framing, lack of clarity in scope and conflicts over problem-solving strategies are a feature. These are complex problems which have often been understood from a simple problem perspective, where linear problem-solving has been tried and has failed or where competing linear understandings of the problem act as spoilers in any co-ordinated problem-solving strategy. While the language of the wicked problem can be helpful in emphasising the difficulties, it may be less helpful in supporting our understanding of complex systems rather than complex problems. The intersecting and tangled systems, issues and questions which coalesce in climate change consistently defy reduction. Understanding climate change as a problem which needs solving puts us in danger of reductive thinking and distracts from the complex systems views which enables us to see and address interconnected elements, relationships, feedback loops within and between systems and emergent changes.

Human services and collaborative complexity

In practical terms, working on climate change as a social justice issue requires us to imagine and realise new cross-sectoral and cross-community relationships. Human service organisations must build collaborative partnerships and processes with those outside the usual remit – environmental organisations, government departments outside the social sector, developers of new technologies, business – as well as groups and communities already working in collaboration. Such partnerships must be much more than assembling different sectors or professions. Collaborations will need to be designed with complex systems thinking at their centre which means building in cycles of feedback and adaptation to ensure learning from the collaboration is able to be incorporated immediately into the next cycle as well as understanding the collaboration itself as a complex system rather than in component sectors (van Tulder et al., 2018). Waddock and colleagues (2015) locate change and adaptation in organisations within a broader context of large-scale systems change linked to climate change.

Action research and complexity thinking

Communities are multilayered and dynamic, simultaneously within a larger system and comprising smaller interconnecting systems. Communities have histories, interactions and energy; they can respond in sometimes unpredictable ways.

Our research with community disaster resilience illustrates how communities, their component parts and the larger systems within which they exist function as complex systems. Working from a theoretical frame of complexity, then, it can be expected that making a small change (such as empowering one individual to advocate for change on a local issue) can have disproportionately large impacts or, equally possibly, little or no impact at all. To understand the different outcomes requires a far more sophisticated understanding than a simplistic analysis might suggest. The individual's own history and characteristics, their relationship with others in the community and a wide range of other factors influence the outcome.

The action research projects that inform this book agree with Rogers and colleagues (2013) in their contention that research founded in complexity thinking must not only be an intellectual exercise but should connect in a meaningful way with lived experience in order to contribute to a positive change. Rogers et al. argue that

> ... the need to adopt a postnormal (Funtowicz and Ravetz 1992) or mode 2 (Nowotny et al. 2001) approach to 'science in the service of society' (Rogers and Breen 2003) is more and more encouraging action research approaches that require researchers and their stakeholder partners to 'live' complexity as a new paradigm for decision making in communities and institutions.
>
> *(2013, p.31)*

This approach positions researchers as walking alongside participants, developing new knowledge together. It is easy to romanticise such an experience; after all, it exhibits the values of respect, power-sharing and working towards a just and equitable society that underpin social work and human service disciplines. However, as researchers who embark on action research with a complexity mindset, we have experienced first-hand the need to clarify expectations of project processes and anticipated outcomes with experienced stakeholders whose worldviews are very likely to be based on reductionist thinking. This involves challenging assumptions held by funding bodies and other organisational stakeholders about the purpose and likely trajectory of action research with communities. In the minds of these stakeholders,

> Any range of solutions can be tried because, if they go wrong, they can be reversed with little consequence for the system. They will expect, consciously or unconsciously, that once the 'real' solution is reached, the problem will go away and they will now have an 'evidence-based' decision that can be applied again should 'the' problem emerge again.
>
> *(Rogers et al., 2013, p.30)*

Implications for social work and human service practice

One of the debates about the usefulness of complexity theory for social work practice has been the abstract nature of its underlying principles (Fish & Hardy,

2015; Pycroft & Wolf-Branigin, 2016), suggesting that the translation of complex theoretical concepts to on-the-ground practice is difficult, particularly in the face of pressures of a neoliberal context within which social and human services operate. However, social work education strives to prepare graduates for practice at multiple simultaneous levels, including work with individuals and engagement with policy and systemic advocacy. Moreover, as we have suggested in this chapter, reframing our understanding towards complexity thinking, rather than complexity theory, allows us to attend reflexively to our position and process, using the conceptual framework as a foundation.

Social work and human services are not limited to a micro/macro binary; rather, they encompass multiple domains simultaneously, including work with individuals, families and other groups and communities as well as wider society (for example, through engagement with policy development). Furthermore, social work and human service practice is not limited to the human sphere but increasingly incorporates a relationship with non-human beings and with the planet that sustains us all. This can be experienced as an additional and onerous demand on practitioners who are already struggling to function under an avalanche of requirements for quality and accountability. Narrowing our lens as practitioners can appear (however erroneously) to be a useful strategy to render the unmanageable into a package that we can work with, allowing us to focus on an identifiable 'client' and establish boundaries around our professional remit. The systems within which we work often encourage this simplification of focus, as it aligns comfortably with the neoliberal frame that shapes much of social work and human service programme delivery.

However, individuals, groups and communities are unquestionably affected by wicked problems including climate change, poverty, health crises including the COVID-19 pandemic and food insecurity. There is ample emerging evidence that climate change affects people in disparate and unjust ways. How, then, might individual social and human service practitioners connect with complexity theory and wicked problems in a way that is meaningful for their work 'at the coalface' (sometimes literally, in the case of communities whose livelihoods depend on fossil fuel industries)? And beyond the individual, how might social work and related disciplines shape themselves to respond to the social, psychological, spiritual, economic and ecological complexities that will continue to emerge over the decades to come?

There are many points of resonance in traditional social work approaches that lay a foundation for a more complex and nuanced relationship with the concepts we have considered in this chapter. Social work has long been concerned with the relationship between people and their environment, either explicitly or implicitly. Practice approaches such as strength-based and solution-focused frameworks speak to a deep desire to confront the problems that face individuals and societies. Critical, transformational and anti-oppressive social work challenge approaches that suggest a 'fix', interrogating the role of power in individual experience. These and other theoretical influences on contemporary social work practice create a diverse and often hotly contested foundation upon which to consider wicked problems, but they also prepare us for an openness to creative responses.

A detailed understanding of complexity, from biodiversity through to network analysis, provides a strong foundation for those working in social justice practice. Arguably, attempting to intervene in the lives of people and environments (as social workers and other human service workers are required to do on a daily basis) without a sincere effort to understand the richness and messy complexity involved is not only likely to be ineffective but also potentially unethical. As Woermann and Cilliers (2012) put it, work with people involves both 'the complexity of ethics, and the ethics of complexity'. In other words, in our professional roles, there are ethical dimensions to our use of complexity thinking as we do not have full knowledge of the whole and must therefore make judgements and choices; at the same time, the suite of ethical frameworks that inform our practice also, in itself, presents us with a layer of complexity.

Complexity thinking threads throughout this book's engagement with the wicked problems of climate change and social justice. For our purposes at this point, the following seven interrelated points provide an overview of ways that we have found complexity thinking to be helpful and hopeful in translating complexity thinking to our own human service practices over many years and in a wide range of personal and professional contexts.

Connections are key to complex systems

Complexity thinking allows us, in fact compels us, to identify, form and sustain connectedness; to avoid working in isolation; and to recognise the connections (or limits of these) for the individuals and communities with whom we work. This leads us to seek out individual networks, not only our own (although these are important) but an awareness of other networks that may not, in a simple linear analysis, appear to be important. In noticing existing networks, it is also imperative that we look for absences. Who is left out? What networks might we expect, but cannot find? What are the possible consequences, both for those who are disconnected and for others in the system?

In our participatory action research with communities, such questions are a common part of initial conversations as we learn about each community's unique characteristics. The conversation goes beyond a simple mapping exercise, although it can be that too; it provides insights into the past and present but also suggests opportunities to develop a richer understanding of potential futures. Above all, it enables action to redress inequities and provide mutual benefit as previously silent voices are brought into the dialogue.

In our work, we are constantly reminded of the importance of relationship and of the dynamic nature of those relationships. Working with humans, individually and collectively, is notoriously messy and requires us to put effort into maintaining relationships over a period of time, but we are not only talking about human relationships here. Broadening our worldview to account for the complexity of systems that include Earth and her more-than-human inhabitants, together with less tangible elements such as what we might call the 'policy environment', we become aware that connectedness is continually operating in diverse and fluid ways and at multiple levels.

Complexity thinking acknowledges and values diverse perspectives

Traditionally, the response to this ever-changing diversity in social systems has been to emulate a scientific model, aspiring to objectivity, clarity, generalisability and a search for perspectives that are considered to be representative. Such methodologies undoubtedly have a place in developing new knowledge on a vast number of topics. However, in research with complex social systems they are, at best, limited in their ability to produce meaningful learnings or frustrated by the messiness they encounter. At worst, their conclusions are erroneous or actively harmful. We have repeatedly heard from communities about experiences of 'being researched' with little or no tangible benefit for the community.

We have also seen a historic inequality in the types of knowledge that are valued, which arguably continues today. For example, colonial settler knowledge in Australia failed to value First Nations people's movement around Country, informed by deep knowledges of Earth and her seasons. Instead, settlers interpreted what they saw through the British worldview of ownership of land, which included sedentary agriculture and industry, and which contributed to their unfounded assumption of 'terra nullius'. The frailty of this worldview is seen in contemporary experiences such as the ownership and property development of flood- and fire-prone environments, in which residents are tied to small parcels of land, economically, emotionally and socially, despite the ever-increasing danger this brings. The wisdom of Indigenous relationships with Country is becoming acknowledged (albeit very slowly) by those whose cultures have historically devalued and silenced such knowledges.

As we broaden our thinking to take in these diverse perspectives, we have an opportunity to identify and challenge hegemony in structures and discourses. Accommodating diverse perspectives must be approached critically in order that we move towards environmental and social justice; we are not arguing for a relativist stance that brings in additional voices but serves to maintain the status quo.

Complexity theory integrates micro-, meso-, macro- and chrono-systems

As we noted earlier in this chapter, complexity thinking represents a development rather than a departure from previous system-focused understandings. In many ways, it is not a big leap for researchers and practitioners who are grounded in ecological systems theory, for example, to take on a complexity perspective. Complexity thinking brings a responsibility to be intentional in considering all layers of a system, regardless of the focus of our action. In our work with communities, we must consider individual diversity and the differential impacts of change on humans, more-than-human inhabitants and on Earth herself. Similarly, work with individuals requires us to actively consider their structural and historical influences, constraints and opportunities. In all this, complexity thinking emphasises the fluidity of every aspect of the system and of its interactions with other systems.

In the life of complex systems and wicked problems, there is no end point, only progression

Unlike simple problems, in which a linear response and solution are possible, our aim in confronting wicked problems is to move towards some sort of positive change. This thought is perhaps at once discouraging and helpful. Discouraging because we usually find satisfaction in solving a problem and moving on. To do otherwise can feel like failure or at the very least like ineffectiveness. At the same time, knowing that we are contributing to progress rather than reaching an end point resonates more closely with our lived experience and may help us to sustain our energy over the long term.

Arising from this, small actions can have large consequences (and vice versa)

Given the influence of time and distance between points in a complex system, as individual practitioners we may not see the consequences of our actions. It is easy to imagine that we have failed to make a significant positive change whether at the level of the individual or more broadly. At the same time, sweeping policy changes can appear to have little impact on the daily grind of people living with disadvantage. Reframing our place and our work through a lens of complexity thinking encourages us that even small acts can have unexpected and maybe long-term impacts, but that we may never become aware of these. At the same time, it emphasises the importance of critical reflexivity in our practice, recognising the uncertainty and messiness of the world in which we live and work.

Social workers and human service practitioners are agents for change

Many of us enter social work and human service careers with a well-established grounding in positivist approaches to learning. Such epistemologies (ways of knowing) focus on objectivity, actively encouraging us to keep ourselves somehow separate and value-free in our professional interactions. Even when a more intersubjective understanding of social work is promoted, we often 'invisibilise' ourselves, if only to ourselves. In an effort to work in a strength-focused way and create space for the autonomy of others, we risk overlooking our own influence or impact. An example of this is the completion of ecomaps and other forms of assessment in work with individuals. As we document a person's relationships, how often do we neglect to include ourselves? And yet, we may wield great power over their futures, through even apparently small acts in the course of our routine working relationships.

Coming back to the wicked problem/s or climate change and social justice, a complexity stance highlights our responsibility to remain mindful of interconnections between land, air, water, humans and more-than-human inhabitants and to act accordingly. We argue throughout this book that it is not possible to work either ethically or effectively if we exclude concern for climate change from our professional lives. Climate action is social justice action, and as social and human service workers, the imperative to be change agents is clear.

Complexity thinking encourages innovation and optimism in an uncertain world

By this point in the book, you will be very familiar with the plurality that is fundamental to complexity approaches. Multiple elements, connections, histories and perspectives contribute to complex systems as we experience them at any point in time. As practitioners in social and human services, we are confronted on a daily basis with wicked and entrenched problems. The environment within which we do so exhibits a range of constraints founded in worldviews that valorise efficiency; evidence-based models that either overtly or implicitly favour quantifiable data and linear logics; and understandings of gender, culture, ethnicity and other characteristics that reflect dominant Western belief systems.

In the face of this seemingly discouraging situation, complexity thinking has the potential to support innovation and optimism. Challenging the limitations of linear 'solutions', complexity thinking presents us with a landscape where our creativity can flourish. As David Byrne (2021) reminds us, 'there is not a single future possible but multiple futures' (p.181). As noted earlier in this section, the impacts of our actions can have effects far beyond their size. This means that whatever we do, however apparently pointless in the face of the larger scheme of things, has the potential to bring about (or at least contribute to) a different future. Having said that, other elements within the complex system are also active. The possibilities of our individual action are strengthened when we undertake them in relationship with others and when we respect and learn from their different perspectives.

Conclusion

In this chapter, we have provided a broad introduction to complexity theory/thinking and the notion of 'wicked' problems, with specific attention to concepts that will be developed further throughout this book. These concepts have been explored on the foundation of diverse knowledges and experiences, most notably the possibilities of learning from both Indigenous and Western ways of knowing, being and doing. Incorporating diversity at every level, from local biodiversity to our conceptual frameworks, is central to our efforts to learn about our world, and our place in it, and how we can engage effectively to bring about a positive change.

Through the remainder of the book, we build on the ideas introduced in these initial chapters, deepening our analysis of the broad concepts introduced here and illustrating their application through our own experiences as researchers, educators, practitioners and human beings. Responding collectively to climate change and other uncertainties makes great sense when we examine it through a lens of complexity, drawing on what we have learned about the important concepts of emergence, self-organisation, feedback loops and adaptation. As you read on, we encourage you to reflect on your knowledge about the ways that Indigenous knowledges, community development and complexity thinking can entwine, assisting you to form your own response to the wicked problems of climate change and social justice in a way that is both ethical and hopeful.

In the next chapter, we will look at everyday life and how things like food, energy and water impact on climate change. In considering these factors, we will look at our relationship with the environment and the intersection of social (in)equality.

References

Anderson, P. (1999). Complexity theory and organization science. *Organization Science, 10*(3), 216–232.

Bronfenbrenner, U. (1996). *The ecology of human development: Experiments by nature and design.* Harvard University Press.

Byrne, D. (1998). *Complexity theory and the social sciences: An introduction* (1st ed). Routledge. https://doi.org/10.4324/9780203003916

Byrne, D. (2021). *Inequality in a context of climate crisis after COVID: A complex realist approach* (1st ed.). Routledge.

Davis, B., & Sumara, D. (2008). The death and life of great educational ideas: Why we might want to avoid a critical complexity theory. *Journal of the Canadian Association for Curriculum Studies, 6*(1), 163–176.

de Vet, E., & Head, L. (2020). Everyday weather-ways: Negotiating the temporalities of home and work in Melbourne, Australia. *Geoforum, 108*, 267–274. https://doi.org/10.1016/j.geoforum.2019.08.022

Fish, S., & Hardy, M. (2015). Complex issues, complex solutions: Applying complexity theory in social work practice. *Nordic Social Work Research, 5*(sup1), 98–114. https://doi.org/10.1080/2156857X.2015.1065902

Green, D., & McDermott, F. (2010). Social work from inside and between complex systems: Perspectives on person-in-environment for today's social work. *The British Journal of Social Work, 40*(8), 2414–2430. https://doi.org/10.1093/bjsw/bcq056

Hager, P., & Beckett, D. (2019). Complex systems and complexity thinking. In P. Hager & D. Beckett (Eds.), *The emergence of complexity: Perspectives on rethinking and reforming education* (pp. 155–183). Springer Nature. https://doi.org/10.1007/978-3-030-31839-0_7

Hartman, A. (1995). Diagrammatic assessment of family relationships. *Families in Society, 76*(2), 111–122. https://doi.org/10.1177/104438949507600207

Healy, K. (2014). *Social work theories in context: Creating frameworks for practice.* Bloomsbury Publishing.

Kauffman, S. A., (1995). Escaping the Red Queen effect. *The McKinsey Quarterly, 1*(Winter 1995), 118.

Lakhina, S. J., Sutley, E. J., & Wilson, J. (2021). "How do we actually do convergence" for disaster resilience? Cases from Australia and the United States. *International Journal of Disaster Risk Science, 12,* 299–311. https://doi.org/10.1007/s13753-021-00340-y

Lorenz, E. N. (1993). *The essence of chaos.* University of Washington Press

Macquarie Dictionary Publishers. (2017). *Macquarie dictionary* (7th ed.). Pan Macmillan Australasia.

McPherson, C., & McGibbon, E. (2014). Intersecting contexts of oppression within complex public systems. In A. Pycroft & C. Bartollas (Eds.), *Applying complexity theory: Whole systems approaches to criminal justice and social work* (pp. 159–180). Policy Press.

Mirbabaie, M., Stieglitz, S., & Brünker, F. (2022). Dynamics of convergence behaviour in social media crisis communication: A complexity perspective. *Information Technology & People, 35*(1), 232–258. https://doi.org/10.1108/ITP-10-2019-0537

MobiSystems, Inc (2022). *Oxford Dictionary of English* (Version 14.3) [mobile app]. https://apps.apple.com/au/app/oxford-dictionary-of-english/id394337484

Morin, E. (1996). A new way of thinking. *UNESCO Courier, 49*(2), 10.

Nowotny, H., Scott, P., & Gibbons, M. (2001). *Re-thinking science: Knowledge and the public in an age of uncertainty.* Polity.

Pycroft, A. (2014). Complexity theory: An overview. In A. Pycroft & C. Bartollas (Eds.), *Applying complexity theory: Whole systems approaches to criminal justice and social work.* Policy Press.

Pycroft, A., & Wolf-Branigin, M. (2016). Integrating complexity theory and social work practice; a commentary on Fish and Hardy (2015). *Nordic Social Work Research, 6*(1), 69–72. https://doi.org/10.1080/2156857X.2015.1123459

Rittel, H., & Webber, M. M. (1973). Dilemmas in a general theory of planning. *Policy Sciences, 4*(2), 155–169. https://doi.org/10.1007/BF01405730

Roco, M. C., & Bainbridge, W. S. (2013). The new world of discovery, invention, and innovation: Convergence of knowledge, technology, and society. *Journal of Nanoparticle Research: An Interdisciplinary Forum for Nanoscale Science and Technology, 15*(9), 1–17. https://doi.org/10.1007/s11051-013-1946-1

Rogers, K., Luton, R., Biggs, H., Biggs, R. (O.), Blignaut, S., Choles, A. G., Palmer, C. G., & Tangwe, P. (2013). Fostering complexity thinking in action research for change in social–ecological systems. *Ecology and Society, 18*(2), 31. https://doi.org/10.5751/ES-05330-180231

Santamouris, M., Cartalis, C., Synnefa, A., & Kolokotsa, D. (2015). On the impact of urban heat island and global warming on the power demand and electricity consumption of buildings—A review. *Energy and Buildings, 98,* 119–124. https://doi.org/10.1016/j.enbuild.2014.09.052

Sun, J., & Yang, K. (2016). The wicked problem of climate change: A new approach based on social mess and fragmentation. *Sustainability, 8*(12), 1312. https://doi.org/10.3390/su8121312

van Tulder, R., Keen, N., Crane, A., & Clarke, A. (2018). Capturing collaborative challenges: Designing complexity-sensitive theories of change for cross-sector partnerships. *Journal of Business Ethics, 150*(2), 315–332. https://doi.org/10.1007/s10551-018-3857-7

Waddock, S., Meszoely, G. M., Waddell, S., & Dentoni, D. (2015). The complexity of wicked problems in large scale change. *Journal of Organizational Change Management, 28*(6), 993–1012. https://doi.org/10.1108/JOCM-08-2014-0146

Warren, K., Franklin, C., & Streeter, C. L. (1998). New directions in systems theory: Chaos and complexity. *Social Work, 43*(4), 357–372. https://doi.org/10.1093/sw/43.4.357

Weiss, C. H. (1998). *Evaluation: Methods for studying programs and policies* (2nd ed.). Prentice Hall.

West, R., Stewart, L., Foster, K., & Usher, K. (2012). Through a critical lens: Indigenist research and the Dadirri Method. *Qualitative Health Research, 22*(11), 1582–1590. https://doi.org/10.1177/1049732312457596

Woermann, M., & Cilliers, P. (2012). The ethics of complexity and the complexity of ethics. *South African Journal of Philosophy, 31*(2), 447–463. https://doi.org/10.1080/02580136.2012.10751787

5
THE BASICS

The volatile dynamics in which social and environmental justice coalesce and through which they can amplify the impacts of climate change are most clear when we start thinking about the basics of living. How do I feed myself and my family? What kind of housing can we afford? How do I keep warm and cool as weather becomes more extreme? What about access to clean water? In this chapter, we will be talking through some of the basic elements of everyday life which fundamentally drive the ways in which we impact on climate change. It is here that we see some of the most vivid intersections of environmental and social justice.

Animal ethicists Fraser and MacRae (2011) remind us of the various ways in which people affect non-human life on Earth. Of particular relevance to this 'basics' discussion is the deliberate harm to animals through activities such as slaughter for food, the unintended harm to animals through crop production and transportation and indirectly through disturbing ecological systems and destroying habitat. How we produce, access and consume food, where we source energy and how much we use and how we utilise water and act in relation to water systems reflect both directly and indirectly our relationship with the environment as well as the contours of social (in)equity. In social work and human services more broadly we have always attended to struggles of people unable to afford food, energy bills and safe housing. For many of us, the focus has been at the crisis end of the spectrum, and our time has been spent making sure the basics for safety and survival can be met. For some of us the broader structural issues of housing, income and social policy have focused our work.

In this chapter, we want to examine the possibility of taking a much more detailed and connected path for meeting basic needs than we have traditionally seen in our field of work.

Let's start with an example from a community where one of us lives. It is an urban community with water on one side, national park on the other and

DOI: 10.4324/9781003146339-5

semi-rural/rural blocks between the town and the national park. In this community, there is social housing which is made up of 40–50-year-old small fibro houses. The local community centre runs a food and clothing distribution hub and sees 40–50 families every week who struggle to afford to pay their bills, buy food and support themselves. The social housing available in town exacerbates this struggle as it is freezing in winter (the area gets regular frosts) and unbearably hot in Summer (in recent years temperatures of above 40 degrees Celsius have been reached on numerous days in January and February). Inefficient but affordable heaters, fans and portable air conditioners provide some relief but result in skyrocketing bills and the lack of insulation in houses as well as poor design means that the level of energy required to heat and cool rooms is high. The two large supermarkets in town provide a range of groceries and fresh food, which is transported from regional warehouses in larger urban centres and capital cities. People who are experiencing poverty in this community do what they can to manage across the areas of basic need but often the action they are able to take exacerbates the poverty cycle while at the same time meeting food, energy, water and housing needs inadequately. What might be some alternative ways of organising for the basics which more thoroughly address both social and environmental equity for this group? Let's work through some of the research and practice knowledge available in relation to this question and then return to the community to discuss possibilities.

Food

Food and food systems are so fundamental to social and environmental justice; it is surprising that more attention is not paid by social and human services to the ways in which food systems permeate the daily life of people experiencing poverty and living in geographically remote or isolated communities just as they do in very different ways, for the affluent. Food, both metaphorically and materially sits at the intersection of social, environmental, biological, economic and cultural life. Food production, in all its forms, has both direct and indirect impact on non-human life. The slaughter of animals for food is startling, with 50 billion chickens, 1.4 billion pigs and 1 billion sheep consumed each year globally. The production of fruit and vegetables is likewise harmful to animals through harvesting, soil tillage and habitat loss (Fraser & MacRea, 2011). Szymanski argues that food is an 'active, multi-directional network' (2016, p. 24) of non-human and human actors, through which power flows (think of the power currently bestowed upon the celebrity or fine dining chef) and social processes are shaped. This network also reveals the ways in which justice and injustice are amplified in the everyday for the environment and for life on Earth.

Our access to different food systems marks our social status, our agency and the structural contours of inclusion and exclusion across society. In Australia, what Booth (2014) has described as 'downstream approaches' to food redistribution has seen a growth in charitable-oriented food systems for those experiencing poverty. Sustainably produced, high-quality food distribution is increasingly the prerogative of the affluent with high prices, increasing household and rental costs and limited access to fresh food resulting in people experiencing poverty relying on poor-quality processed foods which can be bought cheaply (Booth, 2014). This starts and amplifies a vicious circle where poor diet contributes to poor health and obesity. The stigma and social exclusionary impacts which follow are framed as individualised problems within health and medical discourse obscuring the structural factors within unjust food systems which underpin poor food access. Delgado and Delgado (2013) see social work as central in asking questions and reframing this cycle in the context of structural injustice. They argue that social work's role in attending to and acting at this structural level in relation to food justice is critically important.

At a policy and political level, Russell and colleagues (2020) highlight the intersections of ideology and food justice in their research on the construction of junk food marketing by Australian politicians. They found that approaches to policy making in this area followed party lines rather than health or environmental research evidence. Here, the marketing of junk food, which has significant impacts for marginalised communities in terms of food access and affordability, is addressed in accordance with prevailing party ideological positions with no consensus regarding social or environmental impacts outside of these frames. In our case study community over the past 15 years, four multi-national fast-food outlets have opened with local media applauding this as a positive sign for the burgeoning local economy. Local schools are actively engaged in promoting healthy eating and exercise while the availability of fast food any time of the day or night, a perception that fast food is cheap and the employment of many local young people in casual low wage jobs mean that school programs are fighting an uphill battle. There is no local fruit and vegetable shop in the community.

Booth (2014) questions who is benefiting from the increasing number of food banks in Australia. She draws attention to the convergence of complex relationships between waste disposal costs, enhanced reputations for large food manufacturers who donate food, governments who are able to avoid dealing with the impacts of increasing food security and who can outsource debate and food policy and corporations who fulfil social responsibilities through worker volunteering and charities who can easily access food through food bank supply chains and legitimise their work as food distributors without having to address any structural factors. For Booth, food banks represent an array of processes and actors who have created systems which are beneficial for the powerful and ensure the powerless remain locked into the role of grateful recipients of charitable good works. For many, food banks are seen as an excellent way to deal with both food waste in our distribution systems and poverty as they make food available to people with few resources. Booth invites us to look more critically at this system and ask questions about why there is so much waste in food distribution systems, how power is deployed to legitimise and embed food banks as moral and efficient approaches to food distribution, and how this replication of historical charitable institutions distracts us from calling governments to account for poor policy leadership with regard to fair food distribution amongst citizens.

Food insecurity is becoming an increasing problem worldwide and is experienced by many people who come into contact with human services. The work done in addressing food security (as highlighted by Booth) provides an excellent example of how a lack of attention to food systems and a simultaneous focus on alleviating food scarcity as a short-term process, exacerbates both power imbalances and access to healthy sustaining and sustainable food. Remedial and hand-out approaches including food banks, which are constructed around short-term, transactional distribution of 'left over' food to those who have no choice but to accept it, paradoxically demonstrate that collectively there is enough food produced to go around, and that market systems for the fair and equitable distribution of food across the community have failed. The simultaneous over production of particular foods, uneven distribution of food across the system and divergent costs of high value and high nutrition foods and those produced industrially with much lower nutritional value dramatically amplify the injustice in our food systems. Here is a very practical and basic intersection between environmental and social justice.

Alternative food systems and their challenges

As food banks and the proliferation of processed food marketing have grown in their dominance across the world in recent decades, it is easy to become despondent about alternative possibilities for food production and distribution which deliver on social and environmental justice. While organic, local and sustainable food production has also been a growing feature of food systems, this movement has tended to amplify rather than reduce social inequity. Alkon et al. (2019) explore the unintended exclusionary consequences of alternative food movements when communities gentrify resulting in people on lower incomes being squeezed out as the desirability of living with sustainable, local, organic food systems increases rents and property prices. From their research in Oakland, California, they argue that the paradox where communities build local networks, community gardens and food systems, only to have these resources used by developers and real estate agents to sell housing at inflated prices to those with more resources who have not contributed to community infrastructure, must be addressed at a policy and planning level to ensure equity. Provisions for affordable housing, positive employment of local people in local jobs, land use and planning which enshrines community ownership of and access to food-producing land and distribution infrastructure are essential in maintaining and nurturing food justice at a local level. The distortions created by market-oriented processes in this research saw local people on limited incomes who had developed and stewarded local food systems displaced by affluent newcomers attracted by what the existing community had created but unevenly contributing once they arrived. Newcomers inflated prices by their presence and greater resources, and on occasion objected to community food distribution networks where those with the least resources might still access local food. In this example, we see very clearly the importance of social as well as environmental justice being placed at the centre of food systems if they are to deliver both ethical/sustainable food production and fair sharing of food within the community.

Allen (2010) outlines the importance of attending to historical structural inequities in order to ensure that locally focused food systems do not reproduce and amplify existing disparities. Her analysis of some approaches to localising food systems reveals an alignment with neo-liberalism in the entrepreneurial flavour in some food localisation efforts. Allen discusses Community Supported Agriculture (CSA) as an example where environmental issues can be effectively addressed via lower food miles and small-scale organic and sustainable rather than industrial food production, but where social justice goals must be addressed within existing market structures. This means adjusting prices, sharing excess food and employing local people experiencing disadvantage are key social justice strategies but these must all be implemented within traditional capitalist economics, that is, it must generate profit. Institutional food purchase is another example Allen explores. Here, large institutions such as Universities can include social justice goals in their purchase policies. This kind of strategy has proved successful in achieving environmental justice goals through superannuation funds divesting shares in environmentally damaging sectors such as coal mining.

Allen's analysis reveals a number of assumptions in the drive for local food systems including a simplistic understanding of demographic and geographic nuances which mean that for workers and community members, entrenched racism, social exclusion and poor work conditions on farms can be more focused and intense within localised systems than in larger more dispersed systems. She warns us to resist romantic notions of local farming communities reminding us of the often violent and oppressive histories which have shaped land ownership and power. This is certainly the case in Australia where colonial land grabs by well-resourced squatters accompanied by violent destruction, and indeed extermination of First Nations communities, environmental destruction through land clearing, sheep and cattle grazing and killing local plants and animals have pervaded life across the country over the past 230 or so years (Beresford, 2021; Hamilton & Kells, 2021). If these are the contours of the food systems in which we live, we are at best naïve and at worst in denial if we do not consider the impact of this history.

For James (2016), a focus on the relationship between small farmers (particularly in urban and peri-urban areas) and supermarkets is an important but under-researched area in food system scholarship. James argues that a focus on alternative food systems has resulted in a neglect of analysis in the everyday power relations between supermarkets and small farmers. She cites a lack of clear evidence about whether farmers' markets, which have been increasing in numbers across Australia, have had a significant impact on the viability of small-scale farmers even though these and other alternative food systems are viewed as a way for small producers to survive. Her research reveals that the economic viability of small-scale farmers in Sydney faces threats from price squeezing by supermarkets, and land use changes including conversion of market gardens to turf farms or horse grazing. Most of the small farmers she spoke to were first-generation migrants to Australia who were fearful of advocating against or criticising supermarkets in case this impacted negatively on the contracts they did have. For James, structural issues regarding the concentrated power of supermarkets require greater government regulation to ensure a fair playing field for small farmers. Alternative food systems such as farmer's markets will only make a difference if they truly support small producers and create a broad base of regular consumers.

Promising directions

The picture created so far with regard to food systems is one where multi-layered and complex power relations, history, ideology and practice have shaped production and distribution in ways which have paid inadequate attention to connected notions of social and environmental justice. Where the social has been a focus the environment has suffered through industrial food production and expensive polluting distribution networks. Where environmental values have been privileged alone, we have seen an increase in social inequity as only those who can afford high value, locally and organically produced food can tap into the environmental values and credibility available in such a system. There are, however, a number of encouraging examples where both social and environmental justice underpin food systems. In these examples, we see the operation of reciprocity, an ethics of care, self-organising networks and shared learning as central to food production and distribution. Alternative food systems which connect social and environmental justice have often been local, decentralised and community-focused. Sometimes intentionally and sometimes as a result of their community focus, these food systems challenge industrial, competitive and centralised approaches (Migliore et al., 2014), building local distribution networks and behaviour change regarding food choices through sharing knowledge and learning, both in person and online (De Bernardi et al., 2019).

Blake (2019) argues that in spite of the ongoing erosion of community resources and networks undertaken by neo-liberalist policy and processes in the UK, low-income communities continue to self-organise around food security. Using a practice-based approach she connects local self-organising on food use with resilience building in communities and sees this process as vital in supporting both food security and ongoing local resilience. She highlights the ways food parcel activities limited community reciprocity and cast those receiving them as non-contributors, entrenching both food insecurity and isolation. This was contrasted with a different approach which enabled and encouraged a range of reciprocal opportunities and activities to be connected with food support programs. A community pantry where a small contribution enabled access to fresh food worked alongside volunteering opportunities at the pantry and also other activities run alongside the food support. This enabled people to receive and contribute as they could building their social networks and pairing food support with collective cooking and eating which connected people as community members rather than as recipients of charity. Blake also warns of the fragility of self-organising structures such as those described in her research. This warning is a reminder of the discussion in Chapter 7 about the importance of supporting the conditions and contexts in which self-organising can reach its full impact and not become either overwhelmed by expectations or stymied by suffocating structures.

Hasanov et al. (2019) examine self-organising in a community food-sharing initiative in the Netherlands. Here, in the 'Free Café' (p.4) activist politics explicitly frame the purpose and context for food sharing. This is very different from the case studies in Blake's research discussed above. Self-organisation at the Free Café following eviction from its original premises resulted in an interesting self-organising dynamic. Two groups emerged post-eviction, one continuing the original idea of food sharing from waste food while the other developed a project with a broader vision and much stronger ecological focus. A third group emerged over time adopting a more business-oriented approach. Hasanov and colleagues found that intersections of ideology, personalities, organisational styles and vision contributed to both the establishment of the Free Café and its dispersal into three different projects. This example raises a number of important questions in relation to food and climate change. The authors themselves raise the question about whether surplus food initiatives more generally both provide mitigation for the excesses of current food systems and also act to entrench the idea of surplus food as a commodity. The Free Café did very effectively engage in education about food waste, modelled food sharing practices and built nutritional and local food knowledge. More importantly, however, in this research self-organising demonstrated a process for supporting innovation required for broader system change to address the concern about food as a commodity raised by the researchers. In addition, partnerships developed with formal food systems including supermarkets also showed promise in relation to systems change through dialogue and learning with an alternative food system. The dynamic and emerging processes seen in this case study provide a further example of transformation with new initiatives developing from existing iterations. Here, the alternative food system was able to remain fluid and adapt to changing circumstances, participants and ideas. Collective action here is not totalising but instead able to accommodate different options and iterations.

For Picchioni et al. (2020), analysis of food systems with a focus on social reproduction (attending to social relations and processes on which labour is reproduced) and ethics of care, or more specifically geographies of care (particular times and places 'embedded in social connections as well as our relationship with nature' (p.29)) invites us to question the fundamentals of existing food systems. These researchers argue that current food systems reproduce structural inequity based on gender, race, class and citizenship. Their research focused on the food market in Lagos reveals a complex and networked system which blends care work, earning income, food distribution and provision, social and material support. In this system, food is far from a commodity to be bought and sold in a linear exchange. The food system blurs the boundaries between social, economic, private and public activities and relations. The food market is about life in the everyday. Picchioni and colleagues see food systems as enacting social reproduction and an ethics of care which directly challenges purely capitalist framings of food systems and recognises such systems as critical to social health and wellbeing. In this example, we can see a functioning, long-term food system which integrates relationships, care, knowledge sharing and reciprocity as shapers of food production and distribution. This is very different from the commodified food systems in which most of us participate and also different from individualising narratives of self-sufficiency. These approaches align with a First Nations Worldview through their centring of reciprocity and relationships. Food systems are complex and entangled within the broader connection and activities of daily life.

In the next section, we discuss one of the most powerful food system critiques which have emerged in recent decades: food sovereignty. For us, food sovereignty is an important idea and practice in the context of climate change as it draws out the operation of power and the consequences of markets making food into a context-free commodity rather than an embedded part of social and ecological life.

Food sovereignty

The idea of food sovereignty offers a comprehensive critique of capitalist food policy and locates food production and consumption in a political context where power relations have increasingly favoured multi-national corporate and industrial food systems over the rights and livelihoods of local farmers and communities more generally (Werkheiser, 2016). In 1996, the Spanish organisation of farmers, La Via Campesina, introduced the idea of food sovereignty on the international stage at the United Nations World Food summit (von Redecker & Herzig, 2020). They argued that local communities should be the decision makers regarding their own food production and distribution systems, that the rights of local farmers to produce food and receive a decent income and the rights of communities to be able to access locally produced food distributed in local economies must be defended to prevent the exploitative environmental, social and economic practices of large-scale industrial producers and the bias in international trade towards national or multinational corporations, destroying local systems.

Since that time food sovereignty has gained both momentum and diversity as a movement effectively drawing attention to the political landscape in which food production and distribution is shaped. Werkheiser (2016) discusses a number of critiques of the food sovereignty movement which view the diversity amongst those utilising this idea as a problem. For many, food sovereignty has become stretched too thin across a divergent range of issues including international trade, First Nations rights, gender, land use, sustainable farming and fundamental societal change away from capitalism. For advocates of the movement, this diversity symbolises the interconnectedness of food systems with community life in one direction and global capitalism in the other. Food becomes a central focus for work on justice more broadly. So, achieving food justice is not possible without working on social and environmental justice simultaneously. Gendered power imbalances, the ongoing impacts of colonialism experienced by First Nations communities, care and lack of care for the land and environment are played out in food systems. Werkheiser asks how food sovereignty, which has been largely taken up in small-scale farming and First Nations communities where the connection between food production and consumption is linked closely and locally, might be adapted to urban communities where the separation between food production and consumption is the norm. He argues that for people living in urban contexts, food sovereignty has the potential to act as a point of solidarity and connection with farmers and communities seeking local food justice. As a result, it is important to ground action within the ethical framework of food justice. In this context, food sovereignty as food justice must avoid focusing purely on local or organic without considering the cost differences and social exclusion these marketing narratives can inadvertently deliver.

Food sovereignty very effectively identifies the systemic injustices experienced by local farmers in communities across the world. The argument by advocates in the movement that multi-national industrialised farming distorts food production and distribution towards low nutritional value, high environmental impact food types as well as destroying local economies where food cannot be produced at this scale or price has been taken up by farmers in communities and enacted through the kind of networked self-organising that we have seen in small scale examples earlier in the chapter. Critiques of food sovereignty which see it as covering too much ground too thinly may have a point; however, an alternative view is that the idea of food sovereignty, like the Free Café in the earlier example, has become a touch point for farmers and local food systems and adapted to local contexts and priorities. One such example in Australia draws links between uneven power in markets, health and care for local land with practices promoting local farming and food production. Rose (2017) draws links between climate change and obesity describing the production of processed foods through land clearing and industrial monoculture farming as having a destructive impact on earth and climate initially and then on human health through the consumption of processed food. Pressure from supermarkets, as dominant players in Australian food systems, on farmers to grow particular crops or be left out of negotiations while simultaneously having their bargaining power eroded is discussed by Rose as another manifestation of the links between climate and social justice in food systems. Rose reports on the development of Food Hubs in Australia as an intentional way to disrupt neo-liberal market processes. His critical literature review outlines both the potential for food hubs to address sustainability/climate change and social justice but warns that they are not a catch-all solution to food system problems. Rose identifies a number of key success factors for Food Hubs – leadership and creative thinking at Board and operational levels, partnerships and networks with producers preferably building capacity of existing organisations, being credible and embedded in the local community, achieving threshold income through sales and non-sales avenues, supporting policy and experienced and skilled staff. He cautions against looking to the success of Food Hubs in the US advocating for an approach which recognises the significant differences in market size and also in the history of price differences between supermarket and farmer's market produce in Australia resulting in the exclusion of people with less resources for whom supermarket food is both cheap and convenient.

We finish this section on food sovereignty and food justice by returning to the idea of food systems as multi-layer and multi-scalar networks which link humans and the more than human world. Coulson and Milbourne (2020) in their examination of food movements in the UK suggest the concept of the 'justice multiple' (p.43) as a way to analyse and connect plurality, space and time and the more than human in food justice. For us, this is a helpful way to make sense of what just food systems might look like. They draw a distinction between food activism and alternative food movements drawing on Fraser and Honneth's (2003) work on recognition as a critically important dimension of justice. They argue that in food systems disrespect and misrecognition can be seen clearly in the ways that First Nations food systems have been dismissed, disrupted and marginalised. Linking back to Chapter 3, they see emancipatory strategies as imperative for First Nations communities to enact collective decision-making about their own food systems. This goes beyond communities having a voice in decision-making to address structural inequities seen in both misrecognition and uneven distribution of power and resources. Coulson and Milbourne (2020) argue that a plural view sees justice as contextual, situated and embodied, but also operating in a multi-scalar way. Here, environmental and social justice are intricately interconnected across space and time with global food system issues, governance and justice manifesting themselves in very local socio-political ways including workers' rights, supporting diverse local food systems, and sustainable food production. Working on food justice over time includes recognising and addressing historical, environmental and social injustices played out in food systems and looking to justice for future generations. They extend their discussion to the more than human world arguing that this frames food justice within a more complex ecological system where society and nature are not separate but in relationship as part of dynamic, connected, emergent systems. This quote exemplifies a relational understanding of food systems and the way in which we might locate ourselves in this context;

> Food systems, therefore, provide a pertinent, embodied and vital lens to examine how we can/do/do not live responsibly in multispecies worlds at

various 'contact zones'—the places where species meet (Haraway 2008)—such as agrifood systems.

(Coulson & Milbourne, 2020, p.48)

In this first part of the chapter, we have taken a close look at some of the social and environmental dimensions of food systems and suggested some possibilities for those of us in social work and human services to engage with structural as well as impact contours across these systems. In the next section, we look at energy generation, use and governance.

Energy

Similar to food systems, the questions focused on energy include, what kind of energy should we produce and use, what are some of the ways energy systems might be organised and how is fairness achieved through energy generation, use and distribution. For many, growing renewable energy production and access to renewable energy through established energy companies or government energy providers is the preferred approach in addressing the nexus between climate change and energy use. Take up of renewable energy technology at a community level in Australia has outstripped expectations since it has become both more accessible and affordable (Garnaut, 2019). According to the Commonwealth Scientific and Industrial Research Organisation [CSIRO], Australia had the highest global uptake of solar panels by 2021 with over 25% of houses across the country (CSIRO, 2021). In spite of policy confusion and a propensity for current conservative governments in Australia to advocate for coal power even as the coal industry is shifting its production to renewables community enthusiasm for supporting a transformation of the energy sector in line with climate change mitigation is strong. While government rebates such as those on the installation of solar panels linked to the energy grid, alongside falling material and installation costs, have enabled more people across the socio-economic spectrum to make renewable energy choices, those in social housing, renters and low-income households remain more likely to be impacted by both rising energy costs and human-induced climate change and least able to access alternatives. In the scenario at the beginning of this part of the book, the impact of poor and ageing housing infrastructure, such as uninsulated fibro cottages provided as social housing, places those with the least means in the community in the untenable situation of being blamed for both using electricity inefficiently (thus increasing emissions) and being irresponsible with their money as they are unable to pay the skyrocketing energy bills. In this situation, the structural exclusion of particular groups and individuals due to uneven energy costs and distribution, a lack of investment in housing designed to reduce energy costs and individualised approaches to renewable energy infrastructure is transformed into a deficit on the part of the excluded rather than an invitation for comprehensive re design as climate change ramps up.

Globally, energy consumption linked to heating and cooling creates a paradoxical picture where access to air conditioning is largely the privilege of more affluent societies. Here, the inequities which reveal themselves at a local level are hidden as those with resources across the world are able to and do utilise power in ways which maximise emissions while those with less bear the brunt of heatwaves without the means to stay cool. In a typical American home, for example, the air conditioner will consume more electricity than lights, computers and refrigerator combined. Worldwide there are 1.6 billion air conditioners in Japan, US and South Korea accounting for more than 80% of home units. Countries such as Mexico, Brazil, Indonesia, South Africa and India own less with fewer than 20% of homes furbished with air conditioning (Gates, 2021). In Australia, estimates place our ownership at three out of every four homes and rising – along with the costs of running the units (Strengers et al., 2014), with an estimated 1.9 million Australians leaving their air conditioning units running while they are not at home. As temperatures increase, these figures will rise and the carbon-intensive generation of electricity will also rise.

Renewable energy and social justice

Energy consumption, however, is not the only consideration as we think through the relationship between climate change and social justice. As with food systems, energy systems are complex, entangled and shaped by often invisible structural and decision-making dilemmas. While the transition to low emission and renewable energy is welcomed worldwide as both long overdue and hopeful where it has started, a number of researchers have highlighted the reproduction of social injustice amongst renewable energy projects where inequities have not been integrated as core to project development. Levenda et al. (2021) undertook a systematic literature review of renewable energy projects globally examining different forms of justice considered in each project. They found that without a comprehensive and detailed engagement with justice across dimensions of distribution, procedure, recognition and capacity, intersectional inequities were reproduced for communities with the least power. For example, the location of hydro power projects had significant implications for many communities with no decision-making power regarding project location. Goedkoop and Devine-Wright (2016) in their study of shared ownership of renewable energy projects in the UK found that without clear and detailed agreement between developers and communities from the start of a project, exploitative relationships where communities felt used in order for developers to gain approvals for their project, often developed and a lack of trust between players was amplified. In this research, the difference between theoretical shared ownership and the messiness of practice provided important learning for enacting a shared understanding of goals in renewable energy projects. Questions about how to support equitable energy distribution and costs alongside renewable low emissions energy generation invite us to think and plan carefully in relation to the how and who in designing and enacted energy projects.

An *energy justice* framework provides one theoretical co-ordinate for us to work through the relationships and dynamics which shape current and possible future questions of energy sustainability and social justice. *Energy justice* places affordability, supply and social and environmental sustainability within a context of rights, democratic decision-making and inclusion. Rather than seeing our relationship with energy systems as one of consumers only, energy justice locates us as citizens with rights, responsibilities and decision-making power at all stages of the energy life cycle. This means there is an ethical responsibility regarding the way energy is produced which is accompanied by a commitment to equity in the supply and accessibility of energy to all (Fortier et al., 2019). So what might this mean on the ground? If we use *energy justice* to shape energy system design, how might we make it work in practice? McCauley (2017) asked exactly this question citing six considerations in designing a transition to renewable energy founded on *energy justice*. They argue that in order to respond adequately to the combined problem of energy security, the impact of poverty and the imperative to reduce carbon emissions we need to change the ways we think about and behave in relation to energy in fundamental ways. For McCauley, the future of energy production and distribution must be decentralised with 'Communities [involving] themselves as much in energy production as much as they do today on consumption' (p.76). Access rather than only affordability must become a central focus as access covers a range of energy justice challenges of which affordability is just one part. Low-carbon energy rather than only renewable energy is a key consideration. Energy burdens must be shared equally across time as well as space which means we need to consider historical impacts of carbon emissions and burdens experienced across the life of energy cycles. McCauley's fifth consideration involves recognition of the environment which they argue is often not prioritised as it should be in energy justice research and practice. The final consideration in the delivery of energy justice as the world transitions to a low-carbon future is one of inclusion. Here, McCauley emphasises the importance of supporting innovation and decision-making on energy consumption at a household level.

In the context of our discussion in the book so far, McCauley's approach to energy justice is a particularly interesting one as it draws out the potentially significant changes in power relations which may be possible as the world shifts from reliance on fossil fuels to low carbon renewable energy sources such as solar, wind and biomass. The distribution of these resources across the world and the difficulty in maintaining ownership and control of sunlight, wind and biomass potentially changes the way in which energy justice might emerge. As McCauley states:

> The modest nature of infrastructural requirements for a community to purchase, learn sufficient technological knowledge and deliver wind or solar electricity or biomass heating is resulting in globally observable low – carbon social movements.

> (p.81)

Closely connected to self-organising systems, we see collective approaches mobilised to create alternative energy distribution, food production and distribution and alternative economies more generally. Smith and colleagues (2016) argue that this kind of collective innovation has been driven by 'an insistent undercurrent of grassroots activism' (p.408) and rather than broad-based societal change has focused on practicalities of environmentally sustainable living. Spanning focus areas from housing to community energy to eco-farming, the differences between these innovations and those driven by individual entrepreneurial efforts (such as Elon Musk) are located very much in the how rather than the what. Here collective action shapes the development of innovation by ensuring that local place-based community involvement is central at all stages. Smith and colleagues examine Community Energy initiatives in the UK, highlighting some of the dangers for these collective action initiatives as they become more influential at a policy level. They argue that community-led sustainability innovations are characterised by work across the remit of numerous government agencies as community discussions may start with a particular focus then move to other aspects of local sustainability. For example, they suggest a focus on food, might lead to waste which may lead to energy. The compartmentalised structure of government means that the free ranging community initiative fits nowhere neatly and must contend with multiple agencies wanting just one aspect of their work. In addition, as an initiative gains traction a tendency to become a version of an existing energy provider, rather than staying focused on difference and what it does well is a challenge for this type of collective action. In this research, the importance of taking a critical stance which enables community activists and innovators to recognise and maintain their differences and to stay focused on developing innovations in energy thinking rather than only technical innovation is central. This theme is taken further by Cameron and Hicks (2014) arguing that community owned energy initiatives offer the potential for challenging dominant narratives about the importance of scaling up as a prerequisite for success and impact. As with Smith and colleagues' research, the focus here is not on the delivery of technical impacts alone through solar or wind energy, but experimentation with ways of organising collective action which fundamentally reshapes power relations. For Cameron and Hicks, community energy schemes can challenge the discourse that power flows from the top down through large scale influential projects by mapping out an alternative to scaling up. They propose that a proliferation of a 'multiplicity of small initiatives' (p.62) which, though diverse and not necessarily linked, can have a cumulative impact on a broadly shared agenda such as renewable energy. Here collective action is situated and community led. Initiatives multiply through networked sharing with other local groups. They describe an example of a community owned wind farm in Hepburn, Victoria, which shifted from a focus on raising funds with large grants from government and other sources to a strategy to increase membership of the co-operative. This second strategy proved much more successful than the first, and served further to establish new knowledge about how to build resources by multiplying ownership within the situated context of the initiative. Rather than grow larger the project established a process for sharing knowledge and supporting similar community groups exploring local energy initiatives in their own location.

Cameron and Hicks actively critique and dismantle the idea that markets can only operate on the basis of individualised competition. This is a critically important point for us to consider in thinking through the ways in which collective action might reshape the ways we provide social support. Through community energy initiative examples, they describe ways in which markets can be shaped by ethical considerations including price and wage setting and moderation or redistribution of profit to ensure access for those without resources to participate or support local environmental groups. This approach matches the ethos of many social enterprises which operate within markets while both adhering to their own ethical frameworks rather than individualised self-interest, and re-shaping the market through these actions. Kunze and Becker's (2015) survey across the EU, of diverse small-scale renewable energy projects likewise found that across diverse organisational forms and policy contexts, collective renewable energy initiatives, although occupying niche positions in the energy system, had the potential to guide a practical change towards more democratic renewable energy generation. The researchers argue that such initiatives combine decentralised technological capability in energy production with intentionally democratic business and organisational approaches.

If energy justice enables us to shift our thinking on energy away from the market-oriented frameworks which dominate discussion in this area, and towards an approach to energy founded upon rights, recognition and equity for both human and non-human actors in the system, what does this mean on the ground? How might this shift be put into practice, given the opportunity for more de-centralised and community focused decision-making which low carbon energy sources offer?

Community renewable energy projects

Community renewable energy (CRE) projects provide tangible examples of energy justice in action and are creating new opportunities to link local governance, decision-making and community ownership with renewable energy use. CRE projects have emerged across the globe during the 21st century (Hicks & Ison, 2018) and, in a diverse range of forms, have been described as seeking to 'decentralise, democratise and decarbonise electricity while also demonstrating the value of both renewable energy and community involvement' (Hicks, 2020 p.138). In practical terms, these projects are diverse and it is this diversity which is seen by a number of researchers as a key strength (Hicks & Ison 2018; Seyfang & Longhurst, 2013). They are shaped by local context, geography, culture, community dynamics, weather and policy. Hicks and Ison (2018), drawing on over a decade of CRE research, identify five spectrums which are common to CRE projects and explain the process of balancing motivations and context across this diversity of project approaches. Their five spectrums are as follows:

1 The range of actors involved who make up the community
2 Decision-making processes including the distribution of voting rights
3 Distribution of financial benefits
4 Scale of technology and project size
5 Level of community engagement

Projects in their action research study included solar and wind, those in local communities of place as well as more dispersed communities of interest and were diverse in scale and community engagement. Each of the projects was located on different parts of the spectrum depending on context, policy and motivation (for example, while all projects included community engagement, some occupied a position with high levels of engagement throughout while others engaged with a smaller group) but all shared a design which included consideration of the five. Common here is a process which sees reciprocity, shared benefits and decision making, care for the environment, and community involvement as foundational for an energy project. This range of concerns and the accountabilities which accompany them is vastly different to limiting priorities to cost and shareholder profit.

CRE projects very clearly demonstrate ways in which addressing human-induced climate change and participatory, community-led planning and decision-making are closely linked to produce positive social and environmental outcomes. These kinds of projects take up the opportunities created by the availability of renewable energy resources and affordability of technology described by McCauley (2017), developing alternative business and governance structures to those in traditional energy sectors where cost and control of fossil fuels favoured corporate ownership structures. The shift from needing to own a coal mine or even nuclear facility to being able to utilise wind and sunlight to generate energy creates space for diverse processes, people and structures to be developed in local communities as the transition to low carbon energy unfolds.

While for social and human services workers the production and distribution of energy may seem like a long bow, CRE projects illustrate in a very concrete way, the critical role which community development knowledge and skills play in building the context of social support which has been a major contributor to successful CRE projects (Hicks, 2020; Hicks & Ison, 2018; Seyfang & Longhurst, 2013). There is growing research and practical evidence that CRE projects create and support structures and processes which increase community engagement and ownership in local energy production as well we consumption. Hicks (2020) describes two wind energy projects (Hepburn Springs in Victoria and Denmark in Western Australia) where community education, engagement and ownership resulted in strong community support for local wind generators (where these are often met with community opposition due to poor local

engagement) and a strong local sense of connection with renewable energy production. In the Hepburn Springs project, a co-operative governance structure
and ongoing communication, reciprocity (through grants and support for local
projects) and broad-based ownership of energy generation (one vote one share
and large shareholder membership) resulted in a deeper and more sustained sense
of connection with and involvement in renewable energy production and use.
There is significant potential here for environmental and social justice to be
shaped in ways which recognise community reciprocity, care for earth and equitable access to energy resources.

There is still a long way to go, however, with attention to policy settings,
investment support and building capacity in local community development infrastructure required urgently to make the most of opportunities such as CRE
projects. For example, in the UK, Martiskainen (2017) describes such initiatives
as both niche and grassroots, citing challenges in accessing technical knowledge, policy change favouring centralised energy production and the domination
of large corporate players unwilling to let community energy initiatives into
mainstream energy generation as key reasons why this sector remains small. For
Martiskainen, the niche space in which community energy schemes operate is
critically important as it is here where innovation and experimental work can
be put into practice. Like the Free Café innovation described in the previous
section, community energy initiatives in the UK are characterised by an iterative
process where new ideas and practices emerge sequentially as projects take shape.
In two case studies they cited, community leadership and network building were
vital in supporting a negotiated vision and a viable long-term project. Navigating
conflict, negotiating partnerships with organisations and government outside the
community, while building a sustained and practical plan meant that community
energy scheme leaders were required to utilise and/or develop key community
development skills to realise the project.

In the community described in our scenario at the beginning of the chapter,
the acceleration of global and national shifts towards renewable energy has recently created community and renewable energy opportunities which were not
imagined a decade ago. One dominant feature of the local landscape is the number of coal-fired power stations which are dotted around the local waterways.
While some of these have closed due to age, the community is torn between the
role of the remaining power station as a local employer and the environmental
impacts which are felt locally despite the generation of power being distributed
across the State. An unexpected announcement from the power station owner
bringing the closure date forward has opened up local conversations about renewable energy and community energy ownership as this now seems possible
and imminent (the closure is for 2025). If we imagine what might be possible
here for those living in social housing locally and the community more generally the shift to renewable energy locally could either be designed and delivered within existing corporate structures and ownership (the energy company
changes its energy generation but uses the existing site to install a large battery

which it owns exclusively and supplies customers as it has previously with coal), through the development of one or more community energy projects which generate solar or wind energy with local ownership available to community members as per the projects discussed by Hicks (2018, 2020) or through a combination of these strategies. If a community energy scheme developed, the possibility of environmental and social justice outcomes being achieved through affordable, community owned renewable energy generation becomes a very real prospect alleviating both the social and environmental costs currently borne by those least able to afford them. This change has been made possible through new technology and a significant shift in broad community uptake of renewable energy but can only be realised through democratic and community-building processes which are needed to support the germination of a CRE project from an idea to an actual organisation. It would be too simple, however, to argue that Community Energy Projects were the silver bullet or the only alternative in terms of social and environmental justice in energy generation. Creamer and colleagues (2019), in their reflection on a seminal article by Walker and Devine-Wright on Community Renewable Energy (CRE) published 10 years earlier, highlight the ways in which process and outcome have been separated during the last decade of thinking and developing CRE projects which they find unhelpful. For these researchers, there is a need to recognise CRE projects as much more complex and fluid. Entangled and changing dynamics between process and outcomes over time within a project and in relation to local context, they reflect, require a much more considered understanding for those trying to make sense of how a project is evolving. They point to ongoing gaps in knowledge about long-term outcomes and impacts of CRE projects as part of a just energy transition.

In the case of a number of CRE projects in Scotland studied by van Veelen and Haggett (2017), the successful community engagement and ownership processes outlined by Hicks and Ison (2018) were not evident, with local conflicts centred on different understandings of place. Van Veelen and Haggett (2017) warn against assumptions that co-operation in communities can be guaranteed and against simplistic approaches which seek to replicate projects without a detailed understanding of the very different social, cultural, economic and political contexts in which they take place. In our local example, it would be a mistake to assume that everyone will embrace the closure of the power station and welcome the changing environment which it will bring. For many local people, a sense of place and identity may be linked with work at the power station. For others, large energy companies have provided economic stability and growth in the area. While for others the end of the coal-fired power station represents cleaner air, a return to a pre-industrial landscape and possibilities for different approaches to energy generation and ownership. For many the sense of loss, concern about change and shift in social and economic relations can be unsettling. The research we have discussed here suggests that work ahead will bring significant change, but unknowns and the adaptation and learning required to navigate these are likely to accompany us from the start.

So, the picture remains incomplete and there are significant challenges in designing and operating renewable low emissions energy schemes which deliver on climate change and social justice goals. For us, this is not a reason to withdraw from the kind of structural changes possible through CRE and other renewable energy strategies. Indeed, these challenges are arguably amplified in a context where community members are excluded from the process of renewable energy generation entirely or allowed only to be consumers of energy. Rather, research across this area reminds us that energy generation and governance are as much about social and political relations (in this case at both a local and broader level) as they are about engineering and land use.

In this context, one of the reasons we are particularly interested in these kinds of projects is because they demonstrate an emergent alternative which brings together the complex and changing dynamics, which characterises democratic ownership of energy and low-emission renewable energy generation. It is here where we might contribute in a useful way. For those of us in social work and human services work, the participatory processes and governance possibilities in organising energy generation in this way, along with the capacity for dispersed, local renewable energy production through new technology, very practically link climate change action with the everyday social justice work we are involved in. These kinds of projects remind us that in the context of climate change, our work will be more effective if we see it as part of a much broader spectrum of planning and action than within more traditional boundaries at the welfare end of energy consumption. To date, social work and human services workers have had a very limited presence in the area of energy systems, except at the pointy end of supporting people unable to pay power bills. Relations between social justice and climate change in the area of energy are intimate, so it is interesting that workers and researchers in our fields have been so noticeably absent. A vital opportunity exists here for social and human service workers to engage with this field in ways which have not been possible in the past. The next section of the book shifts this thinking towards the *how* of action for change. Before this, however, we examine a third basic of life which has been the centre of debate connecting climate change and social justice – water.

Water

Water is perhaps the most paradoxical of the basics discussed in this section. When we think about climate change, the spectre of rising sea levels and the inundation of low-lying islands and coastal areas are often the first things which come to mind. Images of flooding in South East Queensland and the Northern Rivers are vivid in our minds. Too much water with nowhere to go. But at the same time, access to water, and the impact of drought causing prolonged and critical water shortages, has also been profound for many in recent years. Since the turn of the 21st century, Australia has experienced two severe droughts – the long Millennium Drought between 1997 and 2007 and the more recent 2017–2019 drought (Bureau of Meteorology [BOM], 2022) – which created conditions for the Black Summer bushfires in 2019, the most widespread and intense since records began (Baird et al., 2021). This paradox is acutely felt by the residents of Lismore which despite being the most flood-prone city in Australia cannot guarantee access to fresh water for the region's estimated population of 110,000 people at current consumption levels past 2024 (Clarke, 2022). Local Richard Trevan from Lismore-based community group Our Future Northern Rivers commented

> How is it possible that the most flood affected community in the country cannot guarantee water supply past 2024? NSW does not do water security or flood mitigation well.
>
> *(Clarke, 2022)*

Like others we argue that

> drought and flood adaptation strategies need to co-exist – one should not replace the other as the climate oscillates between its wet and dry phases. This coexistence of strategies is especially important given the anthropogenic climate change projections for Australia which suggest that increases in the frequency and duration of droughts could be associated with increases in the frequency of short-lived but intense rainfall events.
>
> *(Kiem, 2013, p.1616)*

Water is essential to human life, including in the production of food, and water availability is 'looming' as a significant social, cultural, political and economic problem (Mercer et al., 2007). In Australia, agriculture consumes 54% of freshwater, mostly for irrigation (ABS cited in Page et al., 2011). Water scarcity has implications for both food security and environmental sustainability again highlighting the complexities of the challenges created by climate change. Human use of water of course affects animal life on Earth, particularly agricultural practices that degrade soil and water. Fertilisers used in agriculture enter water systems creating 'hypoxic dead zones' resulting in mass fish deaths (Fraser & MacRea, 2011). However, simplistic solutions (stopping growing tomatoes in the Sydney basin) may in fact result in poor ecological, hydrological and economic decisions (Page et al., 2011). Understanding the Water Footprint of the goods we consume requires considering

> not only the direct water use which occurs at the production site as irrigation, but also the volumes of water consumed indirectly in the production of inputs (fuels, fertilisers, machinery, equipment, transport and other inputs) to deliver the product to the consumer.
>
> *(Page et al., 2011, p.23)*

The strategies used in agriculture are likely to be vital in responding to water scarcity in Australia and beyond into the future. Despite this, farmers tend to be less convinced of the dangers of anthropogenic climate change with Wheeler et al. (2013) finding less than one-third of irrigators in NSW and Victoria believed it posed a risk to their region. Following from this, just over half of irrigators in NSW, Victoria and South Australia in the same study were *not* 'incorporating the potential for climate change in [their] farm planning'. Whilst this study is somewhat dated it seems likely that a substantial proportion of farmers continue to be unconvinced of the need for urgent action. Over centuries farmers however have demonstrated the ability to adjust their properties, equipment and productive capacity (Wheeler et al., 2013). This ability to adjust is likely to be tested as water scarcity in the Australian environment requires transformational adaption as

> ecological, economic, or social conditions make existing systems untenable … [demanding] a major change in livelihood, location or identity.
> *(Wheeler et al., 2013, p.537)*

Farmers appear to be adapting to water scarcity in a range of ways: through expansion (buying additional water and land); accommodation (changing farm practices); or contraction (selling water and land). Of these adaption possibilities, Wheeler et al.'s (2013) study found that improving irrigation efficiency and changing crop mix (accommodating) were most widespread. It seems likely that these incremental changes are unlikely to enable farmers to successfully adapt to a drier climate, requiring the design of structural adjustment packages to aid the transition out of farming (Wheeler et al., 2013, p.546). This bleak future is a source of concern in many rural communities already experiencing an ageing population (Kiem, 2013). The success of family farms is essential for rural towns economically and socially. Structural change of agriculture has the 'potential to change rural communities permanently' (Kiem, 2013, p.1624).

The Murray-Darling Basin

Covering 14% of land area in Australia, spanning four states and producing 40% of Australian agricultural produce (Abel et al., 2016), the Murray-Darling Basin represents a complex example of urgent need for comprehensive action at all levels and at the same time, of the challenging context through which this must develop. Water resources are not adequate to meet all competing priorities but without a collaborative plan, the threat of further decline and collapse is imminent.

Access to water only became a focus of government policy relatively recently (Kiem, 2013). Prior to this time drought was framed by policy responses as 'a climatic abnormality' resulting in income support payments similar to floods, earthquakes and cyclones (Kiem, 2013).

During the late-1980s ... the view of drought as a one-off, unpredictable
and unmanageable natural disaster began to be questioned in scientific and
policy circles.

(Kiem, 2013, p.1616)

The policy responses to drought since that time are very revealing of how water is conceptualised not as a basic human right but as commodity to be traded.
Water policy is being developed and debated in the context of less water due to
anthropogenic climate change. The complexity of developing a water policy that
responds to the needs of the environment, humans, agriculture and industries
within Australia's large hydroclimatic variability has led to

widespread acknowledgement that past policy responses to drought and
water resources management have not worked effectively and are unlikely
to do so in the future.

(Kiem, 2013, p.1615)

Although not the only intervention, creating a market for the trading of water
across the Murray-Darling Basin has been a key climate change adaption strategy. This approach, heavily influenced by neo-liberalism, creates competition
for access to water with a market preference to 'high value' users (Kiem, 2013).
In too familiar language, the Rural Industries Development Corporation (2007)
argued that 'reallocating scarce water resources' would be more efficient and
allow 'more productive uses' (cited in Kiem, 2013 p.1622). The Basin is home to
2 million people, including some 40 First Nations tribes, and provides habitat to
over 120 waterbird species and 46 native fish species as well as trees that are hundreds of years old (Murray Darling Basin Authority, 2022). Attempting to find
common ground across such a broad range of 'stakeholder' groups has proven
very challenging for successive Commonwealth, State and Local governments.
This is made more challenging as the existing science of water sustainability
is poor and the social costs difficult to factor. However, evidence is emerging
that the marketisation of water across the region has ironically supported high
emission industries that exacerbate climate change such as mining, manufacturing and electricity generation (ABS cited in Kiem, 2022, p.1622). As discussed
in more detail below, large corporate agricultural producers have also been far
more successful in manipulating the water market than smaller traditional family
farms (Kiem, 2022). The end result of the marketisation of water is no different
to other market interventions: those with resources to use and manipulate the
market are advantaged; those with fewer resources find themselves even more
disadvantaged.

During the Millennium Drought, pressure on the Murray-Darling Basin –
a river and catchment system running from Queensland to South Australia –
became so intense that many feared it may collapse. Public discussion and debate
about the Murray-Darling system during this period highlighted both the sorry

history of exploitation, extraction and greed which this river system has had to endure since colonisation (Hartwig et al., 2020; Lukasiewicz et al., 2013) and the political and management ineptitude of successive Commonwealth and State governments in bowing to particular interests and ignoring the basic environmental requirements for the system to stay healthy. In many ways, the history of the Murray-Darling since Australia was colonised reflects the history of environmental and social justice more generally as a result of colonisation. Combining a wilful ignorance about care for country and the essential work done by First Nations communities for upward of 60,000 years to look after and manage the land in ways which respected the climate, geography and environmental systems held delicately in balance across Australia, with a notion that natural resources were there for the endless taking by those with power and resources, water use over the past 200 years provides some salient and urgent lessons for a future impacted by climate change. The plight of the Murray Darling Basin also provides us with a detailed case study of how social and environmental justice are navigated within complex and layered sets of relationships. Food production, community and cultural life, employment, ecosystem health, corporate economics, social and political dynamics, custodianship and everyday survival are just some of the dimensions in play throughout this large and diverse river system. Walgett, a town of around 2000 people in North Western NSW, experienced 18 months of dry river beds during the Big Dry. Thirty per cent of the Walgett community are First Nations people, and the town takes its name from the local Gamilaraay language meaning 'the meeting place of two rivers' (the Namoi and the Barwon Rivers). The lack of water in the rivers created a 'culture of despair' according to Yuwalaraay man Ted Fields. Dhariwaa elder Virginia Robinson said at the time

> It's a triple whammy – drought, land clearing and climate change – that means no water.
>
> *(Allam, 2019)*

The community like so many others along the Basin were reliant upon bore water, which recorded sodium levels of 300 mg/L. Whilst there is no standard for 'safe' level of sodium in drinking water GPs are advised that sodium levels about 20mg/L are likely to be dangerous for people with severe hypertension or congestive heart failure (Allam, 2019). Walgett's recorded levels were 15 times this, in a community with a significant Aboriginal community with chronic health issues (Commonwealth of Australia, 2010). Local frustrations were exacerbated by the allocation of water resources to cotton irrigation nearby (Allam, 2019). In a shocking indictment of policy failure, bottle water donations were carted from as far away as Sydney, with the community experiencing water shortages during a run of 40-degree days (Fitzsimons, 2019).

Although known as the Blue Planet, less than 3% of Earth's water is fresh and suitable for human consumption (Tamlin, 2019). Rivers, lakes and other bodies of freshwater are threatened by pollution, agricultural practices, population growth as well as climate change (Tamlin, 2019). Research undertaken by the Cooperative Research Centre for Water Sensitive Cities evaluated the effectiveness of community engagement processes to improve project outcomes, build trust in organisations or reform processes, and support transition to water sensitive cities (Dean et al., 2016, p.4). In their work, the CRC identified three approaches: strategies that provide input into the community (e.g., education and information); strategies that seek input from the community (e.g., consultations) and strategies that build active and connected communities (e.g., community stewardship). Whilst evidence was found for each of these strategies stewardship initiatives (restoration and citizen science programs) were found to be very popular with communities, attracting participants and generating social learning (Dean et al., 2016, p.30–37). One highly successful example of citizen science is Streamwatch which started with a trial of 15 NSW public schools in 1990. Now a national program involving citizens from all walks of life, over 1,100 Streamwatch groups monitor water quality at over 1,060 sites contributing nearly 31,000 sets of data to the online database (Greater Sydney Landcare, 2022). The program monitors the health of waterways (large and small) through monthly water quality testing and surveys of aquatic macroinvertebrates (NSW Waterwatch, 2016). The focus is on local waterways, building stewardship between the local community and local catchments. Outcomes from these citizens science initiatives include:

- Providing historical information on how waterways have changed over time and demonstrating natural fluctuations or highlighting local issues (ongoing or emerging)
- Demonstrating whether activities to protect and restore waterways are having the desired effect – i.e., on-ground riparian or instream works have improved water quality and aquatic biodiversity.
- Contributing to catchment planning or reporting (NSW Waterwatch, 2016).

The focus on young people in the early stages of Streamwatch and other citizen science initiatives made sense to educators such as Sue Lennox as

> students were becoming overwhelmed by the negative information on environmental and social issues. I was seeing them shut down, rather than engage with it... [And then] there was a massive fish kill in Curl Curl Lagoon, and the kids were really angry and upset. So we dropped all the other stuff we were doing in class .... And the kids were so enthused— they came up with 100 different ideas of things they could do, they were really switched on to it. And out of that whole process they developed an action plan of conducting interviews with businesses around the school, making a video, and creating a water monitoring program at school. We didn't initially have the skills to do any of those things, but that was part of the learning— to get those skills. The surprise was that the consequence

of doing each of those actions was beyond anything that we would have anticipated. The kids went out and interviewed the businesses and they realized what powerful educators and motivators of adults they could be. The water-monitoring program worked with Streamwatch; the video ended up winning a UN Media Peace Prize.

(Australian Association of Environmental Education
NSW [AAEENSW], 2022)

Again, in this example, we see the surprising, unexpected outcomes of community action. We see the disruption of expected roles, with students becoming the educators. We see crisis as catalyst for change. We see care and connection of people to the environment. We see professionals (in this case teachers) prepared to take a risk and to engage creatively. And we see networks being built at the local and global levels. But mostly we see the possibility of a different way of interacting with country.

Social work and human services

For those of us working in social work and human services, the social issues we engage with every day – ageing populations and outmigration from small communities, unemployment, poverty, family and domestic violence, social exclusion, mental health, racism, gender inequities and social cohesion are all impacted by the role of water in communities. The very real and comprehensive impacts of an event such as the mass fish kills at Menindee (Beresford, 2021) or Black Summer bushfires traverse environmental, cultural, social, economic and political boundaries. The entanglement of social and environmental justice is very close to the surface in events such as these and they remind us that when we think about people in their environments (a basic tenet of social work) we cannot afford to consider only the social environment. The paradigm shift we have discussed throughout the book – from viewing the ecological systems upon which we depend for survival as distant and outside the concerns of social work to locating ourselves and our work in the social world as intimately connected and entangled with the natural world – is particularly relevant to our use of water. As clean water becomes a scarcer resource worldwide, the social implications will become more widespread. Should systems such as the Murray Darling collapse, or even decline significantly communities within its catchments are unlikely to survive, food production in Australia will be profoundly impacted and ecosystems which currently support a myriad of life both within their boundaries and further afield will experience devastation.

In this context, our relationships with water and our understanding of the social contours of our relationship with water is in need of urgent attention. The good news in relation to the Murray Darling system is that thinking is shifting. Planning and policy focused on cultural as well as environmental flows within the system, although contested, introduce a recognition that water systems communities and cultures are connected (Hartwig et al., 2020; Jackson & Barber, 2013). In debates such as these, both an acknowledgement of historical and ongoing power imbalances and pro-active action to address these are being consistently raised in policy, commentary and research as baselines for future action. Here the work of social justice and social justice practitioners including social workers is critical. Lukasiewicz and Baldwin (2017) argue that attention to distributive, procedural and interactive social justice is essential in all water planning with diverse public participation at the centre of the process. Using two case studies – one from the upper end of the Murray Darling system on Queensland and the other much further downstream in south west NSW, these researchers analysed the water planning process against their social justice framework. They found that participation and decision-making processes drew only on historical ownership of water licences (gained largely by irrigators in the past resulting in a context favouring corporate interests) which effectively excluded a wide range of other participants from graziers and croppers to Aboriginal communities to the wider public and through to the environment. Utilising the social justice framework both revealed the often-hidden structural biases and exclusions in water planning in this system and provided guidance for developing a much more participatory and transparent process which includes all interests rather than those with established power. In a similar way, Hartwig and colleagues (2020) apply a social justice analysis of Aboriginal water rights in the Murray Darling Basin to highlight the ways in which neo-liberal marketisation of water in this system, while purporting to create better water management and access, served to entrench existing power imbalances and exclude Aboriginal organisations who had not historically been able to access water licenses. As Hartwig and colleagues conclude:

> our results demonstrate the limits of government approaches that focus on Indigenous consultation and engagement and ignore more substantive redistributive programs or law reform.
>
> *(p.11)*

As with both food and energy systems, there is work for those of us in social work and human services at both a policy and practice level in applying a social justice analysis to questions of water planning, in advocating for and being involved in the application of social justice approaches at a community and broader level in this area and in working alongside groups and communities currently excluded from the planning process. This work requires us to broaden our frame for social justice work and to locate this work in a social, cultural and ecological system rather than one framed only by narrow social concerns.

In this chapter, we have sought to highlight the impact of climate change on the basics of life: food; energy and water. If we do not act for change, we face a future of irreparable damage to Mother Earth. In the next chapter, we turn our attention to supporting action for change.

References

Abel, N., Wise, R. M., Colloff, M. J., Walker, B. H., Butler, J. R. A., Ryan, P., Norman, C., Langston, A., Anderies, J. M., Gorddard, R., Dunlop, M., & O'Connell, D. (2016). Building resilient pathways to transformation when "no one is in charge": Insights from Australia's murray-darling basin. *Ecology and Society*, *21*(2), 23. https://doi.org/10.5751/ES-08422-210223

Alkon, A. H., Cadji, Y. J., & Moore, F. (2019). Subverting the new narrative: Food, gentrification and resistance in Oakland, California. *Agriculture and Human Values*, *36*(4), 793–804. https://doi.org/10.1007/s10460-019-09954-x

Allam, L. (2019, January 2019). *Walgett's water crisis: NSW considers options after 'concerning' sodium levels found*. The Guardian. https://www.theguardian.com/australia-news/2019/jan/22/walgetts-water-crisis-nsw-considers-options-after-concerning-sodium-levels-found

Allen, P. (2010). Realizing justice in local food systems. *Cambridge Journal of Regions, Economy and Society*, *3*(2), 295–308. https://doi.org/10.1093/cjres/rsq015

Australian Association of Environmental Education NSW [AAEENSW]. (2022). Write it up! Sustainability education case study – Youth LEAD: From little things, big things grow. https://www.aaeensw.org.au/sites/aaeensw/files/pages/files/youthlead.pdf

Baird, A., Walters, R., & White, R. (2021). Water theft maleficence in Australia. *International Journal for Crime, Justice and Social Democracy*, *10*(1), 83–97. https://doi.org/10.5204/ijcjsd.v10i1.1604

Beresford, Q. (2021). *Wounded country: The murray-darling basin: A contested history*. NewSouth Publishing.

Blake, M. K. (2019). More than just food: Food insecurity and resilient place making through community self-organising. *Sustainability*, *11*(10), 2942. https://doi.org/10.3390/su11102942

Booth, S. (2014). Food banks in Australia: Discouraging the right to food. In G. Riches & T. Silvasti (Eds.), *First world hunger revisited: Food charity or the right to food?* (2nd ed.). Palgrave Macmillan UK. https://doi.org/10.1057/9781137298737

Bureau of Meteorology [BOM]. (2022). Previous droughts. http://www.bom.gov.au/climate/drought/knowledge-centre/previous-droughts.shtml

Cameron, J., & Hicks, J. (2014). Performative research for a climate politics of hope: Rethinking geographic scale, "impact" scale, and markets. *Antipode*, *46*(1), 53–71. https://doi.org/10.1111/anti.12035

Clarke, T. (2022, March 10). *Lismore transformed into 'warzone' as political bickering, gridlocked bureaucracy leaves flood-ravaged town repeating history*. Sky News Online. https://www.skynews.com.au/australia-news/lismore-transformed-into-warzone-as-political-bickering-gridlocked-bureaucracy-leaves-floodravaged-town-repeating-history/news-story/7bed16b645e2d2992608692d2b946450

Commonwealth of Australia. (2010). Working together to close the gap in Walgett: Remote service delivery local implementation plan. *Department of Social Services*. https://www.dss.gov.au/sites/default/files/documents/05_2012/walgett_lip.pdf

Commonwealth Scientific and Industrial Research Organisation [CSIRO]. (2021, May 13). *Australia installs record-breaking number of rooftop panels* [Press release]. https://www.csiro.au/en/news/news-releases/2021/australia-installs-record-breaking-number-of-rooftop-solar-panels

Coulson, H., & Milbourne, P. (2020). Food justice for all? Searching for the "justice multiple" in UK food movements. *Agriculture and Human Values*, *38*(1), 43–58. https://doi.org/10.1007/s10460-020-10142-5

Creamer, E., Taylor Aiken, G., van Veelen, B., Walker, G., & Devine-Wright, P. (2019). Community renewable energy: What does it do? Walker and Devine-Wright (2008) ten years on. *Energy Research & Social Science*, *57*, 101223. https://doi.org/10.1016/j.erss.2019.101223

Dean, A. J., Fielding, K. S., Ross, H., & Newton, F. (2016). *Community engagement in the water sector: An outcome-focused review of different engagement approaches.* Cooperative Research Centre for Water Sensitive Cities. https://watersensitivecities.org.au/wp-content/uploads/2016/05/TMR_A2-3_CommunityEngagementWaterSector-1.pdf

De Bernardi, P., Bertello, A., & Venuti, F. (2019). Online and on-site interactions within alternative food networks: Sustainability impact of knowledge-sharing practices. *Sustainability*, *11*(5), 1457. https://doi.org/10.3390/su11051457

Delgado, M., & Delgado, M. (2013). *Social justice and the urban obesity crisis: Implications for social work.* Columbia University Press. https://doi.org/10.7312/delg16008

Fitzsimons, D. (2019, January 7). *Bottling generosity: People bring gifts of water to help quench dry, drought-hit Walgett*, The Daily Liberal. https://www.dailyliberal.com.au/story/5839535/gifts-of-water-for-dry-walgett/

Fortier, M.-O. P., Teron, L., Reames, T. G., Munardy, D. T., & Sullivan, B. M. (2019). Introduction to evaluating energy justice across the life cycle: A social life cycle assessment approach. *Applied Energy*, *236*, 211–219. https://doi.org/10.1016/j.apenergy.2018.11.022

Fraser, N., & Honneth, A. (2003). *Redistribution or recognition? A political-philosophical exchange.* Verso.

Fraser, D., & MacRae, A. M. (2011). Four types of activities that affect animals: Implications for animal welfare science and animal ethics philosophy. *Animal Welfare*, *20*(4), 581–590.

Garnaut, R. (2019). Australia can be a superpower in a low-carbon world economy. *2019: Weathering the 'perfect storm' – Addressing the agriculture, energy, water, climate change nexus, 12–13 August 2019.* Crawford Fund. https://econpapers.repec.org/paper/agscfcp19/301970.htm

Gates, B. (2021). *How to avoid a climate disaster: The solutions we have and the breakthroughs we need.* Random House Large Print.

Goedkoop, F., & Devine-Wright, P. (2016). Partnership or placation? The role of trust and justice in the shared ownership of renewable energy projects. *Energy Research & Social Science*, *17*, 135–146. https://doi.org/10.1016/j.erss.2016.04.021

Greater Sydney Landcare. (2022). *Streamwatch.* Retrieved April 8, 2022, from https://greatersydneylandcare.org/streamwatch

Hamilton, S., & Kells, S. (2021). *Sold down the river: How robber barons and Wall Street traders cornered Australia's water market.* Text Publishing Co. ISBN: 9781922458124

Hartwig, L., Jackson, S., & Osborne, N. (2020). Trends in aboriginal water ownership in New South Wales, Australia: The continuities between colonial and neoliberal forms of dispossession. *Land Use Policy*, *99*, 104869. https://doi.org/10.1016/j.landusepol.2020.104869

Hasanov, M., Zuidema, C., & Horlings, L. G. (2019). Exploring the role of community self-organisation in the creation and creative dissolution of a community food initiative. *Sustainability*, *11*(11), 3170. https://doi.org/10.3390/su11113170

Hicks. J. (2020). Generating conditions of strong social support for wind power: Insights from community-owned wind energy projects. *Australasian Journal of Environmental Management*, *27*(2), 137–155. https://doi.org/10.1080/14486563.2020.1758807

Hicks, J., & Ison, N. (2018). An exploration of the boundaries of "community" in community renewable energy projects: Navigating between motivations and context. *Energy Policy*, *113*, 523–534. https://doi.org/10.1016/j.enpol.2017.10.031

Jackson, S., & Barber, M. (2013). Recognition of indigenous water values in Australia's Northern territory: Current progress and ongoing challenges for social justice in water planning. *Planning Theory & Practice, 14*(4), 435–454. https://doi.org/10.1080/14649357.2013.845684

James, S. W. (2016). Beyond "local" food: How supermarkets and consumer choice affect the economic viability of small-scale family farms in Sydney, Australia. *Area, 48*(1), 103–110. https://doi.org/10.1111/area.12243

Kiem, A. S. (2013). Drought and water policy in Australia: Challenges for the future illustrated by the issues associated with water trading and climate change adaptation in the Murray–Darling Basin. *Global Environmental Change, 23*(6), 1615–1626. https://doi.org/10.1016/j.gloenvcha.2013.09.006

Kunze, C., & Becker, S. (2015). Collective ownership in renewable energy and opportunities for sustainable degrowth. *Sustainability Science, 10*(3), 425–437. https://doi.org/10.1007/s11625-015-0301-0

Levenda, A. M., Behrsin, I., & Disano, F. (2021). Renewable energy for whom? A global systematic review of the environmental justice implications of renewable energy technologies. *Energy Research & Social Science, 71*, 101837. https://doi.org/10.1016/j.erss.2020.101837

Lukasiewicz, A., & Baldwin, C. (2017). Voice, power, and history: Ensuring social justice for all stakeholders in water decision-making. *Local Environment, 22*(9), 1042–1060. https://doi.org/10.1080/13549839.2014.942261

Lukasiewicz, A., Bowmer, K., Syme, G. J., & Davidson, P. (2013). Assessing government intentions for Australian water reform using a social justice framework. *Society and Natural Resources, 26*(11), 1314–1329. https://doi.org/10.1080/08941920.2013.791903

Martiskainen, M. (2017). The role of community leadership in the development of grassroots innovations. *Environmental Innovation and Societal Transitions, 22*, 78–89. https://doi.org/10.1016/j.eist.2016.05.002

McCauley, D. (2017). Energy justice: Re-balancing the trilemma of security, poverty and climate change. Palgrave Macmillan. https://doi.org/10.1007/978-3-319-62494-5

Mercer, D., Christesen, L., & Buxton, M. (2007). Squandering the future—Climate change, policy failure and the water crisis in Australia. *Futures: The Journal of Policy, Planning and Futures Studies, 39*(2–3), 272–287. https://doi.org/10.1016/j.futures.2006.01.009

Migliore, G., Forno, F., Guccione, G. D., & Schifani, G. (2014). Food community networks as sustainable self-organized collective action: A case study of a solidarity purchasing group. *New Medit, 13*(4), 54–62.

Murray Darling Basin Authority. (2020). *Why the environment needs water.* Australian Government.https://www.mdba.gov.au/issues-murray-darling-basin/water-for-environment/why-we-need-water-environment

NSW Waterwatch. (2016). *About waterwatch.* Retrieved April 10, 2022, from https://www.nswwaterwatch.org.au

Page, G., Ridoutt, B., & Bellotti, B. (2011). Fresh tomato production for the Sydney market: An evaluation of options to reduce freshwater scarcity from agricultural water use. *Agricultural Water Management, 100*(1), 18–24. https://doi.org/10.1016/j.agwat.2011.08.017

Picchioni, F., Po, J. Y. T., & Forsythe, L. (2021). Strengthening resilience in response to COVID-19: A call to integrate social reproduction in sustainable food systems. *Canadian Journal of Development Studies, 42*(1–2), 28–36. https://doi.org/10.1080/02255189.2020.1858761

Rose, N. (2017). Community food hubs: An economic and social justice model for regional Australia? *Rural Society, 26*(3), 225–237. https://doi.org/10.1080/10371656.2017.1364482

Russell, C., Lawrence, M., Cullerton, K., & Baker, P. (2020). The political construction of public health nutrition problems: A framing analysis of parliamentary debates on junk-food marketing to children in Australia. *Public Health Nutrition, 23*(11), 2041–2052. https://doi.org/10.1017/S1368980019003628

Seyfang, G., & Longhurst, N. (2013). Desperately seeking niches: Grassroots innovations and niche development in the community currency field. *Global Environmental Change, 23*(5), 881–891.

Smith, A., Hargreaves, T., Hielscher, S., Martiskainen, M., & Seyfang, G. (2016). Making the most of community energies: Three perspectives on grassroots innovation. *Environment and Planning A, 48*(2), 407–432. https://doi.org/10.1177/0308518X15597908

Strengers, Y., Maller, C., Nicholls, L., & Pink, S. (2014, January 2). Australia's rising air con use makes us hot and bothered. *The Conversation*. https://theconversation.com/australias-rising-air-con-use-makes-us-hot-and-bothered-20258#:~:text=Three%20out%20of%20every%20four%20of%20Australian%20households, that%20the%20cost%20of%20running%20them%20is%20rising

Szymanski, I. F. (2016). What is food? Networks, not commodities. In M. C. Rawlinson & C. Ward, C. (Eds.), *The Routledge handbook of food ethics*. Routledge. https://doi.org/10.4324/9781315745503

Tamlin, S. (2019, November 8). *How people are resolving to reduce water scarcity*. WaterLogic. https://www.waterlogicaustralia.com.au/resources/blog/how-people-are-resolving-to-reduce-water-scarcity

van Veelen, B., & Haggett, C. (2017). Uncommon ground: The role of different place attachments in explaining community renewable energy projects. *Sociologia Ruralis, 57*(S1), 533–554. https://doi.org/10.1111/soru.12128

von Redecker, S., & Herzig, C. (2020). The peasant way of a more than radical democracy: The case of La Via Campesina. *Journal of Business Ethics, 164*(4), 657–670. https://doi.org/10.1007/s10551-019-04402-6

Werkheiser, I. (2016). Individual and community identities in food sovereignty: The possibilities and pitfalls of translating a rural social movement. In M. C. Rawlinson & C. Ward, C. (Eds.), *The Routledge handbook of food ethics*. Routledge. https://doi.org/10.4324/9781315745503

Wheeler, S., Zuo, A., & Bjornlund, H. (2013). Farmers' climate change beliefs and adaptation strategies for a water scarce future in Australia. *Global Environmental Change, 23*(2), 537–547. https://doi.org/10.1016/j.gloenvcha.2012.11.008

6

ACTING FOR CHANGE

In this and the following two chapters, we shift our focus to acting for change. Whilst we present different 'sites' of action we are aware of the interconnected, dynamic and emergent networks that shape these sites. Thinking about this question demands we think about power in responding to climate change. What is the capacity of the different actors (governments, industry, communities and individuals) to contribute to climate justice? Three 'sites' of change are explored: the local (homes, offices and neighbourhoods); the collective (self-organising systems); and the State (policy). As community development scholars, we are very interested in how social work and human service practice can support social change. Accordingly, in the first section of this chapter, we revisit some of our emerging thinking on useful practice in the context of climate change. We also draw attention to the ways in which acting without a critical analysis of complex power serves largely to reproduce and reinforce existing social and economic inequality.

Community development practice and climate change

Social work scholars have been researching, writing and thinking about climate change for at least the past decade although mostly at the fringes of mainstream social work (Dominelli, 2011; Holbrook et al., 2019; Santha, 2020). In the main, the 'profession has been relatively silent' on climate justice debates, despite obvious synergies between the purpose of social work and the impact of climate change (Dominelli, 2011, p.430). The challenges presented by climate change again will focus the profession's attention to how it relates to the State, communities and individuals. Climate justice demands that the tensions experienced by the profession with 'radical social change' and community development (Hugman, 2015) must be resolved. For us, this can be resolved through a

DOI: 10.4324/9781003146339-6

positioning of social work not as a profession (with all the accompanying power dynamics) but as a social movement. Like Peeters (2012), we despair that social work and human services are

> limited to the role of 'fire brigade', making impacts more bearable through 'end-of-pipe' solutions. … Social work interventions aimed at influencing the environmental behaviour of (poor) people lack legitimacy if they are not part of a context of social action that makes a difference on a broader scale.
>
> *(pp.106–107)*

It will be of no surprise that we are calling for change driven from below, through participation, through dialogue, though connection to Country and through action. Like Peeters (2012), we are hopeful that social work and human service practice can 'contribute to a great social transition, a systemic change' (p.107). Social work and human service worker identities are shaped and constituted through discourse (Thorpe, 2017). Understanding social work and human services as produced through language and knowledge reminds us of the potential to reshape or reconstitute this 'identity'.

> By internalizing these forms of discourse, the everyday ways of thinking students import with them into their professional training are reconfigured and reconstituted in the ways demanded by the profession. … The forms of knowledge – e.g. social work theory, sociology, psychology and so on – construct the category – i.e. 'social worker' – that the people – i.e. 'social work students' – within the discourse come to internalize.
>
> *(Thorpe, 2017, p.97)*

For social work and human service practitioners, climate justice creates some profound challenges as some of our 'go to' strategies may actually work *against* action. A stock in trade approach – influence through communicating information – appears to be having little effect. For some knowing and talking about the science of climate change is an important element of a social work and human services response (Dominelli, 2011; Holbrook et al., 2019; Naranjo, 2020). A 'facts and figures' approach based on scientific knowledge has, as noted earlier, had very limited success in engaging people about climate change (Huntley, 2020). The bombardment of predictions and dire warnings perversely have left many feeling bored and unwilling to listen (let alone act) (Huntley, 2020). Inertia is the worst possible outcome of education on the need for climate action. Another stock in trade approach is case work or individual work – again this is likely to be of limited value. The gradual narrowing of social and human services is unsurprising in the context of neo-liberalism's 'individual choice' mantra. Whilst individually we are able to play a part in climate action, we need to resist being held responsible, allowing the market and the state to disappear from view. Climate justice demands we 'lift our gaze' beyond individuals to the networks through which action is possible. Environmental concerns cannot become just another 'target area' but action for climate justice must underpin all our practices: where we work; how we work; how decisions are made; and how we measure 'success'.

Although it may seem quaintly old fashioned, slogans such as 'the personal is political' and 'act local, think global' may provide some useful directions. There is much to learn from history and the development of 'human services' in the 1970s and 1980s. Non-hierarchical structures developed to enact commitments to equality; some groups of workers allocated a percentage of their wages to social justice outcomes (such as 'paying the rent' to First Nations people); equity was built into wage payments; time was allocated to conscious raising and dialogue; and coalitions were formed across gender, class and cultural differences. As we write this, we are aware of how completely neo-liberalism has quashed these social justice aspirations: they seem so naïve and unsophisticated. We are suggesting that as a form of resistance social and human service workers explore how their personal concerns for climate justice impacts on their practice. As an antidote to the despair of 'facts and figures' we offer an understanding of change that understands history as

> a thickly woven rope, comprising billions of individual threads. Each thread represents an individual story line, but they're so densely braided it's impossible to label any specific era, or predict what's coming next. The combinations aren't random; some patterns seem to come up again and again, but the vast, tangled mass prevents easy characterization.
>
> *(Future Crunch, 2022)*

Some useful conceptual tools

We have written extensively elsewhere about community development practice (see for example Everyday Community Practice; Working with Communities; and Rural Social Work). Whilst we don't want to rehash these ideas in this book, we would like to highlight some specific ideas that we believe will support effective social work and human service practice in supporting action on climate change. In engaging with climate action through a social work lens new insights have also emerged which we lay out here. Climate, our relationship to Mother Earth and action on climate change are interconnected, dynamic, emergent, non-linear and adaptable. It is this complexity that provides both a sense of powerlessness and a sense of hope.

Conceptually, there are a number of useful tools for those interested in action for change and climate justice. These arise from different disciplines at different times. Again, we are not claiming they are the only strategies nor that they are applicable in all settings. We offer them as hopeful ideas.

Understandings of power

The concept of power is of central importance to supporting action for change for climate justice. Unpacking the meaning and operation of power is challenging, with many scholars and activists contributing to our thinking. For us though understanding power is only useful when it allows us to *act*. The extent and ramifications of unabated climate change is overwhelming, often creating a sense of powerlessness. Although understanding how power works is central to climate justice there is no consensus on definitions or conceptualisations of power. Generally, we have been influenced by post-modern perspectives on power: that power is produced rather than owned or held; that language and knowledge are conduits for power; that it is fluid and embedded in relationships or networks; and importantly that it is not a finite resource. Thinking about power in this way is important for social justice practice and community development as it allows for change.

Critical consciousness or conscientisation

Many scholars trace the history of community development ideas to Brazilian educator Paulo Freire. Freire saw the core role of educators as helping people 'read their world' through the development of a critical consciousness (or conscientisation in Portuguese, the dominant language of Brazil). A critical consciousness enables people (particularly groups of people) to ask questions about their histories and social position (Ledwith, 2016). It is this questioning and awareness of the world that enables democratic participation. The learning that supports the development of a critical consciousness is very different from the traditional 'banking' model, where the educator deposits knowledge into the student (Ledwith, 2016). Freire advocated for a critical pedagogy as the foundation for change (Ledwith, 2016, p.68) suggesting:

> if we see the world differently we will act differently in the world ....
> Seeing critically leads us to act critically. Empowerment, as a collective process of becoming critical, opens up the possibility of change through collective action.
>
> *(Ledwith, 2016, p.68)*

Shevellar and Westoby (2016) also argue that the act of joining with others is inherently powerful. It moves us from 'stuck-ness' to a position of being more able to influence decisions, to make choices, to belong to something larger than ourselves. We can only act in the world if we understand how we have arrived at this moment and believe we can play a part in shaping the future. This was evident in research with community members who 'bought back their island' in Scotland. For these community members 'putting your head above the parapet' was recognised as requiring great courage (and time) (Rawsthorne, 2009). Adopting a critical pedagogy (Terare, 2019) has also been shown to be vital to (re)connecting with Mother Earth and engaging with First Nations Worldviews (Terare, 2019).

Recognition

In thinking through how we might act locally to support climate justice, the inter-relationships between distributive justice (who is impacted most, who bears the biggest burden for mitigation and adaptation) and recognition (who is visible in relation to climate justice, how do we ensure justice for Mother Earth, which approaches to care are seen as legitimate?) are important for us to work through. Axel Honneth's (1995) theory of recognition is helpful for us here as he uncovers the cultural and symbolic contours of justice which are intertwined with distributive justice and which fundamentally shape the ways in which we experience justice in the everyday. For Honneth, justice could only be achieved when people recognised each other through love (relationships between people), rights (legal frameworks which create equality) and solidarity (collective connections and work together). Distribution of resources was seen by Honneth as important but not sufficient to really deliver justice in a meaningful way. You may know Honneth's theory of recognition through its application when groups and individuals are misrecognised and disrespected through racism, sexism, ableism and other forms of discrimination. In these cases, Honneth argues, people are rendered invisible and assessed as categories or stereotypes making it impossible for them to be recognised fully through the process of love, rights and solidarity necessary for society to operate ethically and justly. Honneth's ideas were taken further by Nancy Fraser (2007), who argued that distribution and recognition were inseparable elements in working on social justice.

Bulkeley et al. (2014) found in their research about operationalising climate action in local urban environments that recognition was useful in drawing attention to the ways in which historical and ongoing disempowerment, structural misrecognition and exclusion of particular groups might explain the reasons for climate justice to be enacted unevenly. The city, for these authors, is seen as a key site of work to address climate change and climate justice. They argue for the importance of recognising the ways in which existing structural inequalities in the urban context play out culturally and socially to better support planning and action on climate change in the city. Their research found that a focus on recognition added an important dimension to frameworks which focus on rights, responsibilities and distributive justice alone. In one example from their study, an emission reduction program was applied using similar tools and approaches across communities based on the premise of individual responsibility for reducing carbon footprints across the city. As the project unfolded very different patterns of engagement and action became apparent which revealed long-running structural exclusion. A lack of recognition of the very different experiences of participants led to an adjustment in approach but revealed that attention only to distributive justice and one size fits all responsibilities, meant that many were automatically excluded from the program as they became misrecognised as irresponsible rather than recognised as structurally excluded.

Paying attention to recognition enables us to look more closely at the detailed contours of climate justice and include cultural and symbolic injustice as key shapers of climate change impacts and just action. They describe justice as being refracted by both politics and practice. Using a pyramid metaphor, they argue that each different facet of climate change action (for them these are distribution, procedure, responsibilities, rights and recognition) is refracted and reshaped by other facets. This metaphor resonates with our ideas of climate change and climate action occurring within complex systems that are interconnected, adaptable, dynamic, non-linear and emergent.

Dadirri (as practice)

Climate change, responsibility and action have been a source of significant argument and even conflict in Australia (Huntley, 2020). Acting for change at any level will draw on social work and human services capacities to

> Navigat[e] collectively through shared conversations and dialogic processes … embark on an enduring journey where diverse actors would mutually learn, innovate and make informed choices to enhance the safety and security of their lived environment.
>
> *(Santha, 2020, p.2)*

Ensuring open dialogue and active exchange allows for positive transformation of ideas and actions (Crampton, 2015). Dadirri is a form of deep inner listening based on mutual respect and willingness to learn (Baumann & Wells, 2007). Listening is not merely using our ears. It is about using our eyes and our hearts. It is about stillness of mind and body. It is about stepping away from the 'expert' position to one of learner, based on cultural humility. We explore and create new understandings through listening. In our work with students and research with communities we are continually surprised how poorly people listen to each other, how quickly pre-existing assumptions come to the fore in shaping understandings. But also, how significant breakthroughs are possible when people actually listen to each other. In a recent project, community members with deep historical suspicion and dislike of each other were pitted against each other for control of resources. One participant (an environmental activist) decided to step outside their assumed role and deeply listen to the concerns of long-term farmers. They were still, gave their full attention, did not mount counter arguments but sought to understand the others perspective. During the pack up after the meeting the farmer commented to that 'I don't believe I'm saying this but that greenie is ok. It's really exciting to think we might be able to do something together for the community'.

A few words of caution: the 'c' word

Before we continue, a few words of caution about the concept of 'community'. 'Communities' can be a useful concept in terms of understanding patterns and groupings across different sectors of society. However, if we are to explore and recognise the role of communities in acting for change, it's important we attempt to begin from a place of shared understanding around the meaning and limitations of the term 'community'. This is easier said than done and requires we unpack and challenge the sometimes-simplistic notion of what constitutes 'community'. Ife (2012) notes the term, while generally having positive connotations, is used in many different contexts and is therefore problematic. Ife (2012) invites us to think about the context or how the person using the term might mean by this. Given climate change and environmental impact affects us all, in shared and different ways, this proves challenging. In the context of this book, we might be tempted to focus on geographical communities, shared industry communities, such as farmers, lobby groups, or Aboriginal and First Nations Communities and apply the consideration to what might seem 'easily defined' communities. While they may be valid representations of 'community' we invite the reader to explore this further. Members of a rural community for example might have shared and divergent interests and needs. Farmers may have a very different view of the issue of water management than First Nations peoples for example. For the purpose of attempting to gain a deeper understanding of 'community' it is important we explore the oppressive and less positive aspects to this overarching concept.

Indigenous researcher, Frances Peters-Little questions the very term 'community' in relation to its use when referring to First Nations Peoples. In her Discussion Paper, *The Community Game: Aboriginal Self-Identification a local level* (2020), Peters-Little questions the commonly held perception that 'community invokes notions of an idealised unity of purpose and action among social groups who are perceived to share a common culture' (p.5). Peters-Little examines the history of development of Aboriginal 'communities' as politically motivated social constructs, and challenges readers to incorporate into their thinking this issue of displacement and the role governments played in formulating concepts of Aboriginal communities.

One example of the need for care in language use is the First Nations land management practices of cultural burns which have received more recognition over the past few years. The re-emergence of traditional burns reflects First Nations Peoples efforts to reconnect and strengthen cultural practices. Whilst the re-emergence of cultural burns practices is an acknowledgment of leadership in relation to land management of First Nations Peoples, these examples are very specific to Traditional Custodians and can look different depending which Country they are located. Therefore, they are not an 'Aboriginal Community' example, but rather the reclamation of practices by the Dja Dja Wurrung peoples, for example.

We would argue that we need to apply this thinking and reflexivity to all imposed or socially constructed communities. This also demands we cast a critical view over research data that is reported as reflecting the 'community' (think here about the Foundations for Tomorrow research quoted above: who *are* the young people in that study?). As researchers interested in 'communities', we are continually vigilant about the very easy slippage into homogenous, harmonious, depictions. This conceptualisation of 'communities' is mobilised in the common 'bottom–up/top down' metaphor used in community development. Bottom-up processes are said to drive 'community' (Gilchrist & Taylor, 2011; Ife, 2012; Shevellar & Westoby, 2016). This is often contrasted to 'top-down' action which signifies decisions imposed from outside the community most often by government. This chapter was, in fact, initially titled 'bottom-up change'. As we wrote this chapter, reflecting on the complexity of change, we moved away from the 'bottom-up/top-down' binary. We were uneasy about portraying change in such simplistic terms as if 'community' is inherently positive and un-riven by power dynamics. And conversely the all-powerful 'State' thought of as above and separate from everyday life. Our work in communities impacted by disasters has demonstrated how unhelpful the metaphor has become, particularly in our work with those working in the emergency services who straddle community and the State. We were also cautious about unintentionally endorsing the neo-liberal individualising of responsibility. In our disaster research, we repeatedly hear the mobilising of 'bottom-up' metaphor in unhelpful, disempowering ways to blame communities.

In this first section of this chapter, we have sought to highlight some important elements of social work and human service practice to support action on climate change. In the remainder of the chapter, we now shift attention to examples of people acting: at home, at the office and with neighbours.

Acting for change as individuals

Poll after poll highlights the concerns of Australians about climate change and the need for action. Research in 2021 found young Australians are calling for urgent action on climate change and a shift to more sustainable economic and social policies (Foundations for Tomorrow, 2021). Consultations with over 10,000 young people undertaken between 12 April and 7 May 2021 found 93% believed the government 'was not doing enough to address climate change' (Foundations for Tomorrow, 2021, p.9). The research collected data from young people via on-line surveys as well as polls on platforms such as Instagram. Among these young people, there was also strong agreement (80%) that the government should make 'accelerating climate change action a key goal of the economic recovery' (2021, p.9). Of particular relevance to any discussion of acting for change was the finding that 53% of young people felt 'government' was most responsible for addressing climate change, far in excess of large-scale enterprises (15%) and individuals (15%) (Foundations for Tomorrow, 2021, p.62). Conversely, when asked who was making the most positive contribution to action on climate change the research participants identified: not-for-profit organisations (35%); individuals (28%); companies (17%); Federal government (7%); political parties (7%); State government (5%); and Local government (1%) (Foundations for Tomorrow, 2021, p.64). Leanne Smith, Director of the Whitlam Institute sums up the frustration of government in-action identified by the research:

> In this country, the realm of policy has traditionally been a government realm… However, other sectors of society, particularly business and civil society, are beginning to play a much stronger leadership role on a range of policy areas that should be the remit of the government. I think that if government wants to stay in the driving seat when it comes to policy, they're going to actually need to lead, otherwise, others will take the reins.
>
> *(Foundations for Tomorrow, 2021, p.69)*

An Essential Poll commissioned by The Guardian in the lead-up to the COP26 talks in Glasgow (Murphy, 2021) found 68% of those surveyed supported more ambitious emission reduction targets for 2030 and net-zero by 2050. As we have seen repeatedly over the past decade, public opinion does not always lead to policy action. Whilst there were differences by political voting preferences, these were less than is evident in the Federal Parliament which continues to be racked by dissent over climate policy. The survey found that 30% of those surveyed believed 'we are just witnessing normal fluctuations in the earth's climate'. Drawing on ideas of community organising (Walls, 2015), it is this sizeable minority that climate activists must engage with and seek to better understand if we are to achieve inclusive social change.

For those of us who accept the earth's climate is changing due to human action, the urgency of acting can leave us overwhelmed by existential alarm: How do we act? Who can act? When? As we have argued earlier, in this book, we hope to lay out some theoretical ideas that might assist us working through this existential alarm. We wish to challenge the binary of 'government' and 'the individual' as sites of action, instead drawing on complexity theories to lay out a more hopeful future. In exploring acting for change, we accept

> that the signals for disaster are everywhere we look, and so are endless examples of human progress, environmental stewardship, ecological restoration and extraordinary acts of kindness, all densely entwined.
>
> *(Future Crunch, 2022)*

Returning to the insights of Freire, people must first have an understanding of the broader structures that shape their experiences, to *act*. Here we use housing (or more correctly shelter) as an example to demonstrate the relevance of Freire's ideas to action on climate change. As a society, we make decisions about how the need for shelter is met through policies, including subsidies and taxation. If we are asking people to change the way we meet this human need they firstly need to be aware of the structures that shape 'housing choice'. These might be how the profit motive inherent in capitalism influence land use decisions that limit individual choices in relation to housing. And how a smokescreen of 'consumer choice' is used to hide the lack of choice in housing options. In a just and sustainable world, it is unlikely housing options such as those in outer urban fringes of Australian capital cities would be built. This housing often has a very large footprint, with little yard space; pre-development tree cover is removed to facilitate construction; this shelter consumes large amounts of energy to heat and cool; has poor access to public amenities which are often centralised at some distance from neighbourhoods; and demands large commutes for employment. This 'Australian Dream' is sold as the 'only' way into the housing market, locking families into unjust and unsustainable housing options for decades to come. A/Professor Wendy Steele, urban planning at RMIT, argues that more than 80% of Australians live in middle or outer suburbia which can be 'very alienating' and 'homogenous' (Scopelianos & Crothers, 2019). Individualising the responsibility for these housing options obscures the political, economic and social factors that drive these choices. It also obscures the part played by the 'housing market' in embedding spatial inequality in modern cities. Here, the ideas of Freire (and those influenced by his thinking) provide optimism for change through the development of critical consciousness to see the world with all its contradictions (Ledwith, 2016, pp.41–42). Through a critical pedagogy, Freire demonstrates a process that 'creates the context for people to question their everyday experiences' (p.42).

> The purpose of this is to look beyond what we unquestioningly accept and take for granted in everyday life. Seeing situations with fresh eyes lifts the blinkers: we see the contradictions of life that are unjust.
>
> *(Ledwith, 2016, p.2)*

Until people are able to see the contradictions of life that have resulted in climate change any transformation is likely to be shallow and unsustainable (Ledwith, 2016). It is not enough, returning to the housing example above, to build housing on the urban fringes with solar panels, although this is likely to have some minimal benefits. Sustainable change is more likely to arise from asking far more fundamental questions about shelter and its relationship with Mother Earth. For Freire, it is the act of asking these questions that is vital rather than moving quickly to the answer or solution or the 'fix'. Aboriginal Worldviews likewise disrupt assumptions about the 'only way' of 'solving' our need for housing, reminding us also that our right to shelter does not nor should not overrule the rights of other creatures (trees, waterways, animals and birds) to Mother Earth.

An awareness of how structural forces shape our experiences is thus the starting point for action for climate justice. Action in conjunction with others however transforms this awareness into the power to effect change. Our experience suggests that bringing about climate justice will be enhanced through collective action. This working together can be at a wide range of settings: it can be at the household level; the neighbourhood level; the suburb level; the city level; the national level or the international level. It is our argument that due to the complexity of the factors that contribute to climate change we cannot know in advance which action is likely to have the most profound impact. In fact, we would urge resistance to seeking out the quick response with the 'greatest impact'. Drawing again on Aboriginal Worldviews, working together over time, building trust, listening deeply and acting slowly are the foundations of working together for change.

We want also to distinguish 'critical consciousness' from 'resilience'. The discourse of disaster resilience has emerged globally over the past two decades as a way of explaining, exhorting and planning for individuals to 'bounce back', 'bounce forward' or at least recover from a range of extreme weather events and other disasters. These calls for 'resilience' have become louder with the increasing regularity of disasters in countries such as Australia (where fire, flood and drought have been regular events over time) and with sudden extreme impact in Europe and Canada (where extreme heat, fire and flooding are being experienced to an unprecedented degree). As people interested in climate justice, however, we need to carefully examine these demands for 'resilience' which are shaped by neo-liberalism tendencies to heighten individual responsibility (Jolly, 2020). An increasing critique of resilience in policy and practice is focused on the individualised way in which the idea has been framed, diverting responsibility from institutional structures and processes to communities and community members who are framed as responsible for their own resilience. (Atkinson & Curnin, 2020; Crosweller & Tschakert, 2021). Our research (Rawsthorne et al., 2020) with social housing tenants living in high-rise complexes in Inner Sydney highlighted the social and economic inequality commonly overlooked by resilience strategies such as 'Go Bags' (having everything one might need in an emergency always packed):

> They were big on the Go Bags; that you'd have this bag ready so that you're ready to go in an emergency. It did relate more to what people would experience here, because there are a lot of elderly people with health problems. But then again, it didn't have a big understanding of how a lot of people who live here, would live. A lot of people here are on Newstart. They don't have the extra funding to have spare kind of toiletries and things in a bag, ready to go. It wouldn't happen. Or if it did happen, they wouldn't stay there, then they'd be needed. These are people living 100 kilometres below the poverty line.
>
> *(Resident)*

This focus on individual responsibility diverted attention from institutional responsibility. Despite repeated requests from residents and advocacy groups

Housing NSW (the landlord for these tenants) and Fire & Rescue (the relevant Emergency Management Service) refused to lead an evacuation drill of the buildings. Evacuation drills are not required under current legislation in residential high rise. Housing NSW responsibility for placing frail aged tenants with poor mobility on upper floors is also obscured by the focus on individual responsibility. There is little doubt that an evacuation drill, if it occurred, would have highlighted significant challenges facing residents and Emergency Management agencies in moving people out of the buildings in the event of a disaster such as the Grenfell Towers fires in the UK. A failed drill would have created implied responsibility to address the issues that emerged: better not to know. We are not arguing here that all responsibility and power lies with institutions: what we are trying to highlight is the way in which responsibility is subtly shifted away from institutions to individuals through the discourse of 'resilience', with its origins in psychology. Researchers have drawn attention to the ways in which adopting resilience strategies without an analysis of power serves largely to reproduce and reinforce existing social and economic inequality (Ensor et al., 2018).

In the remainder of this chapter, we turn our attention to what we can do as individuals in our everyday lives, in our workplaces and in our neighbourhoods. These ideas are offered with the understanding that small acts are the basis of large change.

At home

The decisions we make in our everyday lives matter to climate change. Australians led the world in the uptake of solar power in homes, creating change in the energy system. Fraser and MacRae(2011) remind us in relation to animal justice

> A key issue will be to make ethical decisions about actions such as driving cars and using paper that may seem innocuous when done by individuals but cause vast harm to animals when done by billions of people.
>
> *(2011, p.585)*

There are hundreds of organisations popping up around the globe providing advice and support for those wishing to act at home for climate change. One of the latest, emerging in the UK, is called The Jump (https://takethejump.org/about) which advocates for 'less stuff and more joy' enabling humans to be in balance with nature (Take the Jump, 2022). A grassroots organisation, they challenge citizens to 'Take the Jump' in our own lives, in a staged way (1, 3 or 6 months). They identify six 'steps' for those of us who live in advanced economies that would lower emissions:

1   Keep electronic products – smartphones, personal computers, smartwatches and TVs – for at least 7 years
2   Get rid of private vehicles (unless absolutely necessary)

3 Limit clothes purchases to three per year (ideally ones that are durable and will last); buy second hand, repair or adjust existing items
4 Making three changes to our diet would dramatically reduce the impact of the food we eat:
   • Move to a mostly plant-based diet.
   • Eat everything you buy.
   • Eat healthy amounts.
5 Reduce air travel committing to one short-haul return flight every 3 years or one long-haul flight every 8 years
6 Change the system through actions such as
   • Changing to a green energy supplier.
   • For those who can afford it, installing energy efficiency measures at home such as insulation and heat pumps.
   • Switching your superannuation to a green investor.
   • Using ethical and green banks.
   • Using energy efficiently at home.
   • Pushing for change through activism or peaceful protest or writing to your MP (Taylor, 2022).

Others such as Dave Goulson, a professor of biology at the University of Sussex advocate for action in our gardens. Professor Goulson laments the 'alarming rates' at which insects are disappearing from the Earth they have played a vital role in for 400 million years. In Germany, there has been a 76% decline of flying insects over the past 26 years, in the UK 13 bee species have gone extinct and in the US, the monarch butterfly has declined 80% since the 1980s) (Goulson, 2021). Like many of the changes we are witnessing to Mother Earth there is no simple, single, cause (or solution) for the loss of insect life. How we live and how we grow food are critically important though: insects have lost habitat from intensive farming, housing and development; have been collateral damage from the 'blizzard of pesticides' we use; have suffered the effects of invasive species due to disturbance of ecological systems and are feeling the impact of global warming. In a dire warning Goulson argues:

> Our tidy, pesticide-infused world is hostile to most insect life, save for the toughest, most adaptable species, such as cockroaches, mosquitoes and houseflies.

In the face of such a desperate and distressing future, how do we act? Do not despair, Goulson implores. Even the smallest space can help insects thrive and rebalance the ecological system; a single marjoram pot plant will bloom attracting bees, butterflies and hoverflies. In our private gardens, we can create sanctuaries for insects, we can lobby our local government to cease the use of pesticide creating 'swathes of wildflowers' and through our food behaviour (buying local, seasonal, organic produce, buying loose fruit and vegetables and reducing our meat consumption) reduce the need for intensive farming (Goulson, 2021).

Herring et al. (2013) argue that educating yourself is the first step to repairing the damage of colonisation. We draw on this to argue that this education needs to include educating ourselves about the Country we live and work on, that we take time to notice the other creatures that we share with, that we seek to understand how the land has nurtured First Nations peoples, that we take responsibility for caring for this place and demonstrate reciprocity to Mother Earth in our day to day lives.

At the office

Environmental concerns cannot become just another 'target area' but action for climate justice must underpin all our practices: where we work; how we work; how decisions are made; and how we measure 'success'. We are suggesting here that social and human service workers explore how their personal concerns for climate justice impact on their workplaces. A useful starting point may be to undertake an Environment Audit of the office. Groups such as CitySwitch Green Office (https://cityswitch.net.au/Resources) provide resources to support you 'do it yourself'. Alternatively, you could partner with a university to offer a placement for a student studying sustainability. However you approach the audit, this data will provide specific strategies for reducing your office climate footprint. This can be small actions such as reflecting on their workplace energy use, consumption choices and recycling. Reducing consumption of paper, using recycled paper on both sides and recycling toners are all achievable steps at work. Increasingly offices are moving away from plastics, providing cups, cutlery and dishwashers. It can be larger actions such as actively participating in local climate action with schools, councils and environment groups. Applying analytical mapping skills to local issues will quickly identify climate-related challenges affecting the community in which you work, be it waste management, waterway restoration or heat sinks. In the next chapter, we discuss in detail the possibilities created through collective action.

Placed-based organisations are increasingly being recognised as key resources in responding to climate-related disasters (Park & Yoon, 2022). In our research, we have seen NGOs playing important roles in each stage of disasters, from preparedness to response to recovery. It seems likely that this trend will continue and, for these agencies, expectations will grow that being engaged in climate change at the local level will become core business. In one community impacted by regular disasters the organisational decision to install solar power (with assistance from government subsidies) had very unexpected benefits:

> [The] main centre is now kind of self-sufficient for energy – we've got water tanks installed and we have a big power ball battery there, if for example in the event of a fire or a flood, and the poles and wires go down but our solar panels are okay, we are now kind of – I think we're registered as a safe place in the event of like a blackout or a storm surge or what have you.

>So what that means is the local community can come to our main cen-
>tre and we'll still have power on, so people can make phone calls, they
>can – we've got a pantry with blankets and food and nappies and things
>like that, so families could come to our centre for shelter. We could feed
>people for a couple of nights if necessary. And we would hopefully have
>power on.
>
>*(Community worker)*

Holbrook and colleagues (2019) illustrate how a commitment to climate justice in our work may play out at the micro, meso and macro levels of practice. For example, supporting low-income people impacted by heat could include providing information about ways to passively reduce heat infiltration of their apartment (keeping windows closed during hottest times of days, closing shades on sunny windows during the day, improving sealing around windows and doors), low-cost ways to cool (strategic placement of fans, adjusting direction of ceiling fans) and connection to community resources such as energy assistance, community cool places or any local programs (Holbrook et al., 2019, p.957).

Contributing to 'a great social transition' invites us to consider our work as social work educators and researchers (Holbrook et al., 2019; Naranjo, 2020). As educators, rather than teaching about boundaries, we can teach about connection. Rather than keeping a 'professional distance' from our 'clients' we can demand students walk with others they share the world with, both human and non-human. In this way we disrupt the power and privilege of the 'profession' and tap into the desire that brings many people to the field in the first place: to work with people, to make social change and to make a difference. Rather than positioning these ideals as naïve and childlike requiring abandonment in 'becoming professional', education could focus on harnessing these ideals and building social change skills and capacities.

With our neighbourhoods

The local or neighbourhood level is an important site for social action and change (Howard & Rawsthorne, 2019; Vinson & Rawsthorne, 2013). There are many, many examples of local communities connecting together. One grassroot group, Climate for Change (2022), deliberately focuses on conversations as a tool for change adapting the Tupperware party-plan model to support meaningful discussions among people with pre-existing relationships. Climate for Change (2022) argue that action is enabled through conversations with people we know and trust. People can either participate in Climate Conversations as a guest or become a host of conversations. An evaluation of the Program by the Global Consulting Group found that over 7,500 people participated in conversations in 3 years; 58% had not previously engaged with environmental organisations; most left feeling more empowered and committed to acting for change. The evaluation of Climate Conversations found they are a unique organising tool within the climate movement. It demonstrates the ability of our Climate Conversation model to reach new audiences that other environmental organisations have historically found challenging to tap into, including the "wavering middle". Most importantly, this evaluation showed the ability for this organising tool to build the capacity of the climate movement as a whole.

(Climate for Change, 2022)

A long way away from middle class Australian suburbs, another example of neighbourhood level action is evident in the actions of Citizens' Groups in the *ger* districts of Ulaanbaatar, Mongolia (Terbish & Rawsthorne, 2020). Mongolia is a vast landlocked country in East Asia with a unique ecosystem and culture that are 'highly vulnerable to climate change risks' (World Bank, 2021). Blizzards and extreme weather known locally as 'dzud' have decimated herds forcing many nomadic herders to shift to the capital city Ulanbataar looking for work and education opportunities (Terbish & Rawsthorne, 2020). Conversely, Mongolia has endured some of the world's fastest rates of historical climate warming of over 2°C and declines in rainfall reported between 1940 and 2015 (World Bank, 2021). Without significant action on climate change, Mongolia faces a grim future with the possibility of a 5°C increase by the end of the century, increased climate-driven hazards including heat wave, drought and river flood (World Bank, 2021). Rapid urbanisation has seen the growth of urban fringe 'ger' districts (named after the traditional felt dwellings) with limited physical infrastructure. Ger districts are now home to about 60% of Ulaanbaatar's population with limited access to roads, electricity and water. Some ger areas are located in riverbanks or known flood-prone lands.

In the absence of government and institutional investment in the ger districts, Citizens' Groups have emerged, often with a strong focus on addressing environmental problems. Citizens' Groups have been involved in planting trees, removing rubbish, stabilising land through road and footpath construction (Terbish & Rawsthorne, 2020). They have also driven the construction of water wells, scattered throughout the ger districts and often shared by dozens of families. The experience of Citizens' Groups does however provide a stark example of how individuals are able to respond differently to climate change due to the power they hold in society and where they are situated in accessing resources. Tuya, a Citizens' Group leader, told researchers how her Citizens' Group received an international grant to establish an additional water well in their local area but when this needed repair the horoo (local government) cut the power to the well and fenced it off to prevent it being fixed by the Citizen's Group. In this example, community action was stymied by government, potentially corruptly, as it was in competition with the for-profit water providers operating in the ger districts. She wryly noted '*water is money in the gers*'.

The activities of groups such as the Citizens' Groups in Mongolia illustrate how local community action can link up to a broader climate change agenda. The very particular histories, cultural threads, social and environmental contexts for this kind of collective action, however, need to be recognised. We need to guard against the temptation of transplanting knowledge from one context in a cookie cutter style. Locally emerging new ideas are often morphed into franchises unintentionally. The danger here is that the particular contours of diverse community contexts can be unintentionally driven over or sidelined in favour of the large-scale agenda. Ideas for collective action which have been successful where they grew, fail to survive being transplanted into contexts where things are very different.

Research by Marta Kolářová (2020) on the take up of Transitions Towns in the Czech Republic highlights this danger of 'rolling out' initiatives across communities. The Transition Towns initiative, started by Rob Hopkins to design and implement life after peak oil in local communities, is very popular and extensive in the UK (Smith, 2011). Transition Towns aim to reduce their dependence on fossil fuels and mitigate climate change be re-localising, shifting production closer to home and creating strong neighbourhood networks. The movement has grown since 2005 to include thousands of people, in over 50 countries, but failed in Czech Republic despite a common enthusiasm for permaculture. The history of socialism where state sanctioned collectivism discouraged the development of civil society, a perception that Czech society was transitioning towards Western capitalist style prosperity from relative poverty rather than needing to move in a direction that they had been experiencing for decades already, strong climate change scepticism in government and the broader population and a lack of genuine local adaption of the Transition ideas are some of the intersecting local contextual issues which meant that Transition Towns did not fall on fertile ground in the Czech Republic. In Kolářová's research, permaculture ideas interestingly had taken hold even though they, like Transition Towns, originated outside Czech communities. Research findings attributed this difference to the resonance with existing values in the community (care for nature, care for earth, self-reliance) and adaptability to local context of permaculture and the very local focus. For those involved in permaculture in the Czech Republic, there was a reluctance to engage with large-scale climate change politics which was central to Transition Towns and which was experienced as imposed from elsewhere rather than home grown. Collective action in the Czech permaculture movement was found to be dispersed with connections between members founded on education and shared approaches which were enacted in the lives of individuals and families. The imposition of what was perceived as a ready-made pathway to act together which did not resonate with local communities was both resisted and ultimately ignored. Local ownership, adaptation and development in line with what was important to people materially, ethically and culturally were key to building long-term collective action here and that collective action was fundamentally shaped by history and circumstances situated in that place. In thinking about shared knowledge and approaches for local action the room to adapt, reshape and integrate that action in ways which are credible, authentic and practical for communities provides us with an additional dimension to consider.

Acting for change in homes, offices and with neighbourhoods is neither simple nor quick. Whilst acknowledging the confusing, emotionally distressing and politically divisive nature of climate action (Huntley, 2020, p.14) we have argued here for the need to *act*. In the following chapter, we continue to explore opportunities for acting for change through self-organised collective action. We will consider and celebrate the capacity we have to grow and sustain through creative collaboration.

References

Atkinson, C., & Curnin, S. (2020). Sharing responsibility in disaster management policy. *Progress in Disaster Science, 7.* https://doi.org/10.1016/j.pdisas.2020.100122

Baumann, M.-R. U., & Wells, J. T. (2007). Education is for living and for life. In P. Duignan & D. Gurr (Eds.), *Leading Australia's schools.* Australian Council for Educational Leaders.

Bulkeley, H., Edwards, G. A. S., & Fuller, S. (2014). Contesting climate justice in the city: Examining politics and practice in urban climate change experiments. *Global Environmental Change, 25*(1), 31–40. https://doi.org/10.1016/j.gloenvcha.2014.01.009

Climate for Change. (2021). https://www.climateforchange.org.au

Crampton, A. (2015). Decolonising social work "Best Practices" through a philosophy of impermanence. *Indigenous Social Development, 4*(1), 1–11. https://scholarspace.manoa.hawaii.edu/bitstream/10125/37624/v4i1-03crampton.pdf

Crosweller, M., & Tschakert, P. (2021). Disaster management leadership and policy making: A critical examination of communitarian and individualistic understandings of resilience and vulnerability. *Climate Policy, 21*(2), 203–221. https://doi.org/10.1080/14693062.2020.1833825

Dominelli, L. (2011). Climate change: Social workers' roles and contributions to policy debates and interventions. *International Journal of Social Welfare, 20*(4), 430–438. https://doi.org/10.1111/j.1468-2397.2011.00795.x

Ensor, J., Forrester, J., & Matin, N. (2018). Bringing rights into resilience: Revealing complexities of climate risks and social conflict. *Disasters, 42*(S2), S287–S305. https://doi.org/10.1111/disa.12304

Foundations for Tomorrow. (2021). *Awareness to action: A youth-informed proposal for a more just, equitable and sustainable Australian future.* https://aware.com.au/content/dam/ftc/digital/pdfs/member/factsheet/Awareness-to-Action-Report-FFT-Aware-Super.pdf

Fraser, N. (2007). Mapping the feminist imagination: From redistribution to recognition to representation. *Estudos Feministas, 15*(2), 291–308. https://doi.org/10.1590/S0104-026X2007000200002

Fraser, D., & MacRae, A. M. (2011). Four types of activities that affect animals: Implications for animal welfare science and animal ethics philosophy. *Animal Welfare, 20*(4), 581–590.

Future Crunch. (2022). *Good news.* https://futurecrun.ch/goodnews

Gilchrist, A., & Taylor, M. (2011). *The short guide to community development.* Policy.

Goulson, D. (2021, September 21). Insects are vanishing from our planet at an alarming rate. But there are ways to help them. *The Guardian.* https://www.theguardian.com/commentisfree/2021/sep/21/insects-vanishing-alarming-help?CMP=Share_iOSApp_Other

Herring, S., Spangaro, J., Lauw, M., & McNamara, L. (2013). The intersection of trauma, racism, and cultural competence in effective work with aboriginal people: Waiting for trust. *Australian Social Work, 66*(1), 104–117. https://doi.org/10.1080/0312407X.2012.697566

Holbrook, A., Akbar, G., & Eastwood, J. (2019). Meeting the challenge of human-induced climate change: Reshaping social work education. *Social Work Education, 38*(8), 955–967. https://doi.org/10.1080/02615479.2019.1597040

Honneth, A. (1995). *The struggle for recognition: The moral grammar of social conflicts.* Polity Press.

Howard, A., & Rawsthorne, M. (2019). *Everyday community practice.* Allen & Unwin.

Hugman. R. (2015). *Social development in social work: Practices and principles.* Routledge. https://doi.org/10.4324/9781315780337

Huntley, R. (2020). *How to talk about climate change in a way that makes a difference.* Murdoch Books, Allen & Unwin.

Ife, J. (2012). *Human rights and social work: Towards rights-based practice* (3rd ed.). Cambridge University Press.

Jolly, M. (2020). Bushfires, supercyclones and "resilience": Is it being weaponised to deflect blame in our climate crisis? *Scottish Geographical Journal, 136*(1–4), 81–90. https://doi.org/10.1080/14702541.2020.1863607

Koláŕová, M. (2020). Climate change and the transition movement in Eastern Europe: The case of Czech permaculture. *Sociologický Časopis, 56*(3), 363–386. https://doi.org/10.13060/csr.2020.022

Ledwith, M. (2016). *Community development in action: Putting Freire into practice* (1st ed.). Bristol University Press. https://doi.org/10.2307/j.ctt1t895zm.10

Murphy, K. (2021). Guardian Essential poll: most Australians want Morrison to set a higher emissions reduction target. Guardian Australia, 12 October. https://www.theguardian.com/australia-news/2021/oct/12/guardian-essential-poll-most-australians-want-morrison-to-set-a-higher-emissions-reduction-target

Naranjo, N. (2020). Environmental issues and social work education. *The British Journal of Social Work, 50*(2), 447–463. https://doi.org/10.1093/bjsw/bcz168

Park, E.-S., & Yoon, D. (2022). The value of NGOs in disaster management and governance in South Korea and Japan. *International Journal of Disaster Risk Reduction, 69*, 102739. https://doi.org/10.1016/j.ijdrr.2021.102739

Peeters. J. (2012). A comment on "Climate change: Social workers' roles and contributions to policy debates and interventions". *International Journal of Social Welfare, 21*(1), 105–107. https://doi.org/10.1111/j.1468-2397.2011.00847.x

Peters-Little, F. (2020, December 31). The community game: Aboriginal self-definition at the local level. *Research Discussion Paper No. 10.* Australian Institute of Aboriginal and Torres Strait Islander Studies [AIATSIS]. https://aiatsis.gov.au/publication/35754

Rawsthorne, M. (2009, October 25–November 5). *Creating inclusive rural communities: Grass roots perspectives on the opportunities and challenges* [Conference presentation]. 11th Australian Social Policy Conference [ASPC] – An Inclusive Society: Practicalities and Possibilities. Sydney, Australia. https://www.aspc.unsw.edu.au/sites/www.aspc.unsw.edu.au/files/uploads/aspc_historical_conferences/2009/paper273.pdf

Rawsthorne, M., Howard, A., & Joseph, P. (2020). *Redfern Surry Hills Community Resilience Committee, "We've got our act together": Towards shared responsibility", Final Report.* Inner Sydney Voice.

Santha, S. D. (2020). *Climate change and adaptive innovation: A model for social work practice* (1st ed.). Routledge. https://doi.org/10.4324/9780429203138

Scopelianos, S., & Crothers, J. (2019, July 13). Living on the fringe can erode our sense of community. Here's how we fix that. *Life Matters* [Radio broadcast] ABC Radio National.

https://www.abc.net.au/news/2019-07-13/living-on-the-fringe-can-erode-our-sense-of-community/11287330

Shevellar, L., & Westoby, P. (2016). *Learning and mobilising for community development: A radical tradition of community-based education and training.* Routledge. https://doi.org/10.4324/9781315591889

Smith, A. (2011). The transition town network: A review of current evolutions and renaissance. *Social Movement Studies, 10*(1), 99–105. https://doi.org/10.1080/14742837.2011.545229

Take the Jump. (2020). *About.* https://takethejump.org/about

Taylor, M. (2022, March 7). *Six promises you can make to help reduce carbon emissions.* The Guardian. https://www.theguardian.com/environment/2022/mar/07/six-promises-you-can-make-to-help-reduce-carbon-emissions

Terare, M. (2019). Transforming classrooms: Developing culturally safe learning environments. In D. Baines, B. Bennett, S. Goodwin, & M. Rawsthorne (Eds.), *Working across difference: Social work, social policy and social justice* (pp. 26–39). Bloomsbury Publishing.

Terbish, B., & Rawsthorne, M. (2020). The state and civil society: The case of citizens' groups in the ger districts of Ulaanbaatar, Mongolia. *Community Development Journal, 55*(3), 382–398. https://doi.org/10.1093/cdj/bsy063

Thorpe, C. (2017). *Social theory for social work: Ideas and applications.* Routledge. https://doi.org/10.4324/9780203529638

Vinson, T., & Rawsthorne, M. (2013). *Lifting our gaze: The community appraisal and strengthening framework.* Common Ground Publishing.

Walls, D. (2015). *Community organizing: Fanning the flame of democracy.* Polity.

World Bank. (2021). Mongolia. *Climate Change Knowledge Portal.* Retrieved April 7, 2022, from https://climateknowledgeportal.worldbank.org/country/mongolia

7

ACTING FOR CHANGE TOGETHER

Collective action

In this chapter, we want to explore a number of different shapes which collective action can take, draw out some of the reasons why we think acting together not only matters but is becoming increasingly needed and suggest that we need to change the direction we have been heading in social work and human services work to be equipped for working on social justice as the climate changes. Rather than provide a unifying definition of collective action, and consistent with our approach throughout the book, we draw on existing published research and our own research, experience and reflection to mark out some of the parameters for thinking and action we think are useful. One of the reasons we have included a chapter focused on what it is to act together and why we would do this is that we see and experience the alternative in many of the systems in which we work and research and this alternative leaves us fearful that we are not currently prepared for the work that is here now and that which is to come.

The dominance of individual choice and why we need to reconnect collective networks for action

In many ways, the title for this chapter could be 'why collective action matters'. The power of individualising narratives and processes over the past three decades to render any preference for acting collectively at a policy and organisational level, as a kind of threat to freedom or choice, or a cumbersome dinosaur unable to adapt to the agile and fast-moving pace required for survival, has been impressive and alarming (Dawson et al., 2020; Mladenov, 2015). We have seen many of the mechanisms within human services which encouraged deliberative approaches to funding and policy design streamlined into tendering processes where individual organisations compete for available resources with no recourse to communities or those impacted for consultation (Bamforth et al., 2016). Collaborative

DOI: 10.4324/9781003146339-7

processes across organisations where knowledge is shared, networks form and integrated systems of support are co-ordinated across organisational borders are actively discouraged. Market-oriented governance processes designed to keep the balance of competition in place, view such collaborations as anti-competitive and against the interests of the marketplace into which human services have been thrust (Baines et al., 2019; Lazzarato, 2009). In order to address the long-term and very real need to shift from service-centred to person-centred approaches, to shape support for people in a way which prioritised their experience and needs rather than system-centric concerns, policy and practice seem to have corrected towards individualised ways of working to the exclusion of all else. Alongside this, we have seen the success of neo-liberal programs in relation to housing, people living with disability, out of home care, health and mental health (Baines et al., 2019; Connell et al., 2009; Dawson et al., 2020; Mladenov 2015) skilfully acquire person-centred narratives and subsume these into a worldview in which competition between services in a constructed market is the only possible way for choice and person-centredness to be delivered. This narrowing of focus in human services, in our experience, has resulted in a narrowing of our understanding of the life experiences of those we work with, and of our relationship with the place we have in the world. We see climate change as fundamentally challenging this worldview as individualised approaches on their own become increasingly inadequate. We do not argue here that a shift to person-centredness in human services is a problem, but rather, that such a shift must be accompanied by a shift to planet-centredness as well and that acting together is as essential as individual choice and dignity in shaping social justice as climate change unfolds. The erosion (and we use the term intentionally) of structures, processes, language and even consciousness through which we might act together within social work and human services, we have observed over the past four decades, leaves us less equipped to work creatively in the face of complex problems which require not only action amongst us, but a concerted effort across professional, geographic, political and cultural boundaries. Students we work alongside speak about working for companies rather than organisations casting those who receive services purely within a transactional and narrow customer frame. In the lifetime of this group, individualised and transactional arrangements between human services and those they support have been the only available experiences. Rights and reciprocity as a citizen or community member have been very successfully reduced to those of a customer. If we can just get value for money or what we paid for, this is the extent of our power. Surely this is better, you might argue, than previous arrangements between social workers in human services and clients which have historically included approaches infused by benevolence, charity and State regulation. At least now, people have some choices about what is provided rather than having to put up with a one size fits all approach which certainly, people living with disabilities were subject to in Australia. We wonder if this is the case in practice and we also wonder about the proximity between individual choice and individual blame within current policy settings. If I am seen to be given a choice (often within very limited options), then I am also to blame for any consequences which emerge. We would question and invite you to question how these parameters of individual choice are constructed and how an individualised worldview locates other people, structural factors and the world we all engage with. Where, if anywhere does relationship and reciprocity sit within this worldview? What are some of the issues which emerge when we design and deliver socially focused support purely within this view?

The idea of individual choice has been and continues to be a powerful one driving action. Recent anti-vaccination protests emerging as a result of the COVID-19 pandemic draw effectively on a narrative which sees individual choice as our primary human right. Here the tensions between our recipro-cal rights and responsibilities to each other and those of individual choice are becoming visible in public discussions in a practical and hopeful way, as the consequences of my individual choices are not mine alone but potentially life threatening for us all. This debate highlights the importance of thinking through reciprocity and relational ways of being which are at the heart of First Nations Worldviews and which enable us to question the primacy of individual choice across a range of areas.

Collective action persists and re-emerges

Interestingly, alongside the various demonstrations of individualism appearing locally and on the world stage, collective action, in a range of different forms, persists and is growing in civil society. School Climate Action Strikes emerged from Greta Thunberg's solo Friday protests growing into a global movement in 2019/2020 gaining and sustaining momentum across the world. This is an en-couraging sign that the collective spirit is alive and well for young people across the world. Local food networks and community energy schemes, as we saw in earlier chapters, provide an approach for organising the basics of life in a way which resists the message that there are no viable alternatives to what we have. In our research with communities, we see examples of collective action both in the long term and during crises mobilised by community members and locally based groups. Self-organising processes and systems have consistently emerged during disasters both in Australia and across the world largely directing first responses in floods, fires, earthquakes, cyclones and tsunamis (Shepherd & Williams, 2014; Wukich & Steinberg, 2013). The power, flexibility and adaptive capacity of this kind of self-organising has the potential to make a significant contribution to climate justice and climate change mitigation/adaption more generally, and it is here that we see encouraging learning to support reconnection, as well as making new connections, infrastructure and processes to support effective action where social and environmental justice meet.

Formal policy, management and service systems consistently struggle to make sense of, engage and collaborate with this kind of collective action and this dilemma poses a major risk to the success of climate change strategies which require planning and action at a local, national and international level. Atkinson and colleagues (2018) argue that an emphasis on markets and government has failed to address climate change adequately while many of the collective self-organising efforts which exist have been neglected in work on climate change and governance. This has certainly been our experience working alongside local informal community networks in disaster preparedness, response and recovery. The role of local, informal collective action promises to become increasingly important as climate change impacts intensify and we will spend some time in this chapter exploring this phenomenon.

At a broader level, even with the success of neo-liberalism, we are seeing a turn towards collective action on climate change amongst politicians and policy makers. Global agreements, with all their inconsistencies and challenges, signify a recognition that the dire progress of human-induced climate change can only be addressed effectively through nations acting together. Over 10 years ago, Robertson and Choi (2010) argued that governance systems worldwide were shifting from a mechanistic to an ecological worldview in which self-organising, interconnectedness and collaboration between diverse groups were key. Drawing on a range of thinkers from the 1960s onward in science and social science, they see a paradigm shift taking place in how we organise and govern action at all levels, driven by the complexity and dynamics of global issues and specifically, climate change. The imperatives of modernism and particularly neo-liberalism which have shaped bureaucratic structures through an emphasis on control, self-interest and competition, they argue, are inadequate to effectively address current and future challenges. As we have seen in earlier chapters of the book, the development of complex systems thinking provides a language and theoretical system which supports a very different way of understanding and acting in the world. Robertson and Choi draw on this thinking along with systems approaches and social construction (Berger & Luckmann, 1967) to outline an ecological governance system emphasising interconnectedness and interdependence, self-organising and self-managing and a co-evolutionary dynamic where ongoing interactions and feedback between systems and their environments facilitate change over time. Atkinson and colleagues (2018) similarly propose the development of self-organisation as a method for future local governance where repeated reciprocal practices support the emergence of shared understanding and decisions.

Increasingly, dominant discourses which locate competition at the core of human survival are being questioned. Attention is being paid to collaboration as key to human as well as planetary futures. The Global Assessment Report produced by the Intergovernmental Science-Policy Platform on Biodiversity and Ecosystem Services (UN, 2019) highlighted the fraying of the interconnected web of life on Earth. Of particular concern was the rate of extinction: around 1 million animal and plant species are likely to be lost within decades. It calls for urgent collective action at all levels, from the local to the global. Christens (2020) draws on the notions of ultrasociality and intersubjectivity in evolutionary theory and social science to argue that human patterns of thought and action may be better understood in the collective than individually. For Christens, it is the human capacity to create, grow and sustain ideas through collaborative processes centred on imagination and story which has consistently been overshadowed by a focus on individual rational thought, but which provides a framework for social action and change more reflective of human evolution.

Swimming against the tide not in a good way

We see a change developing towards collective action at local and global levels as the complexity of climate change responses become more apparent and the relative ineffectiveness of individual approaches on their own is much clearer as noted above. What worries us is that human services seem to be working increasingly in the opposite direction. In NSW, where we live, local neighbourhood centres which previously worked in a universal way supporting a range of community-based initiatives from community gardens to cultural projects to food and emergency support to community connecting activities are now funded under a much narrower scope. Targeted service provision and risk management focused on child protection are changing the breadth and impact of their work with communities, replacing it with more individualised and some argue, punitive approaches. A similar shift in disability support demonstrates a move away from community and collective thinking and practice to a more individualised and risk management-oriented regime. In Australia, the introduction of the National Disability Insurance Scheme (NDIS) heralded a major change in approach towards individualised funding. This was a long-awaited and long-lobbied for change which provided a process for people living with disability with control over the supports they received. As the NDIS has rolled out, however, the replacement of community support systems with purely individualised support has unintentionally undermined local support networks or recast these as purchased individual support in a community setting. An example here is locally run inclusion-focused playgroups in regional NSW. Our research found that these groups (previously funded under government block funding arrangements and now unsupported following a competitive tendering process) provided a unique point of access and inclusive support for First Nations families, those experiencing domestic violence, socially isolated families and for children who were not diagnosed but were experiencing learning and development challenges. The place based and collaborative design of the playgroups with a range of services, partnering with local families in rural areas to provide low key regular support in local community venues including schools, did not fit with competitive tendering guidelines and relied on collective effort between communities and services. Research findings here indicated that following the change children who were involved in the playgroup have not connected with individualised supports and in many cases were not eligible (Howard & Allison, 2018; Howard et al., 2017).

For us, this is a retrograde step in a context where engagement with the global shift towards collective approaches is emerging. If questions of climate change provide an invitation to complexity thinking and to re-orient human-centric individual approaches towards a collective ethics and practice; those which draw on First Nations knowledge about respect and custodianship for earth and all who live here (non-human and human); then this opportunity is one that will shape future support systems for human and other communities in new and generative ways.

It may seem like a long bow to draw a connection between approaches to child protection, disability and climate change; however, as the social justice impacts of both market-oriented service systems and climate change fall most heavily on those already experiencing social exclusion, poverty and isolation, we see questions about the way support systems are designed and implemented, and particularly the impacts of different Worldviews, as central for everyone working in social work and human services. A number of studies highlight the unintended consequences of targeted, individualised approaches which fail to recognise the structural issues faced by marginalised groups and communities (Campbell et al., 2016; Corrigan, 2016). If systems are in place which accentuate individual change (and blame) and minimise the impacts of structural inequity across human services, the unintended and negative impacts of such systems will be amplified in the face of a challenge as complex as climate change. Collective action, in its many diverse forms is, for us, critically important for social and human services workers to understand and re-engage with as we generate new ideas to maximise social justice as climate change begins to bite.

What are we talking about when we say, 'collective action'?

Academic literature examining collective action in the context of climate change spans the disciplines of geography (Dufour, 2021), organisational theory (Arguello, 2021), social science (Kjeldahl & Hendricks, 2018) and environmental science (Kallhof, 2021). Rather than providing one definition here as noted earlier, we walk through the ideas of a range of thinkers as well as drawing on our own research in order to get a sense of the diversity in approaches and practice to guide us.

In thinking through what collective action means in relation to climate change and social justice, and how it might be enacted, Ostrom (2010) provides us with a useful frame of reference and we invite you to think through her approach, as we work through the how, what and why of collective action in this chapter. Ostrom describes climate change as a 'global collective action problem' (p.550) arguing that rather than waiting for decisions and action by global authorities, collective action for climate change can be more effectively mobilised through 'polycentric systems' (p.552) where multiple systems of different sizes act and interact cumulatively towards change. Ostrom draws from complexity theory and sees collective action as a multiple and multiplying process. For us, this concept of multiple systems working in their own ways towards cumulative change is a useful one as it enables us to think about collective action as having diverse dimensions, scales and timeframes. Although Ostrom's focus is on multiple agencies, organisations and governments working in a polycentric way (that is working from different perspectives, within different remits but focused on the same issues and part of a larger complex system), self-organising community-led groups and networks fit well into this system. Ostrom's thinking and research is important for us in a social work and human services context as she argues that rather than chaos and duplication shaping the work of multiple players and systems in the same space (for example, within a city or region), the diverse polycentric systems converge through their work to produce outcomes more efficiently and effectively. In addition, Ostrom found that the polycentric systems she studied, although sometimes in competitive relationships, worked co-operatively and built trust by focusing their independent efforts towards a shared outcome and at the same time gaining knowledge through shared learning from others in close proximity but in different domains. Each system has its own space and parameters, where norms are set but interact with systems in other domains to learn. Here, collaboration and trust are developed to achieve a collective benefit at different scales.

Let's look at an example from our own research, in a region where cascading natural disasters have occurred over a short period of time. Through the ongoing work of local community members, community organisations, local and State government, the health system, formal and informal networks and large organisations, a number of polycentric systems have emerged to focus on recovery from recent events and planning for future disasters. Diverse but connected systems including those around individual and family well-being, community planning and recovery, disaster preparedness, support for marginalised communities impacted by disaster, infrastructure and environmental work, resilience building and community connectedness all work within their own parameters but are jointly focused on improving disaster and climate change resilience. In line with Ostrom's discussion, it is the multiplicity of these systems working around different specific focus areas but with the same overarching direction, which creates a greater collective impact at all scales. It doesn't matter if we are working in different ways on the same issue, if there is duplication and redundancy across the smaller systems or if there is cross over in the ground we are covering. Instead, taking a polycentric system view (that is, one which embraces complexity) builds connection and potential as we are working on dilemmas together bringing critically different perspectives.

Ostrom's analysis runs in stark contrast to the imperatives of competitive funding policy which works actively to ensure no duplication takes place and undermines trust between those seeking resources for their work by reinforcing individual rather than collective approaches across communities. In the region where our research took place a rapid influx of this kind of funding after the numerous local disaster events served to distort relationships between different local systems and create resentment between groups and organisations who were asked to compete to provide the one solution/innovation/answer which deserved to be supported. This process has significantly undermined trust locally and impacted on collective initiatives at a time when a concerted effort across connected systems was sorely needed. The result has been fragmented rather than polycentric activity with organisations focused only on their own piece of a large and complex system.

So, in terms of our understanding of collective work, an important component is focused on thinking and action which builds trust, knowledge and action both within and between systems. The character, and history of complex problems related to climate change are additional key shapers of action. For Groulx and colleagues (2017), climate change is bound by processes for mobilising social action, identifying the collective creation of the issues as needing a collective approach in both mitigation and adaptation. In their systematic review on citizen science as a collective action strategy, Groulx and colleagues argue that climate change issues have been collectively produced, and in response, it is imperative that we design processes to collectively act to address these. Citizen science, for these researchers, provides a structure and process for supporting increased engagement and communication on climate change issues as participants have agency to act together to build knowledge as well as building trust and connection with others in a shared project.

In our research with communities living in flood plains, we heard from farmers who very clearly understood that collectively generating and sharing information about river levels with each other as a flood came down the system was an essential part of both their animals and their own survival. This issue was one which required collective action at every stage given that both response times and action were available to community members at different times and relied on information being passed on so that it could be immediately acted upon. Community members joined together to raise funds for state-of-the-art measurement and communication equipment at different points in the river, which they monitored and maintained. Using a long-established neighbourhood network, they utilised this information to ensure everyone who needed assistance getting animals or themselves to higher ground was able to get support. In this example, the problem was collective in character. Individual approaches would be ineffective in ensuring safety for all the farmers along the river system. Collective action was required to adequately address farmer and livestock safety when the river flooded so farmers self-organised in this context to look after each other. Here we see that collective problems and dilemmas invite collective action so the way in which we understand the impacts and parameters of a problem directly shapes the approach to action we need to take (Howard et al., 2016).

Self-organising systems

In our research, collective action has been both ephemeral –responding to a crisis or disaster – and long term – community members have engaged in slow, small actions which build community and act on issues over decades and drawn on the relationships and social capital built over time when a crisis or disruption happens. In both cases, groups and networks have operated largely informally. This informality usually results in action and relationships being well known in local communities but invisible or little known by formal systems including human service systems. Here, the character of collective action is shaped by local relationships and concerns and sometimes linked nationally or globally to shared concerns. Large-scale complex issues including climate change and disasters are acted on in very local ways where impacts are felt and where change happens through intimate conversations and small-scale initiatives.

People organise themselves into informal organic systems every day. Whether it is connecting with a few people for a walk, sharing an interest or working together on a common cause. Self-organising is such a ubiquitous part of life that we often don't even notice it is happening. Self-organising systems challenge hierarchical structures fundamentally drawing a long history from First Nations communities. Relationships are reciprocal and built through mutual support, shared connections and belonging. Knowledge is generated and shared laterally with different members of the group and utilised collaboratively. Roles and expertise are largely fluid with different people making contributions in line with their skills, time, knowledge and capacity. Community-led observations and self-organised collective action on climate change are ongoing in First Nations communities (Maclean, 2015; Nursey-Bray et al., 2019) and also more broadly. Nursey-Bray and colleagues (2019) found that communities in the Torres Strait, Arabana Country, central Australia and north Queensland were making detailed observations and taking action in relation to changes to Country including increased flooding, sea level rise and cyclones. In our research, we have found community members in regional NSW who observed collected and shared flood information locally dating back to 1840. Detailed records were kept, well known and utilised amongst community members. These observations and actions, however, in the case of First Nations communities and flood-impacted communities in our research remain largely unrecognised and unutilised in formal climate change mitigation and adaptation systems.

The role of self-organising systems, as a fundamental element of survival regularly emerges during a crisis. In times of disaster, communities organise themselves with remarkable speed and capacity. In our research, we have seen local residents during a flood when cut off from town and before formal assistance arrived (some days) identify all those who needed urgent medications, co-ordinate prescriptions, contact the local pharmacist (after ascertaining which mobile phones amongst community members were still working), then have prescriptions transported by a community member's kayak, back to those in need.

We also see self-organising in action as part of larger movements or events such as school climate strikes where local informal relationships and communication connect in a networked way to produce large-scale (in this case global) mobilisation of people (Boulianne et al., 2020). This form of self-organised collective action emerges from the multiple localised sites of action networked through shared ideas, sometimes through formal organising systems, and often through rapid informal sharing of information through social media and online communication more generally.

These very visible examples of self-organising systems sometimes seem to emerge from nowhere but when we trace that emergence backwards, there has often been local self-organising activity going on for some time creating an organised foundation for action (Hutton, 2012; Luke, 2017), there is a level of trust and goodwill amongst community members creating everyday relational and social capital (as in the earlier pharmacy example), or there is a shared frustration and motivation for action with others. Each and all of these underlying contextual factors are then drawn on to mobilise a collective response when a catalyst or crisis arrives. In some cases, this process results in global movements such as the School Climate Strikes, while in others it is made up of small groups of people acting in dispersed local ways but loosely connected to a broader issue. As part of our research on informal local networks, we spoke to community members who were part of very small local groups (3–8) people acting together to work on national and global environmental issues including coal mining and coal seam gas exploration, deforestation and land clearing, climate change overall, water and food security. Often part of very informal groups and not officially affiliated with specific social or environmental movements, we have seen this small–scale but linked self–organised action operating in a range of communities and underpinning response, support and recovery when disaster occurs.

Drawing down on social capital and local networks

One of the questions we want to discuss in this chapter is how we can nurture and safeguard these stores of relational and social capital which underpin self-organising collective action. For communities who experience cascading crises and disasters these resources can become depleted. Governments, paradoxically, rely on informal self-organising systems in times of crisis when their own resources are stretched, but have consistently failed to invest in long-term support of such systems and often frame self-organising collective action as interfering or hindering institutional efforts. While self-organising collective action is often characterised by governments as ephemeral, unpredictable and chaotic in the face of efforts to restore control, reliability and certainty, such action is, in reality, far from any of these attributes. Rather, such action is a consistent feature of community life guided by relational values and processes which ebb and flow, change direction and emerge in new forms over time. This shape and flow in collective action sits in tension with institutional parameters sometimes precipitating conflict with these parameters and at other times working in parallel. In looking closely at collective action in this chapter, we need to grapple with these tensions, resisting the temptation to advocate for such action as *the answer* to addressing climate change impacts, while arguing that acting collectively remains essential in response as it is in other aspects of life. Whether it is reaching agreement on climate change mitigation and adaptation globally, ensuring accountability for policy and resource allocation nationally or organising local work on environmental and social justice, we are interested in understanding the role of collective voices, practices and actions. Self-organising systems may well be the most ubiquitous systems of human organisation on the planet, and they are also, arguably the most invisible and poorly understood.

Online communication, including the proliferation of social media use provides an opportunity for self-organising systems to both increase their own participants and to connect with other systems forming networks which operate both locally and globally (e.g., Knitting Nannas). Song and colleagues (2020) argue that crowd-sourcing during disasters very effectively taps into existing self-organising systems and enhances capacity at all levels in the context of disasters. In their case study research spanning 12 disasters and locations across the globe, they found that multi-directional communication was key in realising self-organising processes where trust, identity, culture, language, skills and knowledge were central elements interacting as a complex adaptive system. They describe the ways in which self-organising systems disrupt hierarchical communication where one authority transmits information and others are cast only as recipients and responders. In studying crowdsourcing, they found that communication efficiency was enhanced when people involved operated from multiple perspectives as producers, conduits, designers and recipients within the communication process. This disruption of hierarchical decision making and chains of command which we see in self-organising systems in the context of disasters as well as recurring argument in research on collective action regarding the importance of multiple perspective systems draws our attention to the paradox between self-organising and formally organised systems (Le Roux & Van Niekerk, 2019). In social work and human services, self-organising community systems provide vital local knowledge, relationships, social capital, support capacity, energy and creativity. Unfortunately, with increasing targeted and deficit-oriented programs and services, this critical social infrastructure is becoming increasingly depleted at a time when climate change impacts and the need for action are making self-organising systems more critically important than they have ever been. Community development approaches enable effective support for and capacity building in relation to self-organising systems as these approaches make space for new networks and informal reciprocity to emerge and grow.

Widening and deepening the view: collective action at multiple scales

So, at a very localised level, we see collective approaches adopted and sustained consistently. What does this look like at a broader level where divergent interests, conflicts and parameters are multiplied? In Australia, a key example where collective action at this level has been desperately required but rarely seen is the Murray-Darling Basin. We discussed this extensive river system earlier in Chapter 5.3, and it is worth revisiting here as an example of potentially operationalising collective action at a regional level, and with multiple, often conflicting agendas in play. The Murray-Darling system has seen and continues to see the worst impacts of colonisation, extractive agriculture, ignorance and wilful disregard for climate and environmental characteristics within and impacting on the system and competing interests (Beresford, 2021; Hamilton & Kells, 2021).

Abel and colleagues (2016), in their work focused on the Murray-Darling River system, argue for the development of a collective action approach which works across levels of decision making and stakeholders at a regional scale. Examining how their collective action strategy works provides us with important information and insight into what we might build into collective structures and processes where fundamental conflict exists and where urgency for change is pressing. In their approach, human and environmental systems as equal and diverse stakeholders (First Nations communities, farming, mining, environmental activists, tourism, State and Federal government, recreation and researchers) are engaged within a region to work through ongoing and detailed analysis, negotiation and problem-solving. Interestingly, for these researchers, the success of collective action in this complex context is best supported when equity is central and is able to support social cohesion. They see environmental and social justice convergence as essential if negotiated and collective work is to be successful in this context. Their approach marks a distinct break from the focus on water markets and water license holders which has dominated planning in this system.

Those participating bring their own perspective and values but work with others to develop a shared vision for the region which includes practical consideration of what needs to change for the vulnerabilities in the system to shift towards resilience, the thresholds which will tip the system into decline or collapse, changes which will create positive feedback loops able to mitigate future shocks, and implementation pathways for agreed change.

Abel and colleagues' (2016) plan for collective action here requires time and resources and is ongoing rather than contained. They propose a process where values, knowledge and learning are navigated and negotiated where both power and responsibility are shared. They argue this process has the potential to shift the current conservative system where layered checks and balances reinforce business as usual and make transformational change very difficult.

Here, regional collective action is neither simple nor short term. It matches the complexity and ongoing realities of caring for environmental, social, cultural and economic systems and is deliberative, detailed work undertaken by diverse groups and interests. The history of the Murray-Darling system since colonisation of Australia illustrates very clearly the need to match action with the scale and complexity of issues. Previous approaches where individual States made policy and practice decisions which were in their own interest but did not consider the parts of the river running through neighbouring States have resulted in near system collapse on more than one occasion and continue to threaten the life and health of the Murray-Darling (Beresford, 2021). In this example, we see alternative processes and structures developed intentionally and together to work on what can only be called a wicked problem. Collective action here is both detailed in its implementation and accounts for a range of players and agendas. It offers multi-way accountability but also collaborative support as new ways of working emerge, conflicts are unpacked and the complexity of the issues is recognised in the planning process.

Regional collective action has also been examined closely by climate change researchers drawing on community-led decision-making processes more generally. For example, Pavel (2015) describes the importance of collective action on climate change to be carried out at a regional level which recognises the impacts of structural inequity while supporting the development of collective alliances focused on justice for earth. For Pavel, this kind of collective action built from coalitions and alliances signifies a shift from fragmented individualism offering structure and processes for addressing existing problems at the same time as climate change.

As with regional systems, collective action is being designed and undertake within local systems where structural change along with local food sustainability is the desired goal. Here we take a deeper view, unravelling the way in which producers and consumers interact in the food market. Again, we draw from earlier discussions in Chapter 5.1 on food systems as these provide interesting sites for different forms of collective action which disrupt dominant approaches and provide alternatives. This form of collective action is focused in place based local economies where social enterprises or locally based businesses such as community-supported agriculture are growing. At first glance, this way of organising food production may not seem like collective action, but a closer look reveals a radically different set of relationships between growers of food and community members which reflect collective agreement across shared values as well as practicalities. Beacham and colleagues (2018) call these 'tantalisingly different forms of organisation' (p.533). Here we see collective action as transformational, where producer/consumer relations are re shaped as close and reciprocal rather than distant and transactional. Both food producers and community members act collaboratively to create a local food system where agreed values of local production, equity and sustainability are the drivers of economic and social life. This reciprocal and relational approach challenges the binary narrative of people as producers or consumers drawing on First Nations ways of being to transform the activities of daily living. It is important to note here that changing the structural and operational relationships between different participants in a system such as food production, actively supports the practice of Worldviews different from that of capitalism and challenges business as usual by reframing food systems as collective rather than individualised enterprises. Transaction is replaced by relationship and reciprocity in an ongoing process of deliberation and negotiation. The change in relations signifies a systems transformation at a structural level.

These kinds of transformational shifts are supported by both deconstructing what we take for granted in the structures and interactions of life and re-imagining existing systems using different parameters. Robertson and Choi (2010) focus this thinking on governance and human services systems, suggesting we replace hierarchies with networks as the central form in organisations with multiple nodes forming different networks depending on focus and continuous adaptive collaboration. They suggest, participative and consensus-based processes for making decisions where all those impacted by decisions take part in making that decision. Leadership approaches here reflect a stewardship orientation and authority is fluid and focused on specific tasks. This is a considerable shift from current approaches based on stable and pervasive authority invested in positions.

Shaw and colleagues (2018) focus on the imperative to scale up experienced by many small initiatives seeking funding support. They critique climate change exhortations based on individual changes in behaviour while highlighting a number of challenges for local community initiatives in scaling up effectively. Their research is focused on community garden groups in the UK. The practical challenges including land security, development pressure in cities and resources to support projects illustrate a larger structural conflict between the imperatives of cities and those of sustainability. Their use of MacKinnon's (2011) multi-scalar politics critiques linear notions of 'scaling up' and the link with more efficiency and effective impact promoted as part of this push. For these researchers, scalar politics are socially constructed and operate in a fluid way. At a local government level, they argue that a transformation is required which frames climate change action as connected with food security, local land use and community but also addresses the competition for space and resources which besets local collective gardens. Presenting an alternative to scaling up through multiple, networked local projects links back to Ostrom's polycentric systems and allows us to re-imagine activities, organisations and initiatives in very different ways.

In our research with communities experiencing disasters, we have also seen collective action approaches work effectively to generate new shared knowledge which has been utilised effectively by people impacted by a range of extreme weather events. We have seen Participatory Action Research (PAR) support local decisions and initiatives by engaging directly with community members, organisations and government in joint learning, data collection, analysis and planning. Formulating questions, designing work, acting together on a jointly developed agenda and then analysing results before planning the next cycle have created a structure where collective action can practically bring together those with diverse interests to work on local issues. This process supports joint learning and a do-able process for collaborative decision making, where everyone is included in planning, decisions, consequences and refinement. Like Campos and colleagues (2016), who argue that PAR along with scenario planning provides a critically important process for accelerating climate change adaptation, we have found this process for co-designed research and action works well in framing collective action and putting into practice. For example, as part of a PAR project, we were involved in, a group comprising State and Local government staff, emergency management agencies, community housing providers, non-government organisations and social housing tenants worked collectively to generate and share new information about the practical support needed by both services providers and tenants to prepare for floods. In working collectively group members were able to challenge their own and others' assumptions about disaster preparedness, clarify roles and work on new systems for support and communication, as well as developing a much deeper understanding of gaps in the systems which were obscured for most before the group came together.

In advocating for and designing collective action approaches in practical climate justice across social work and human service, then, we are not in entirely new territory. Guidance is available, as we have seen in examples discussed here, which puts collective strategies on the ground at local and regional levels across a range of challenging focus areas.

Collective action: not as simple as it looks

We see considerable promise in collective action at every level of work on climate change and social justice and have seen the very different processes and outcomes when these approaches are adopted. However, it is important not to view collective action naively. A critical analysis of power relations and the operation of power both within and between groups provides the social justice dimension of any collective effort. In our research, we have seen significant differences in power between groups and as a result, local collective action has been undermined. In one example, a local community meeting to discuss disaster resilience was attended by a very organised group from a neighbouring community. The visiting group, who came in numbers and with a well-developed local political agenda dominated discussion and focused plans for local action on their own community rather than on the one where the meeting was taking place. In a creative approach to resisting the takeover, a small group of local community members, who saw their community as perpetually left out, made sure they had members in each of the small planning groups raising local environmental issues in each group so that when the larger group reconvened, local issues were raised by all small group increasing the importance of these issues. Here we see a quite sophisticated operation of power between neighbouring communities, both intent on their own local agenda. Collective action on ground in these communities is far from utopian. It is, however, deliberative and negotiated. In this example, we can also see how collective action can be undermined from outside as the interest of the neighbouring community was piqued by the possibility of funding for community projects. The promise of funding, and the experience in both communities of competitive funding processes resulted in an amplification of conflict rather than an opportunity for joint collective action. In this case, funding was available to one community and not the other, which in the end led to the organised community losing interest in any action and feeling that they had been denied resources in an arbitrary way. An alternative way of supporting collective action required the organisation of structural support (funding in this case) to encourage collaboration rather than competition, and also required a process for building shared power and a shared agenda between local groups.

If collective action is a promising direction for working on either mitigation or adaptation to climate change, it is also challenging to develop and sustain. Collective action requires ongoing attention, negotiation, care and creativity, but also a recognition that conflict or potential conflict is never far from the centre.

McVicker (2012) maps out the fundamental tensions in relation to land management between increasing numbers of competing groups seeking to influence decision making about access to and use of land in the US. It can be tempting to frame these conflicts as binaries between those who see land as primarily for use by humans and advocate for all land to be available for this use, and those who see land as part of ecological systems which must be protected at all costs. This kind of binary is, of course, part of our everyday conversations, of media debate and discussion and of the way we organise much collective action; however, it hides a much more complex picture of competing interests and power relations. McVicker argues for the development of 'Community Based Ecological Stewardship' (p.382) which is community- or citizen-led and local but which builds connections, communication and networks with groups and individuals outside the community, and also works closely with government agencies. For McVicker:

> Lack of trust and distance from the land are big enemies of stewardship. They tend to push power upwards in the system and demand more from government, not less. Somehow, more effective linkages between local people and others concerned about public land health – people who can literally be scattered from coast to coast – need to be secured. The current system is not succeeding in doing that. Rather, it seems only capable of exacerbating the problem.
>
> *(p.380)*

What we see here is a good example of the ways in which conflicts can be constructed in relation to collective action but also the emergence of new understandings and possibilities by diverse interests which stem through the negotiation process. Collective processes are often critiqued for their propensity for conflict and more protracted decision making than hierarchical and/or competitive ways of organising. However, in our experience with communities and organisations that seek to act collaboratively, it is this process of negotiation which most often yields unexpected and creative collaboration. The visibility of conflicts in collective action may be more productive in terms of effective deliberation than when such conflicts are rendered invisible via power imbalances and hierarchical structures.

In this chapter, we have examined and discussed the role, contours and scope for collective action in working on climate justice. We see collective approaches as offering promise in working on complex issues in complex systems, which are at the centre of social work and human services. The individualising trajectory on which social policy and practice has been designed over the recent decades means that any change requires an intentional shift at all levels of the system. Work across a range of disciplines and contexts focused on addressing climate change offers us hopeful and practical guidance in making such a change and outlines how we might more effectively engage in connecting social work and human services more fundamentally with complex issues such as climate change. In the next chapter, we broaden our view further exploring the role of policy and approaches to policy which provide a way forward globally as well as locally.

References

Abel, N., Wise, R. M., Colloff, M. J., Walker, B. H., Butler, J. R. A., Ryan, P., Norman, C., Langston, A., Anderies, J. M., Gorddard, R., Dunlop, M., & O'Connell, D. (2016). Building resilient pathways to transformation when "no one is in charge": Insights from Australia's Murray-Darling Basin. *Ecology and Society, 21*(2), 23. https://doi.org/10.5751/ES-08422-210223

Arguello, G. (2021). Large-scale collective action in the Arctic Ocean: The role of international organizations in climate governance. *Ocean & Coastal Management, 211*, 105706. https://doi.org/10.1016/j.ocecoaman.2021.105706

Atkinson, R., Dörfler, T., & Rothfuß, E. (2018). Self-organisation and the co-production of governance: The challenge of local responses to climate change. *Politics and Governance, 6*(1), 169–179. https://doi.org/10.17645/pag.v6i1.1210

Baines, D., Bennett, B., Goodwin, S., & Rawsthorne, M. (Eds.). (2019). *Working across difference: Social work, social policy and social justice.* Macmillan International Higher Education/Red Globe Press.

Bamforth, J., & Gapps, B., Gurr, R., Howard, A., Onyx, J., & Rawsthorne, M. (2016). *Planning, funding, and community action: The area assistance story.* Common Ground Publishing LLC.

Beacham, J., Nyberg, D., Wright, C., Freund, J., & Rickards, L. (2018). Organising food differently: Towards a more-than-human ethics of care for the Anthropocene. *Organization, 25*(4), 533–549. https://doi.org/10.1177/1350508418777893

Beresford, Q. (2021). *Wounded country: The Murray-Darling Basin: A contested history.* New South Publishing.

Berger, P. L., & Luckmann, T. (1967). *The social construction of reality: A treatise in the sociology of knowledge.* Allen Lane.

Boulianne, S., Lalancette, M., & Ilkiw, D. (2020). "School Strike 4 Climate": Social media and the international youth protest on climate change. *Media and Communication, 8*(2), 208–218. https://doi.org/10.17645/mac.v8i2.2768

Campbell, M., Thomson, H., Fenton, C., & Gibson, M. (2016). Lone parents, health, wellbeing and welfare to work: A systematic review of qualitative studies. *BMC Public Health, 16*(1), 188–188. https://doi.org/10.1186/s12889-016-2880-9

Campos, I., Vizinho, A., Coelho, C., Alves, F., Truninger, M., Pereira, C., Santos, F. D., & Penha Lopes, G. (2016). Participation, scenarios and pathways in long-term planning for climate change adaptation. *Planning Theory & Practice, 17*(4), 537–556. https://doi.org/10.1080/14649357.2016.1215511

Christens, B. D. (2020). Ultrasociality and intersubjectivity. *American Journal of Community Psychology, 65*(1–2), 187–200. https://doi.org/10.1002/ajcp.12391

Connell, R., Fawcett, B., & Meagher, G. (2009). Neoliberalism, new public management and the human service professions: Introduction to the special issue. *Journal of Sociology, 45*(4), 331–338. https://doi.org/10.1177/1440783309346472

Corrigan. (2016). Lessons learned from unintended consequences about erasing the stigma of mental illness. *World Psychiatry, 15*(1), 67–73. https://doi.org/10.1002/wps.20295

Dawson, L., River, J., McCloughen, A., & Buus, N. (2020). "Every single minute and hour is scrutinised": Neoliberalism and Australian private mental health care. *Sociology of Health & Illness, 42*(2), 277–292. https://doi.org/10.1111/1467-9566.13009

Dufour, P. (2021). Comparing collective actions beyond national contexts: "Local spaces of protest" and the added value of critical geography. *Social Movement Studies, 20*(2), 224–242. https://doi.org/10.1080/14742837.2020.1732199

Groulx, M., Brisbois, M. C., Lemieux, C. J., Winegardner, A., & Fishback, L. (2017). A role for nature-based citizen science in promoting individual and collective climate change action? A systematic review of learning outcomes. *Science Communication, 39*(-1), 45–76. https://doi.org/10.1177/1075547016688324

Hamilton, S., & Kells, S. (2021). *Sold down the river: How robber barons and Wall Street traders cornered Australia's water market.* Text Publishing Co. ISBN: 9781922458124

Howard, A., & Allison, J. (2018). *Mapping local networks for disaster resilience evaluation report.* Dungog Neighbourhood Centre. Funder by CRIP, Office of Emergency Management.

Howard, A., Agllias, K., Barrett, K., Stansfield, I., Gissane, J., & Murphy, B. (2016). *Southlakes connections project: Networks, resilience and actions in Southlakes community post April 2015 storms.* NSW Department of Justice through the Community Resilience Innovation Program.

Howard, A., von Meding, J., Blakemore, T., Heinsch, M., Allison, J., & Cavaliere, S. (2017). *Stronger for the storm: Community responses and recovery from the April 2015 storm event* [Unpublished Report]. NSW State Emergency Service [SES] & NSW Department of Justice.

Hutton, D. (2012). Lessons from the lock the gate movement. *Social Alternatives, 31*(1), 15–19.

Kallhoff, A., (2021). *Climate justice and collective action.* Routledge.

Kjeldahl, E. M., & Hendricks, V. F. (2018). The sense of social influence: Pluralistic ignorance in climate change. *EMBO Reports, 19*(11). https://doi.org/10.15252/embr.201847185

Lazzarato, M. (2009). Neoliberalism in action: Inequality, insecurity and the re-constitution of the social. *Theory, Culture & Society, 26*(6), 109–133. https://doi.org/10.1177/0263276409350283

Le Roux, T., & Van Niekerk, D. (2020). Challenges in stakeholders self-organising to enhance disaster communication. *Corporate Communications: An International Journal, 25*(1), 128–142. https://doi.org/10.1108/CCIJ-07-2019-0078

Luke, H. (2017). Social resistance to coal seam gas development in the Northern Rivers region of Eastern Australia: Proposing a diamond model of social license to operate. *Land Use Policy, 69*, 266–280. https://doi.org/10.1016/j.landusepol.2017.09.006

Maclean. K. (2015). Crossing cultural boundaries: Integrating Indigenous water knowledge into water governance through co-research in the Queensland Wet Tropics, Australia. *Geoforum, 59*, 142–152. https://doi.org/10.1016/j.geoforum.2014.12.008

McVicker, G. (2012). Community-based ecological stewardship: A concept for productive harmony on the public lands of the western United States. In H. A. Karl, L. Scarlett, J. C. Vargas-Moreno, & M. Flaxman (Eds.), *Restoring lands – Coordinating science, politics and action: Complexities of climate and governance* (pp. 365–402). Springer. https://doi.org/10.1007/978-94-007-2549-2

Mladenov, T. (2015). Neoliberalism, postsocialism, disability. *Disability & Society, 30*(3), 445–459. https://doi.org/10.1080/09687599.2015.1021758

Nursey-Bray, M., Palmer, R., Smith, T. F., & Rist, P. (2019). Old ways for new days: Australian Indigenous peoples and climate change. *Local Environment, 24*(5), 473–486. https://doi.org/10.1080/13549839.2019.1590325

Ostrom, E. (2010). Polycentric systems for coping with collective action and global environmental change. *Global Environmental Change, 20*(4), 550–557. https://doi.org/10.1016/j.gloenvcha.2010.07.004

Pavel, M. P. (2015). A climate justice compass for transforming self and world. *World Futures, 71*(3–4), 96–113. https://doi.org/10.1080/02604027.2015.1092790

Robertson, P. J., & Choi, T. (2010). Ecological governance: Organizing principles for an emerging era. *Public Administration Review, 70*(s1), s89–s99. https://doi.org/10.1111/j.1540-6210.2010.02250.x

Shaw, D., Cumbers, A., McMaster, R., & Crossan, J. (2018). Scaling up community action for tackling climate change. *British Journal of Management, 29*(2), 266–278. https://doi.org/10.1111/1467-8551.12274

Shepherd, D. A., & Williams, T. A. (2014). Local venturing as compassion organizing in the aftermath of a natural disaster: The role of localness and community in reducing suffering. *Journal of Management Studies, 51*(6), 952–994. https://doi.org/10.1111/joms.12084

Song, Z., Zhang, H., & Dolan, C. (2020). Promoting disaster resilience: Operation mechanisms and self-organizing processes of crowdsourcing. *Sustainability, 12*(5), 1862. https://doi.org/10.3390/su12051862

United Nations. (2019, May 6). UN Report: Nature's dangerous decline 'unprecedented'; Species extinction rates 'accelerating'. *Sustainable Development Goals United Nations.* Retrieved from https://www.un.org/sustainabledevelopment/blog/2019/05/nature-decline-unprecedented-report/

Wukich, C., & Steinberg, A. (2013). Nonprofit and public sector participation in self-organizing information networks: Twitter hashtag and trending topic use during disasters. *Risk, Hazards & Crisis in Public Policy, 4*(2), 83–109. https://doi.org/10.1002/rhc3.12036

8

ACTING FOR CHANGE

Mobilising policy

It would seem remiss to write a book on climate justice and social work without a chapter focusing on policy. Understanding, influencing and implementing policy (particularly social policy) are core aspects of social work and human service practice (Fawcett et al., 2009). Traditionally it is through policy practice that social work and human service practitioners seek to effect structural change (although we would also argue that research practice can be as effective). There are hundreds if not thousands of public policy experts across the globe focusing every day on climate change policy. In this chapter we will draw on and make reference to some of these experts but we do not claim climate policy expertise. Like other elements of this book, we are aiming to bring a social work and human service practice lens to this work.

Public policy

There is ongoing debate about the definition of 'policy', with Fenna (2004) suggesting that 'conveniently vague definitions (include) virtually everything and anything 'society' does' (p.322). Howlett and Cashore (2014) avoid the debate about definition and rather argue that public policy is both a 'technical and political process' (p.17). This technical and political process involves the development and implementation of an actor's goals and means. Fawcett et al. (2009) argue that social policy is concerned with the principles and practices of pursuit by government of social, political and economic outcomes. Policies can be legislated through parliament, made through courts and given expression through procedures. Sometimes policies gain power or traction through compliance to social norms, rather than through legislation. Policies can be understood as social products, produced through human action. Goodwin (2011) and others (most notably Carol Bacchi) interrogate policy as *discourse*, starting with

DOI: 10.4324/9781003146339-8

the assumptions that all actions, objects, and practices are socially meaningful and that the interpretation of these meanings is shaped by the social
and political struggles in specific socio-historical contexts.

(p.168)

Policy making is not of course value-free but involves choice or the 'selection of
goals' as well as decisions about the means of implementation. There is a significant scholarship that focuses on the stages or policy cycle, attempting to identify
how policy is made. This scholarship views policy making as 'applied problem
solving' that moves logically from agenda setting, policy formulation, decision
making, policy implementation and policy evaluation. More recently scholars
have shifted their focus to the 'choice' of goals or the *why* of policy. Scholars
such as Bacchi seek to unearth assumptions about the 'problems' that give rise to
policy interventions (discussed further below).

Policy is developed and enacted in most institutional settings (universities,
non-government organisations, activist groups); however, in this chapter we are
primarily focusing on governments or the State policy. Howlett and Cashore
(2014) highlight that

governments enjoy a special status in public policy-making due to their
unique ability to make authoritative decisions on behalf of citizens; that is,
decisions backed up by the potential for sanctions for transgressors in the
event of non-compliance.

(p.17)

In democratic countries such as Australia it is only governments that have the
ability to sanction transgressors of policy. For example, government policy requires those travelling on public transport to pay set fares and failure to provide
evidence of payment may result in a fine. In relation to climate change, only
governments can force individuals and businesses to change their behaviour and
demand that they publicly report on their actions. Whilst governments have
an especially powerful role in policy making, many other 'actors' are active in
the policy process. Policy actors include political advisors within government,
activist NGOs, international institutions and frameworks, industry lobbyists,
professional associations and even the general public (Howlett & Cashore, 2014;
Nulman, 2015).

Not only do policies arise from human action, they are also influenced by human action. In exploring the policy-making process researchers routinely identify a 'gap' between policy intent and policy impact (Truscott & Malcolm, 2010;
Watkins & Meijer, 2016). In one example research explored health policy in relation to acute care of post-operative pain in the UK (Powell et al cited in Tolfree,
2016). Despite long-term recognition of the 'problem' and general agreement
about the 'solution', pain management in most hospitals did not improve following the introduction of a new national policy. The research identified a range of

social barriers to policy uptake including: lack of agreement that the improvement was necessary; poor fit with local organisational priorities; conflict with longstanding professional boundaries; and divergent views among health professionals. It was noted

> These factors did not just impact as single factors, but also worked in combination and impacted on each other in complex ways.
>
> *(Tolfree, 2016)*

Other scholars point out that policy is made not only by action but also inaction (Fawcett et al., 2009). We have seen policy by inaction very clearly in the Australian context over the past decade in relation to climate change (Zhang et al., 2018). In the results of a 2021 Lowy Institute Climate Poll (Kassam & Léser, 2021), three quarters of Australians reported that the benefits of government action on climate change outweighed the costs and 60% of the population perceived global warming as a serious threat. This poll, along with a number of others, also records a change in public perceptions and priorities with increasing numbers seeing government action on reducing carbon emissions as a priority. Health scientists Rhonda Garad and Joanne Enticott (2021) colourfully suggest that

> [r]ather than leading our country to safer waters, the government is like an officer on the Titanic, telling passengers to return to their rooms and relax.

The political contestation, the range of actors and context highlight the complexity of policy making. Policy making occurs within a network of many interconnected elements which interact with each other in changing or adaptive ways (Pycroft, 2014). This complexity also gives rise to surprising change from seemingly minor policy shifts. By engaging with policy (through our practice or through research and analysis), we are participating in the political processes of democratic polities (Goodwin, 2011, p.168). Our argument is that 'policy' is core work for social workers and human service workers, regardless of their day-to-day job title.

Wicked social problems

The concept of 'wicked social problem' was coined in 1973 by Horst Rittel and Melvin Webber. They sought to highlight the complexities and challenges of addressing certain social problems through policy interventions as well as critiquing traditional 'engineering' approaches to problem solving (Head, 2008). Many areas of social policy are now understood as 'wicked' including Aboriginal incarceration rates, mental health and domestic violence. When a problem is described as 'wicked', it flags the challenge of not only the solution to the problem but also identifying the cause of the problem. Rational-technical solutions are poorly suited to respond to the complexity of the social issue and, perversely, can at times make the problem worse or more entrenched. Think here of the social called 'Basics Card' required of certain income support recipients aimed apparently at supporting 'better money management'. Research suggests that instead the Basics Card exacerbates financial stress and entrenches poverty (Marston et al., 2020). Wicked social problems, such as addressing climate change,

> are seen as 'ill-defined', interlinked, and relying on political judgments rather than scientific certitudes.
>
> *(Head, 2008, p.102)*

The severity and hence challenge of wicked social problems arise from three components:

- *Complexity* of elements, subsystems and interdependencies
- *Uncertainty* in relation to risks, consequences of action and changing patterns
- *Divergence and fragmentation* in viewpoints (Head, 2008, p.103).

As discussed earlier in this book, policy response to climate change is undoubtedly a preeminent wicked problem at a local and global level. The production of fuel is not simply a technical task of closing coal mines and shifting to low-emissions technology. Attention needs to be paid to the subsystems, convergence and interdependencies impacted by policy shifts, including the unintended consequences. We need to be mindful of the risks, consequences and changing patterns of behaviour, particularly bringing a social justice lens. Who might benefit and who may have experiences of exclusion further embedded? We need to be respectful of the divergent voices as well as protective against social fragmentation arising from conflict. Whilst culturally and spiritually connected to the Land, many Aboriginal people benefit socially and economically from coal mining as part of the fly-in-fly-out workforce. Binary or simplistic rational-technical solutions are of limited value in responding to the policy challenge of climate justice. Again, whilst this book is a call to act on climate justice, we draw on the insights provided by complexity theory to guide that action. In acting we need to be cognizant of the possibility of the emergence of new patterns of injustice. This highlights the fallacy that policy intervention takes place within a stable system, naturally recalibrating to an equilibrium. This is not to argue though that those interested in climate justice should not be at the policy table. It is to suggest instead that it is *how* we are at the table that is important. In the next section, we draw on the work of Carol Bacchi and others to provide some more hopeful ways of being at the policy table. Post-modern understandings, particularly those influenced by Foucault, provide some useful tools for those wanting to engage with climate change policy. Goodwin (2011) argues that thinking about policy as discourse captures the ways in which policy shapes the world through the framing of social 'problems' and government 'solutions' and the construction of concepts, categories, distinctions and subject positions.

(p.170)

Thinking about policy as produced through discourse challenges and disrupts the 'taken-for-granted' nature of social problems. Carole Bacchi (2022) has led the development of a methodological approach to interrogating policy as discourse called 'What's the Problem Represented to Be?' (WPR). WPR starts with the policy text and tracks back to unearth assumptions about the 'problem' and thus make visible the logics for the policy 'response'. A WPR approach to policy analysis

> challenges the conventional view that public policies are responses or reactions to problems that sit outside the policy process, waiting to be discovered and solved. By contrast, the WPR approach argues that policies contain implicit representations of the 'problems' they purport to address. ... The goal of the WPR approach is to treat these problem representations as problematizations that require critical scrutiny.
>
> *(Bacchi, 2022)*

There are an increasing number of policy areas subjected to analysis using WPR, in fields such as juvenile justice (Yassine, 2017) and Aboriginal child protection (Briggs, 2019). Bacchi and others argue that policy failure to address 'wicked problems' results from the construction of the problem in the first place: that is, the way we understand the problem (Manning, 2019). McInerney in 2008 (cited in Goodwin, 2011) analysed Howard Government policies in relation to education disadvantage. His research found that under the influence of conservative government education disadvantage was 'radically reframed' as a problem of individual deficits in literacy and numeracy skills. Framing of the 'problem' in this way led to solutions such as an extension of compulsory school years, increased use of standardised testing and prescriptive curriculum. If the 'problem' is located in the individual student, other responses (such as the previous Disadvantage Schools Program that directed additional resources to schools) are outside the frame or unthinkable. Manning (2019) used WPR to critically unpack early childhood policy initiatives in New Zealand and Australia. She demonstrated the way in which early childhood education interventions are represented as addressing economic or labour market 'problems'. This representation positioned early childhood education as primarily of benefit to adults and accordingly was silent on the citizen rights of children. A focus on how 'problems' are framed by policy actors in climate change is emerging highlighting that 'many environmental problems are not decomposable, yet they are often treated as such' (Park, 2022, p.3).

WPR asks six questions of policy texts

1 What's the *'problem'* … represented to be in a specific policy or policies?
2 What *presuppositions and assumptions* underlie this representation of the 'problem'?
3 *How* has this representation of the 'problem' come about?
4 What is left *unproblematic* in this problem representation? Where are the silences? Can the 'problem' be thought about differently?
5 What *effects* are produced by this representation of the 'problem'?
6 How/where is this representation of the 'problem' *produced, disseminated and defended*? How could it be questioned, disrupted and replaced?

This approach to thinking about and analysing policy foregrounds power, bringing a critical perspective to who benefits and who does not from particular problem representations. This focus on unjust outcomes from policy interventions makes it highly relevant to this book and the work of those working in social work and human services. Bacchi argues

> to create real change, the representation of policy 'problems' needs to change.
>
> *(cited in Manning, 2019)*

In the following section we seek to employ some of these broader ideas about 'public policy', how and why it comes about, the policy actors and the debates to take stock of the current state of climate change policy in Australia as well flagging potential future directions.

Climate change and policy

Natural scientists have been seeking to influence public policy in relation to climate change for decades, well before it was taken up by environmental activists (Nulman, 2015). Evidence of the impact of human activity of the earth's climate has been documented by natural scientists since at least the 1970s (Huntley, 2020). Journalist Nathaniel Rich notes that the physics hasn't changed since that time and wryly comments

> nearly every conversation that we have [now] about climate change was being held in 1979.
>
> *(cited in Huntley, 2020, p.21)*

The latest version of Intergovernmental Panel on Climate Change (IPCC) report (2022) again reports the urgency of comprehensive action to slow emissions and temperature rises. It is clear that the impacts of climate change are not being shared evenly, with highly vulnerable countries already experiencing climate-related mortality *15 times higher* than other countries (UN, 2019). The science is depressing, leaving many unable to 'get off the couch' (Huntley, 2020). Whilst attention is being paid to the mental health impact on scientists (Huntley, 2020), spare a thought for those working at the front line of public policy development!

Climate change policy suffers all the difficulties flagged by Fenna (2004) when he bemoaned the tendency of "policy" to include 'virtually everything and anything "society" does'. Even if we strictly focus on policies in relation to the reduction of greenhouse gas emissions from human activities, a wide range of policy areas are relevant, including: taxation, energy production, transport, research and development (R & D), employment, land use and food production to name just some of the most obvious. Unsurprisingly, the Organisation for Economic Co-operation and Development (OECD), a key international economic development institution, argues that

> Climate change concerns should be integrated in all areas of public policy, particularly economic and social policies. Mainstreaming climate change adaptation into all relevant areas of public policy is a priority. It is a long-term process including awareness-raising, integration into sectoral planning and implementation of specific adaptation options. Integrating climate change risks requires more flexible, preventive and forward-looking approaches, and will involve legal, institutional and policy changes.
>
> *(2007, pp.4–5)*

Despite global pressure (discussed below), the Australian government has been reluctant to accept the responsibility for 'authoritative decisions' in relation to climate change, instead highlighting the responsibilities of 'private interests'. The Council of Australian Governments' (COAG's) Select Council on Climate Change in 2012 agreed Roles and Responsibilities for Climate Change Adaptation in Australia, declaring that

> local initiative and private responsibility will be at the forefront of climate change adaptation in Australia ... It is not feasible, nor appropriate, for governments to bear all the costs of adapting to the impacts of climate change.
>
> *(COAG, 2012, p.1)*

Mobilising WPR assists unearthing how framing the 'problem' in particular ways leads to particular 'solutions'. In this document COAG adopts a risk management frame, affirming that parties other than governments are 'usually best placed to manage risks to their own assets and activities from climate change impacts' (2012, p.2). The framing up of the impact of climate change in economic terms ('costs' and 'own assets') demonstrates the economic/social binary so at odds with a First Nations Worldview perspective. Whilst articulated in

2012 this understanding of roles and responsibilities remains in place, informing governments policy interventions . Interestingly, even if we frame up climate change in economic terms, there are still counter arguments to the 'too high' costs argument prosecuted by some conservative politicians such as Senator Matt Canavan who argues:

> Talk of the immediate importance of reducing our small carbon footprint now sounds like a dis-cordant echo from a bygone era. With millions out of work, and our major trade partner threatens our economic security, why would we continue to self-flagellate by imposing the additional costs of reducing carbon emissions for no environmental benefit?
>
> *(Canavan, 2020)*

The OECD, hardly a left-wing organisation, argues that the 'cost' of stabilising greenhouse gas concentrations can be achieved at costs of less than one-tenth of a percent of gross domestic product (GDP) growth per annum, or less than a 3% loss in GDP by 2030 (OECD, 2007). Like other debates in the climate change field, there is an emerging consensus that the cost of inaction is likely to be economically crippling (Treasury, 2011). For non-humans the 'cost' of human action/inaction is already great: over 500,000 ground dwelling creatures have insufficient habitat for long-term survival; over 40% of amphibian species are threatened with extinction; and about one third of reef forming corals, sharks and marine mammals are threatened with extinction (UN, 2019).

It is important as people critically engaged with issues of climate change, we avoid simplistic portrayals and explanations (and to get off the couch). Despite the public perception of inaction, there are many examples of government policy changes that both positively and negatively impact on the climate. Some of these changes can appear quite small but have much larger impacts. Complexity theory has explanatory value in understanding this through highlighting the messiness and uncertainty of social life. Government policy making, whilst portrayed as logical and simple providing 'us with at least the illusion of control' (Pycroft, 2014, p.15), is in fact marked by complexity. As such due to its non-linearity, the cause-and-effect relationships are difficult to track. Furthermore, the non-linear nature of interactions results in consequences that may be disproportionate and difficult to predict.

In the 1980s and 1990s climate activists and environmentalists focused their efforts on international co-operation and treaties, seeing the nation state as having limited traction (Nulman, 2015). With the lack of global progress however more attention was turned to nation state policies. This increased attention at the local (or national) level, whilst frustrating for many, has given rise to a huge array of policies and action on climate. Insights from complexity theory suggest small policy steps should not be dismissed. A good example of this disproportionate effect of government policy change is the Norway electric vehicle policies (Shields, 2021). Through small acts of direct civil disobedience, setting national goals, a raft of incentives (such as toll reductions, parking fee exemptions, access to bus lanes and taxation relief) and infrastructure investments, Norway has become a world leader in the transition towards low and zero-emission cars. Whilst progress was initially slow, the past decade has seen extraordinary change. In 2011 75% of new car sales were diesel; by 2021 this had dropped to 2.3% (Shields, 2021). It is anticipated that Norway will reach its goal of no new high emissions car sales by 2025. This example also reminds that transition will occur over time, not overnight!

National policy

Despite the Australian 'climate wars', many State and Territory Governments as well as businesses have developed and implemented policies aimed at addressing the adverse impacts of climate change (Flannery et al., 2021). Clearly government policy is vulnerable to morphing into rhetoric or political expediency along similar lines as business 'greenwashing' (Gelmini, 2021). Setting tangible and transparent goals is vital in holding governments and businesses alike accountable for their public commitments. The Climate Council argues that the science demands that Australia reduce its emissions by 75% (below 2005 levels) by 2030 and achieve net zero by 2035 (2021, p.45). One important shift identified by the Climate Council is demanding a move away from the use of 'dubious carbon offsets' with the real impact of activities hidden behind accounting procedures (Gelmini, 2021). That real change is possible is evident in the success of Tasmania and ACT. The ACT achieved its goal to source 100% of its electricity from renewable energy by 2010 (Flannery et al., 2021, p.44). This was supported by a staggered emission reduction plan. After achieving 100% self-sufficient renewable energy, Tasmania has doubled this target and is aiming to generate 200% of their current electricity needs by 2040 from renewable energy (Marchant, 2020). Change at the State and Territory level does not just 'happen' but is driven by political will and vision. The Premier, for example, envisages Tasmania as not only 'Australia's renewable energy powerhouse' but also 'a world leading provider of clean, reliable and affordable energy' (Barnett, 2020). In NSW a similar hopeful picture of State Government policy action has emerged under then Environment Minister, Matt Kean (Raper, 2021). Key government action includes investment in renewable energy infrastructure and more supportive electric vehicle policy. What all these States and Territories have in common is a plan of action, again as advocated by the OECD

> Phasing-in the policies according to a clear timetable, and helping workers to retrain or move to other forms of employment, are examples of measures that can help to smooth the transition to a low-carbon economy.
>
> *(2007, p.4)*

However, van Holstein (2020) in their study of community gardens in Sydney, identified the impact of policy, resource availability and changing neighbourhoods in shaping gardeners and gardens to comply with neo-liberalism and the policy directions of local government. Van Holstein reports on the tensions experienced by community gardeners to continually adapt their self-organising to external pressures in the face of – "the ability of institutions and governments to reach into garden spaces to control objectives and functioning of community projects" (p.1286). In this study of three community gardens in the Inner West of Sydney, the actions of local government and the different relationships between Councils and community gardens precipitated a competitive culture between the gardens and fostered the idea of the 'good' community garden which meets with the aesthetic and entrepreneurial preferences of Council in an area which is rapidly gentrifying.

Global policy making

Global action on climate has been formalised through various United Nations forums, commencing with what is now known as the First World Climate Conference in 1979. This forum was the precursor to the United Nations Framework Convention on Climate Change in 1992 aiming to 'avoid dangerous climate change'. The UN hosts an annual 'conference of parties' (COP) often marked by debate and disagreement particularly in relation to enforceable targets (Nulman, 2015). Progress has been slow, and some commentators see COP as another example of the 'horse-trading that characterises international negotiations' (Evans & Gabbatiss, 2019). The Climate Action Network (formed in 1989 with the co-operative leadership of the World Wide Fund for Nature, Greenpeace International and the Environment Defense Fund) was the first civil society co-ordinated effort to pressure governments for global action to address climate change (Nulman, 2015, p.12). Civil society organisations are now key participants in global policy making, across the whole policy spectrum (Nasiritousi et al., 2014).

COP21, which was held in Paris in 2015, saw a positive shift in acceptance of the need to act and resulted in what has become known as the 'Paris Agreement'. In that landmark agreement 197 countries agreed to work together to limit global warming to well below 2 degrees and aim for 1.5 degrees, to adapt to the impacts of a changing climate and to finance this action (Evans et al., 2021). Under the Paris Agreement, countries committed to bring forward national plans setting out how much they would reduce their emissions – known as Nationally Determined Contributions or 'NDCs'. Parties to the Paris Agreement also agreed to come back together every 5 years to update their commitments. As we are writing this book, the world was planning the latest 5-year meeting to update the Paris Agreement and importantly to agree on the 'rules' that would enforce the Paris Agreement. As the Glasgow COP26 Climate Summit approached, the Australian government continued to prevaricate about attending (initially) or agreeing to climate action targets. These targets only aspired to keeping the impacts of human-induced climate change at a significant rather than catastrophic level. None of the agreements made through the UN COP process are legally binding, countries are 'requested' or 'strongly encouraged' to act and language is highly contested with environmentalist noting the

> glaring disconnect between the jargon-filled negotiating halls and the increasingly alarmed populace in the outside world.
>
> *(Evans et al., 2021)*

UN discussions focus on three pillars of international action on climate change: mitigation; adaption; and more recently loss and damage (i.e. financial compensation for those bearing the brunt of climate change). Like many global negotiations, there is strong debate about the 'success' or 'failure' of the COP26 Pact, however, some progress was made with:

- 151 countries submitting new climate plans to slash their emissions by 2030
- The first explicit reference to shifting away from coal and phasing out fossil fuel subsidies
- Agreement to continue, increase and re-calibrate climate-related finance arrangements
- Pledges on deforestation, land clearing and methane reduction on the sidelines
- Meet again next year with a view to increasing short-term emission reductions and long-term strategic plans (World Resources Institute, 2021)

The UN Intergovernmental Science-Policy Platform on Biodiversity and Ecosystem Services has identified a range of policy innovations to support the transformation of consumption-driven growth aimed at addressing the profound impact of human action/inaction on life on Earth (UN, 2019). These require the convergence of agricultural and agroecological practices through 'multifunctional landscape planning' and 'cross-sectoral integrated management' responding to complexity and respecting First Nations Worldviews. This would require all actors to be engaged: in the food system, for example, this would include producers, the public sector, civil society and consumers. Innovation in food production policy would enable greater integration of landscape and watershed management; conservation of the diversity of genes, varieties, cultivars, breeds, landraces and species; the empowerment of consumers and producers through market transparency, improved distribution and localisation (that revitalises local economies), reformed supply chains and food waste reduction (UN, 2019). Transformation enabled through policy innovation has also been mapped out for fresh water, cities and marine environments.

Despite its challenges, co-operation at a policy level both nationally and globally is vital. The actions of individual nations, in the context of climate change, are intimately entangled with each other and the imperative for collective agreement globally is both apparent in commentary and analysis at all levels and urgent as international patience with hesitant countries such as ours is wearing very thin. Although we don't necessarily frame the development of climate change policy as a collective action initiative, the processes we see here provide an important example of how to navigate collective action amongst those with conflicting or divergent interests. The layers of negotiation within the national political system between climate action advocates and sceptics, those with fears about short-term local impacts of shifting away from coal, those who have embraced renewable energy and are already investing, those with interests in business as usual and a reluctance to change, play out in a context where global issues and trends can no longer be ignored. For Australia, calls to take up responsibilities expected of a global citizen are intensifying. A combination of encouragement, cajoling, deal making and peer pressure are deployed to achieve a collective agreement. The social and economic consequences for countries seem to be creating the problem but not participating in the solution, including Australia, may, in the end, be the factor which pushes the government to join the collective process. At a global level, what is possible to get agreement on is very different to the aims of many and may or may not be enough to prevent significant climate change impacts. This form of collective action provides an important example for us to think through as it reflects the contested spaces and dynamics through which agreements on complex issues must traverse.

Positive steps

Future Crunch (https://futurecrun.ch/) has taken up the challenge of telling a different climate story to the dominant 'doom and gloom' stories (https://futurecrun.ch/). These 'good news' stories are powerful tools in 'getting people off the couch' to participate in campaigns, recognising the importance of story-telling to humanity. Future Crunch aim to 'give people hope for the future' (2022), noting:

> Progress isn't a straight line and it doesn't happen by magic. It depends on people who, even during the darkest of times, believe that it's possible to make the world a better place and who are willing to roll up their sleeves to do the work, even when the cameras aren't watching.

The 'good news' in Australia arising from policy action on climate included:

- We now have 25 GW installed solar capacity – the most per capita in the world! In 2021 more than 3 GW of rooftop solar was installed
- Wind and solar provided five times more power than gas in 2021. Coal power is at lowest since 1999 at 62.8%
- The giant Adani Coal Mine in Queensland has been abandoned by Convex, a global reinsurance company, which has signaled a permanent move away from coal-related infrastructure.

- Some of Australia's most beautiful natural sites, including the Daintree, the oldest tropical rainforest in the world, were returned to their traditional owners this year: four parks, covering more than 160,000 hectares, will now be managed by the Eastern Kuku Yalanji people.
- Internationally there is good news on a wide range of fronts, often in surprising contexts. These changes reflect sustained work and when taken collectively point to a more hopeful future – visit the website to be inspired but here are a couple of our favourites:
- Ecologists reported that the Mississippi River is the cleanest it's been in more than a century, with pollution down to 1% of what it was in the 1980s, while the most comprehensive survey of the Thames in 60 years found that the river, once declared biologically dead, is now "home to myriad wildlife as diverse as London itself." The biggest river success story however came from China, which passed a landmark environmental law protecting the Yangtze, one of the country's two 'mother rivers', banning all industrial projects, sand mining and all fishing, including in tributaries and the estuary (more than 400 million people live in the Yangtze basin).
- Three different sites – an Alaskan archipelago dubbed the 'Rat Islands', Lehua Island in Hawaii and Redonda Isle in the Caribbean – were all declared rodent free this year after decades of conservation efforts. In all three locations, the pace of ecosystem recovery and increase of native wildlife populations has shocked even the most cynical of conservationists, shining examples of how quickly nature can bounce back if given a chance.
- Barcelona announced a new scheme to give citizens free, unlimited public transport for 3 years in return for giving up their private vehicles, Paris took back space from cars, opening linear parks on old highways along the Seine, phasing out diesel cars, opening bus lanes, raising parking meter prices and plowing bike lanes down hundreds of streets, and the UK's second largest city, Birmingham finalised a plan to divert car traffic out of the city and introducing zero-emissions cross-city buses, cycle ways and pedestrian lanes.
- In North Cyprus, nest counts of green turtles have increased by 162% and loggerhead turtles by 46% since 1993 and in Cape Verde, the number of nests has increased from 10,000 to almost 200,000 in the past 6 years, thanks to conservation measures and new laws to criminalise the killing, trade and consumption of sea turtles.

Social work and human service practitioners as policy actors

How, then, might social work and human service practitioners *act* in relation to policy? Nasiritousi and colleagues (2014) identify elements of the policy process that appear particularly relevant, including: providing information and expertise; influencing decisions and policymakers; raising awareness of climate change among the public; and representing public opinion and marginalised voices. Lena Dominelli argues

> Social workers, the professionals charged with enhancing human wellbeing from a human rights and social justice framework (Ife, 2003), are well placed to contribute to climate change policy discussions and interventions.
>
> *(2011, p.430)*

Whilst we are 'well placed' to engage with the policy-making process, this needs to go beyond 'speaking about policies' if we are to take 'the challenge of the struggle for ecological justice seriously' (Peeters, 2012, p.107). Like Peeters, we argue that climate justice is not only about lessening the impact on specific groups of the community but about taking sides (with Mother Earth). It involves resisting and rejecting a social and economic system based on continuous growth and exploitation (Peeters, 2012). We wonder if it might be worth us taking a much broader view than traditional social work and human service practice. When we look at the skill set, knowledge and value base, capacity to negotiate in complex systems and relational focus of those working in the world of social justice and social processes, we wonder why there are not more of us involved in policy work shaped by climate change. One factor that may play into social work and human service reluctance is the common portrayal of climate change activists as naïve, ill-informed and performing 'identity politics' which is at odds with professional identity. Additionally, climate activists have had a fraught relationship with the formal institutional frameworks of government policy making, with Corry and Reiner (2021) noting

> radical climate activists who distrust politicians and governments might also be expected to dismiss the idea that policy changes could make a real difference to a problem as intractable as climate change.
>
> *(p.206)*

As argued previously, social workers and human service workers have the opportunity to play diverse roles in the policy process: building capacity; creating democratic structures that support participation; negotiating conflict; highlighting inequality; influencing policymakers; and taking action independent of states (Nasiritousi et al., 2014). In thinking about policy change, Nasiritousi et al. (2014) argue that the capacity of non-state actors derives from different power sources. These include: the ability to invoke moral claims (*symbolic power*); expert knowledge (*cognitive power*); access to networks (*social power*); access to key decision makers and processes (*leverage*); and access to resources (*material power*) (2016, p.113). It is our argument that social work and human service practitioners are well placed to produce and mobilise these forms of power, particularly through collaborative action. In relation to policy change, the Community Tool Box notes

> Changing policy is a step on the road to changing social conditions and real community development ... It's usually the shortest road to permanent social change ... The ideal policy change agents are broad-based coalitions.
>
> *(Rabinowitz, 2022)*

Broad-based coalitions in the climate change arena often take the form of a social movement. A key question for researchers and the participants in these social movements is *what, when* and *how* change has been achieved (Nulman, 2015). These questions are the focus of Nulman (2015) in discussing in-depth case studies of three climate change policy campaigns in the UK: the *Big Ask* Campaign led by Friends of the Earth arguing for the introduction of a Climate Change Act with emission reduction targets; the campaign against the Heathrow third runway, in opposition to investing in carbon-intensive infrastructure; and the campaign to establish a Green Investment Bank as a means to support clean investment. Rather than a simplistic 'success/failure' measure of these campaigns to achieve policy change, Nulman's research provides extensive details of the *what, when* and *how* of these campaigns. In answering the *what* questions, he deploys a Policy Outcomes Model (Nulman 2015, pp.58–86) that examines:

- the extent to which pro-movement policies are considered (policy consideration)
- the extent to which policymakers ally themselves with pro-movement policies (political support)
- the extent to which political action is taken to deliver pro-movement policies (political action)
- the extent to which policy change is formulated and functions to serve movement goals (desired change) and
- the extent to which the policies achieve a movement's broader goals (desired outcome) (2015, p.6).

The three case studies employed a range of tactics (the how), to varying levels of success. Again, complexity theory here brings to the fore the dynamic, emergent, nature of policy practice. Common mechanisms (causal processes that produce an effect) involved in achieving policy change included: public preference; political access; disruption; judicial mechanism; and international politics.

The *Big Ask* campaign had a strong and long focus on shifting public preferences and increasing political access. It built unlikely coalitions (cross party), placing pressure on local MPs, working with parties to develop policy as well as utilising party and parliamentary procedures. During what was called the *Big Autumn Push* (September–November 2007), Friends of the Earth were involved in: 46 public meetings; 58 film screenings; 163 meetings with individual MPs; 445 street stalls; 94 media stunts; and 25 training events. After 3 years of active campaigning, the Climate Change Bill received royal assent on 26 November 2008.

In the Australian context there is a growing willingness to use judicial mechanisms to force policy action. These include legal challenges in relation to Commonwealth government's duty of care in relation to young people and Torres Strait Islanders among others, invoking human rights legislation in Queensland to prevent the expansion of coal mining and holding corporations to account for their emissions reduction claims (Pender, 2022).

Disruption has been mobilised through direct action successfully to influence policy outcomes, often through coalitions of socially progressive groups such as Traditional Owners, Unions, Environmentalists and youth groups. One well-known example was opposition to the expansion of the Ranger Uranium Mine in the Kakadu National Park in the Northern Territory at Jabiluka (Hintjens, 2000). The Jabiluka Action Group opposed the expansion and joined forces with the Mirarr People, the Traditional Owners of the land on which the mine was to be developed and their representative organisation, the Gundjeihmi Aboriginal Corporation. The campaign was marked by non-violent civil disobedience at the site of the proposed mine and most State capitals. Over 8 months some 5,000 people joined the protest camp at the site and police made over 500 arrests despite the peaceful protests (Australian Nuclear and Uranium Sites, 2014). Footpath 'camps' were also established in major cities outside the companies offices to raise public awareness of the opposition of the Mirarr People and the environmental dangers of the mine. Shareholders also become involved in direct action against the companies. Writing in the early days of the disruption, Helen Hintjens notes

> Indigenous people's concerns have for once been made absolutely central to an environmental campaign: in many parts of rural Australia this is now recognized as the *sine qua non* of effective environmental protest (Howitt, 1998). It is this inclusion of the indigenous perspective as central, rather than as a cultural after-thought that marks the anti-Jabiluka campaign out from many previous environmentalist protests in Australia.
>
> *(2000, p.389)*

Those who participated in the direct action, influenced by Aboriginal Worldviews, said: this is ours to look after, to care for and not to destroy. For the Mirarr People the land was sacred, not something to profit. Jeffry Lee, Djok Senior Traditional Owner, said

> I could be a rich man today. I could be a rich man. Billions of dollars…you know, you can offer me anything but my land is a cultural land.
>
> *(Sweeney, 2016)*

For those of us who work in social work and human services, international co-operation and negotiation may seem far from both our experience and far from the work that we are involved in. The process of setting emissions targets, winding up coal mining and developing renewable energy sources seems to lie a long way from where we have influence. In many ways, the only obvious link between global climate agreements and the social can be found in the social impacts which will accompany the transition. Dealing with the social fall out of unemployment, following along to support those who will miss out. In many ways, fulfilling the same role we play in capitalist society more generally.

We are, however, used to occupying contested spaces within the realms of the social. This is why it is important for us to find a place around the table in a world where social dynamics and social justice form part of a much larger and more entangled set of relationships set in an environment of rapid and unpredictable change. There is no doubt that in the short term, emissions reductions will have a disproportionate impact on those already experiencing poverty or in low-income precarious jobs (Park, 2022). In the longer term climate change impacts will also fall disproportionately on those already struggling. Without well-designed and implemented policy and practice to mitigate these impacts and to ensure changes in emissions can be afforded by everyone, this seems like a no win for social justice. Collective action at this global policy level has both direct and indirect knock-on effects all the way to the local and individual. From the price and availability of food, affordable energy, housing and transport, to employment opportunities, health and wellbeing. Global policy frameworks are a 'call for action … [that will] enable us to live within the Earth's carrying capacity' (Park, 2022, p.6).

> In fact, global collective efforts are well underway across a range of domains in both a recognition of the global scale through which action on climate change and sustainability must be acted upon, and in an effort to link global policy with local impact in a consistent way. In 2015, the 2030 Agenda for Sustainable Development marked a milestone with world leaders all supporting an agreement which encompasses 17 Sustainability Goals and 169 targets across diverse countries.
>
> *(Caron et al., 2018)*

We are not so naïve to leave this discussion here. Policy making inherently is shaped by and shapes economic, social and cultural power. Additionally, there is often a (large) gap between policy and practice. Ethicists have also given greater weight to intentional harm than unintentional harm, resulting in a lack of recognition of non-human suffering (Fraser & MacRae, 2011). Those interested in climate action are not immune from human-centric views, conflict nor are the dynamics of power magically harmonised through a shared value base. Research on advocacy in policy forums suggests that competition and self-interest can hinder policy outcomes. McAllister and colleagues (2014) examined the ways in which organisations interact at regional climate change policy forums in Queensland. Through network analysis and interviews, they found that organisations often used policy forums to advocate for their own interests which both narrowed the scope of learning for policy networks and hindered co-operation and collaboration. They argue that while individual advocacy by organisations is an important element of all policy debate, the collaborative work required to develop effective policy within the uncertain context of climate change, means that this advocacy must be managed to create co-operative processes where information can be utilised in learning within a less biased and competitive framework.

There is much to learn from examples such as the *Big Ask* for those interested in action on climate change in Australia. Policy change becomes possible through grass roots activism and sustained engagement. Clearly politicians and the mechanisms of government are vitally important in the policy-making process in liberal democracies. Much can be done between elections, through dialogue and advocacy. Groups like Climate for Change (https://www.climateforchange.org.au/) provide advice and resources to support individual and group activities. They focus on creating opportunities for conversations that support local action, particularly engaging with politicians. Emails, phone calls and meetings with your local Member of Parliament (MP) are known to be highly effective in raising awareness within political parties. MPs recognise that for each constituent who has taken the time to contact them there will be others who feel similar but haven't made contact (yet!). Resources are available to support policy advocacy on: opposing gas investments; reducing emissions; protecting the climate and environment; supporting climate justice and democracy; and enabling a sustainable economic recovery. Advocacy is targeted at local, state and commonwealth governments. Importantly, resources and suggestions are provided to keep a dialogue open with the local MP rather than viewing the engagement as a one-off to maximise accountability (Climate for Change, 2021). MP Engagement Groups creates a supportive environment for action with others who share your concerns, providing a space for sharing and learning (Climate for Change, 2021).

Resources such as those of Climate for Change are useful not only for our own action but also for supporting the people we work with to participate in policy advocacy. Organisations can make available information for face-to-face service users as well as on their digital sites. Conversations identifying local climate change priorities can support local action, remembering that many land use policies are determined at the local government level. Joining local action to larger coalitions also builds power for change.

How then do we engage with insights from First Nations Worldviews, complexity and community development in our policy work? Returning to the lessons from the Jabiluka mine campaign, the inclusion of First Nations people's perspective is vital. Dadirri, deep listening, provides a framework for learning together about the land and care for Mother Earth. Whilst it is easy to feel desperate for action, it is important to remember that policy change is (mostly) slow change. There is time for listening, learning and dialogue: in fact, without this, we risk rushing to the 'easy' answer that over time may create other problems or challenges. This brings us to the insights of complexity theory. Contrary to traditional understandings of policy, complexity theory highlights the dynamic, emergent, convergent, uncertain nature of change. We cannot predict in advance what, how or when our work will have effect. What we can predict however is that this will take time, be built on trust and enabled through coalitions with others. The community development skill set will support this work through respectful engagement, dialogue, dealing with conflict and facilitating participation.

The following chapter shifts our attention to those moments when climate change impacts bubble up into daily life to disrupt and destroy, often referred to as 'natural disasters'. These moments provide us with a window into possible futures and opportunities to learn and make change in the here and now.

References

Australianmap.net. (2014). *Australian nuclear and uranium sites: Jabiluka*. Retrieved from 3 April, 2022, https://nuclear.australianmap.net/jabiluka

Bacchi, C. (2022). *Introducing WPR*. Carol Bacchi blog. https://carolbacchi.com/about

Barnett, G. (2020, December 19). *Continuing our plan to be a renewable energy powerhouse*. [Press release]. https://www.premier.tas.gov.au/site_resources_2015/additional_releases/continuing_our_plan_to_be_a_renewable_energy_powerhouse/continuing_our_plan_to_be_a_renewable_energy_powerhouse

Briggs, C. (2019). *Where was Aboriginal self-determination in the wood inquiry? A policy analysis of child protection 'Reforms' in NSW, Australia* [PhD Doctoral thesis, University of Sydney]. https://ses.library.usyd.edu.au/handle/2123/21929

Canavan, M. (2020, May 27). *The coal, hard fact is we must put jobs first in this economic climate*. The Australian. https://www.theaustralian.com.au/commentary/the-coal-hard-fact-is-we-must-put-jobs-first-in-this-economic-climate/news-story/de84f2b7a8cfb74559afbc00c2308f02

Caron, P., Ferrero y de Loma-Osorio, G., Nabarro, D., et al. (2018). Food systems for sustainable development: proposals for a profound four-part transformation. *Agronomy for Sustainable Development, 38*, 41. https://doi.org/10.1007/s13593-018-0519-1

Climate for Change. (2021). https://www.climateforchange.org.au

Corry, O., & Reiner, D. (2021). Protests and policies: How radical social movement activists engage with climate policy dilemmas. *Sociology, 55*(1), 197–217. https://doi.org/10.1177/0038038520943107

Evans, S., & Gabbatiss, J. (2019, November 29). *In-depth Q&A: How 'Article 6' carbon markets could 'make or break' the Paris Agreement*. CarbonBrief. https://www.carbonbrief.org/in-depth-q-and-a-how-article-6-carbon-markets-could-make-or-break-the-paris-agreement

Evans, S., Gabbatiss, J., McSweeney, R., Chandrasekhar, A., Tanden, A., Viglione, G., Hausfather, Z., You, X., Goodman, J., & Hayes, S. (2021, November 15). *COP26: Key outcomes agreed at the UN climate talks in Glasgow*. CarbonBrief. https://www.carbonbrief.org/cop26-key-outcomes-agreed-at-the-un-climate-talks-in-glasgow

Fawcett, B., Goodwin, S., Meagher, G., & Phillips, R. (2009). *Social policy for social change* (1st ed.). Palgrave Macmillan.

Fenna, A. (2004). *Australian public policy* (2nd ed.). Pearson Education Australia.

Flannery, T., Hughes, L., Steffen, W., Morgan, W., Dean, A., Smith, R., & Baxter, T. (2021, October 21). *From Paris to Glasgow: A world on the move*. Climate Council of Australia. https://apo.org.au/sites/default/files/resource-files/2021-10/apo-nid314678.pdf

Fraser, D., & MacRae, A. M. (2011). Four types of activities that affect animals: Implications for animal welfare science and animal ethics philosophy. *Animal Welfare, 20*(4), 581–590.

Future Crunch. (2022). *Good news.* https://futurecrun.ch/goodnews

Garad, R., & Enticott, J. (2021, August 13). *Climate change: Collective action a counterpoint to Australian government inaction.* Monash University. https://lens.monash.edu/@medicine-health/2021/08/13/1383634/climate-change-collective-action-a-counterpoint-to-australian-government-inaction

Gelmini, S. (2021, June 29). *We're living in a golden age of greenwash.* Greenpeace. https://www.greenpeace.org.uk/news/golden-age-of-greenwash

Goodwin, S. (2011). Analysing policy as discourse: Methodological advances in policy analysis. In L. Markauskaite, P. Freebody, & J. Irwin (Eds.), *Methodological choice and design* (pp. 167–180). Springer. https://doi-org.ezproxy.library.sydney.edu.au/10.1007/978-90-481-8933-5_15

Head, B. W. (2008). Wicked problems in public policy. *Public Policy, 3*(2), pp. 101–118.

Hintjens, H. M. (2000). Environmental direct action in Australia: The case of Jabiluka mine. *Community Development Journal, 35*(4), 377–390. https://doi.org/10.1093/cdj/35.4.377

Howlett, M., & Cashore, B. (2014). Conceptualizing public policy. In I. Engeli & C. R. Allison (Eds.), *Comparative policy studies: Conceptual and methodological challenges* (pp. 17–33). Palgrave Macmillan. https://doi-org.ezproxy.library.sydney.edu.au/10.1057/9781137314154_2

Huntley, R. (2020). *How to talk about climate change in a way that makes a difference.* Murdoch Books, Allen & Unwin.

Intergovernmental Panel on Climate Change [IPCC]. (2022). Climate change 2022: Impacts, adaptation and vulnerability. IPCC. https://www.ipcc.ch/report/ar6/wg2

Kassam, N., & Léser, H. (2021, May 26) *Climate Poll 2021.* Lowy Institute. Retrieved from https://www.lowyinstitute.org/publications/climatepoll-2021

Manning, S. (2019, June 9). 'What's the Problem Represented to Be?' A policy analysis tool designed by Carol Bacchi and some recent applications in the area of early childhood education policy, Ipu Kererū New Zealand Association for Research in Education. *Thinking About Ideas.* https://suzannemanningblog.wordpress.com/2019/06/09/whats-the-problem-represented-to-be-a-policy-analysis-tool-designed-by-carol-bacchi-and-some-recent-applications-in-the-area-of-early-childhood-education-policy/

Marchant, N. (2020, December 9). *Tasmania is now powered entirely by renewable energy.* World Economic Forum. https://www.weforum.org/agenda/2020/12/tasmania-renewable-energy-sustainable-hydropower/

Marston, G., Mendes, P., Bielefeld, S., Peterie, M., Staines, Z., & Roche, S. (2020). *Hidden costs: An independent study into income management in Australia.* The University of Queensland. https://social-science.uq.edu.au/article/2020/02/hidden-costs-independent-study-income-management-australia

McAllister, R. R. J., McCrea, R., & Lubell, M. N. (2014). Policy networks, stakeholder interactions and climate adaptation in the region of South East Queensland, Australia. *Regional Environmental Change, 14*(2), 527–539. https://doi.org/10.1007/s10113-013-0489-4

Nasiritousi, N., Hjerpe, M., & Linnér, B.-O. (2014). The roles of non-state actors in climate change governance: Understanding agency through governance profiles. *International Environmental Agreements: Politics, Law and Economics, 16*(1), 109–126. https://doi.org/10.1007/s10784-014-9243-8

Nulman, E. (2015) *Climate change and social movements: Civil society and the development of national climate change policy*. Palgrave Macmillan.

OECD. (2007). *OECD observer, 2007(5)*. OECD Publishing. https://doi.org/10.1787/observer-v2007-5-en

Park, S. (2022) The politics of 21st century environmental disasters. *Environmental Politics, 31*(1), 1–7. https://doi.org/10.1080/09644016.2021.2024718

Peeters. J. (2012). A comment on "Climate change: Social workers' roles and contributions to policy debates and interventions". *International Journal of Social Welfare, 21*(1), 105–107. https://doi.org/10.1111/j.1468-2397.2011.00847.x

Pender, K. (2022, February 12). The environmental activists bringing the climate crisis to the courtroom, *The Guardian*. https://www.theguardian.com/environment/2022/feb/12/the-environmental-activists-bringing-the-climate-crisis-to-the-courtroom

Pycroft, A. (2014). Complexity theory: An overview. In A. Pycroft & C. Bartollas (Eds.), *Applying complexity theory: Whole systems approaches to criminal justice and social work*. Policy Press.

Rabinowitz, P. (2022). Changing policies: An overview. *Community tool box*. Centre for Community Health and Development, University of Kansas. Retrieved from April 10, 2022. https://ctb.ku.edu/en/table-of-contents/implement/changing-policies/overview/main

Raper, A. (2021, September 29). NSW government sets more ambitious 50pc emissions reduction target for 2030. *ABC News*. Australian Broadcasting Corporation [ABC]. https://www.abc.net.au/news/2021-09-29/nsw-new-carbonemissions-reduction-target-for-2030/100498444

Rittel, H., & Webber, M. M. (1973). Dilemmas in a general theory of planning. *Policy Sciences, 4*(2), 155–169. https://doi.org/10.1007/BF01405730

Shields, B. (2021, October 13). The electric car revolution putting Australia and the rest of the world to shame. *Sydney Morning Herald*. October 13. https://www.smh.com.au/world/europe/the-electric-car-revolution-putting-australia-and-the-rest-of-the-world-to-shame-20210930-p58w9s.html

Sweeney, D. (2016, January 1). We stood with the Mirarr people to stop the Jabiluka uranium mine. *Australian Conservation Foundation*. Retrieved from https://www.acf.org.au/jabiluka

Tolfree, R. (2016). Equality, equity and policy: Problems with policy implementation. *Public Health Textbook*. Retrieved from https://www.healthknowledge.org.uk/public-health-textbook/medical-sociology-policy-economics/4c-equality-equity-policy

Treasury. (2011, July 10). *Costs of inaction*. Australian Government. Retrieved from https://treasury.gov.au/publication/p2011-sglp-overview/costs-of-inaction

Truscott, A., & Malcolm, I. (2010). Closing the policy–practice gap: Making Indigenous language policy more than empty rhetoric. Sydney University Press. http://hdl.handle.net/2123/6949

United Nations. (2019, May 6). UN Report: Nature's dangerous decline 'unprecedented'; species extinction rates 'accelerating'. *Sustainable Development Goals United Nations*. Retrieved from https://www.un.org/sustainabledevelopment/blog/2019/05/nature-decline-unprecedented-report/.

United Nations (2019, October 8). *Unprecedented Impacts of Climate Change Disproportionately Burdening Developing Countries, Delegate Stresses, as Second Committee Concludes General Debate*. Retrieved from https://press.un.org/en/2019/gaef3516.doc.htm

van Holstein, E. (2020). Strategies of self-organising communities in a gentrifying city. *Urban Studies, 57*(6), 1284–1300. https://doi.org/10.1177/0042098019832468

Watkins, A., & Meijer, C. J. W. (Eds.) (2016). *Implementing inclusive education: Issues in bridging the policy-practice gap* (1st ed.). Emerald Group Publishing Limited.

World Resources Institute. (2021, November 17). *COP26: Key outcomes from the UN climate talks in Glasgow.* Retrieved from https://www.wri.org/insights/cop26-key-outcomes-un-climate-talks-glasgow

Yassine, L. (2017). *Governing through 'neutrality': A poststructural analysis of risk assessment in the NSW juvenile justice system* [PhD Doctoral thesis, University of Sydney]. https://hdl.handle.net/2123/21228

Zhang, Y., Beggs, P. J., Bambrick, H., Berry, H. L., Linnenluecke, M. K., Trueck, S., Alders, R., Bi, P., Boylan, S. M., Green, D., Guo, Y., Hanigan, I. C., Hanna, E. G., Malik, A., Morgan, G. G., Stevenson, M., Tong, S., Watts, N., & Capon, A. G. (2018). The MJA–Lancet countdown on health and climate change: Australian policy inaction threatens lives. *Medical Journal of Australia, 209*(11), 474–474. https://doi.org/10.5694/mja18.00789

9
EMERGENT MOMENTS

When it all goes wrong

One of the most challenging aspects of climate change for many has been the day-to-day invisibility of impacts. For four decades a diverse range of thinkers, researchers, activists and people attuned to the environment from all walks of life have been aware of and have been warning others that humans are inducing a warming of the atmosphere which ultimately may wipe us and many other living things out (Cohen & Wadell, 2009; Sorlin & Lane, 2018). For most people these warnings have seemed abstract and distant compared with the struggles and challenges of everyday life. Through this period, however, there have been what we are calling emergent moments when the impacts of climate change become all too visible. In this chapter we want to take some time to think through those moments when climate change impacts bubble up into daily life to disrupt and destroy. These moments provide us with a window into possible futures and opportunities to learn and make change in the here and now. We usually refer to these moments as natural disasters although increasingly research and analysis of the dimensions of so-called natural disasters have questioned how natural these are and how much the work of humanity shapes the precipitating contexts, impacts and unequal burdens which accompany such events as bushfires, floods, storms, heatwaves and droughts (Blaikie et al., 2014; McKinnon & Cook, 2020; Tierney, 2015).

McKinnon and Cook (2020) argue that disasters are created by humans, in that the significance of the event (bushfire, flood, earthquake, cyclone) is only realised when it has an impact on human beings. For these researchers, referring to disasters as 'natural' dilutes, or even denies, the human role and decision-making before, during and after a disaster. For both McKinnon and Cook (2020) and Blaikie et al. (2014), it is more accurate to understand disasters as a complex array of natural hazards and human action where unequal patterns of experience and exclusionary structures play out as they do in other aspects of life. The focus

DOI: 10.4324/9781003146339-9

on human impacts of natural hazards again reminds us of how human-centric our experience of the world is, although there is a slow awakening of the profound impact on wildlife and vegetation through disasters. Our research has revealed how the social, economic and cultural contours in disaster preparedness, response and recovery are interconnected with natural hazards. Tierney (2015) takes this further in her analysis of resilience discourses in the aftermath of Hurricane Katrina in New Orleans. She argues that the impacts of the disaster, created by a long-term withdrawal of State support and a resulting acceleration of poverty for many, were further exacerbated in the recovery. Here, a neoliberal agenda encouraged citizens to be more entrepreneurial while simultaneously decreasing social housing to provide more opportunities for corporate providers to rebuild and sell new housing. For Tierney, the natural element of the disaster was the least impactful for the community.

In many ways, disasters provide a critically important context in which we see social justice and climate change playing out. Drawing back to Chapter 2 of the book, Tierney's discussion of resilience reminds us of the ways disaster resilience is constructed and shaped by ideology and applied to individuals and communities through intersections of poverty, race, gender and other structural factors. For this reason, we have argued throughout the book, that analysis of the impacts of, and action options for, climate change must acknowledge pre-existing social structures which make it harder for some people, by virtue of gender, religion, culture, race, education, (dis)ability and economic means.

So, if we make sense of disasters as complex constructed phenomena, as events where we see climate change in action in real time, what is some of the learning we might glean from what happens before, during and after a disaster?

Drawing from our research to make sense of ideas, context and action when disasters bring climate change to our attention

Over the past decade, we have been undertaking research with different communities in different locations in Australia mapping, documenting, analysing and sharing the knowledge gained with people seriously impacted by disasters. In the following context studies, we utilise some of the data gathered across communities during this time. For those interested in more detail about our documented research, we refer you to a number of publications which detail the methods, all of the findings and recommendations which have been formulated from this research (Howard et al., 2014, 2017, 2020a, 2020b; Rawsthorne et al., 2019).

This body of research comprises data collected with ten communities across seven disasters ranging from drought to bushfire, storm/cyclone, flood and pandemic between 2014 and 2022. The information we draw on here includes interviews, focus groups, Participatory Action Research meetings, observations, workshops and documentary analysis. In our research we have been able to gather data across formal and informal systems at a community, regional, State and national level, to map change over time with communities and service systems, and document disasters over their cycles from preparedness, through response, into recovery and back through the cycle in many communities.

So, in the bulk of this chapter, we draw from this data, creating three context studies in which we saw key concepts outlined in Chapter 2 (responsibility, risk, resilience) play out in very particular ways. We want to work through these examples, which bring together many of the dimensions and relationships we have discussed throughout the book. In doing this we hope to illustrate how we have observed climate change and social justice impacts flow in local communities when things go wrong, that is when disaster hits.

From here we apply a contextual analysis in each example which draws on First Nations Worldviews and complex system thinking to imagine how things might be different if we take these paradigms seriously in our work. Each contextual study provides a window of learning and a process for reflection and analysis which we hope is useful for you in making sense of the very different ways in which the social contours of disasters highlight challenges and generative possibilities as we act together on climate change.

Context 1 – coastal communities

A group of neighbouring communities are impacted by a cyclone which brings high winds, torrential rain and flooding, leaving each of these communities isolated for some days. Low-lying areas near the creek and wetlands are flooded for the first time in decades. For many residents this was the first time their street had flooded since many moved to the area. The communities in this coastal and hinterland area are diverse and include a major tourist town which has become fashionable and attracted significant investment from outside the area, a hinterland community with a long history as both a rural and alternative lifestyle area, a small industry focused community on the floodplain with strong historical ties to the surrounding rural area, a large regional town and a coastal suburban community which includes low-lying beachfront suburbs, streets on high ground overlooking the ocean and houses located along waterways and near local wetlands which have been altered due to housing development.

The experience of this last community provides a number of salient lessons for us in thinking through and acting on climate change. Let's look at how some key ideas played out. Firstly, this community was comparatively more affordable than those which surrounded it and as a result was the place where those who could not afford surrounding towns, particularly as prices rose with the influx of seachangers and city investment, had moved to. Traditionally resources had been deployed disproportionally to the more affluent communities where high tourist financial return was guaranteed and where the local Council wanted to make a good first impression. Our focus community, by comparison, was much further away from the tourist town than mere kilometres. High unemployment and under-employment, an ageing population and the migration of young people (not helped by the absence of a high school) created distance between communities as well as stratification within. Community members here felt the disparity keenly and viewed themselves as perpetually missing out. This impression was also held by many outside the community who viewed the area as neglected compared to other towns.

Responsibility and risk in this community played out in a number of complicated ways. Long-term and ongoing tensions between a key community group and Council fed into an adversarial cycle of blame and avoidance regarding a range of community issues including disaster preparedness, housing and environmental planning. Some community members felt that Council's decision decades earlier to preserve creek areas, wetlands and conservation zones where water flowed during heavy rains, rather than allowing development of these areas, had put the community at greater risk of flooding. Council's planning process argued that natural water flows needed to be preserved to avoid high impact flood events which would be created if flows were diverted and constructed waterways and development allowed. These ongoing tensions regarding risk and responsibility came to a head during the cyclone when a number of areas were cut off and others flooded. The whole community was also isolated from neighbouring towns during this period which meant that assistance was not forthcoming from local government and emergency management agencies until the flood had subsided. Some community members experienced this as another example of responsibility and risk being placed only on community members rather than shared with government and emergency agencies.

Drawing on their own resources was viewed by community members as a sign of their resilience and a source of community pride. However, this was also experienced as further evidence that the community was invisible and let down by those they expected to help them over the crisis. During the recovery period after the cyclone, a number of overtures were made by emergency management agencies to support the community in resilience building. Unfortunately, these were framed unintentionally in ways which served the needs of the agencies but did not acknowledge long-term community anger or respond to what the community were saying they needed. One example here was the provision of equipment to assist with flood preparation and clean up (including pressure washers, signs for roads under water, etc.). Emergency management agencies were keen to provide these as a donation but communities were then asked to store, manage and be accountable to the agency for the equipment. This was experienced as a burden for community members rather than a support for resilience building. Interestingly, little attention was given to supporting the extensive and long-term resilience initiatives which were already in place in the community. In one case, a local business owner whose premises regularly flooded expressed their frustration as they already had a plan in place where local community members came, assisted in clearing low furniture and equipment, sandbagging and then cleaning up after the flood had gone. They had asked for additional assistance to be given to support this voluntary effort, which had been in place for over 40 years, and were told they could only have the equipment, and then only as long as they provided appropriate storage above the flood level. The property was on the floodplain and completely under water even a minor flood level. Here resilience building initiatives imposed from outside the community consistently failed to acknowledge community context, community-led initiatives already in place and the frustration of community members who had tried and failed to access support during and after the disaster.

Along with resilience, community members in this area had also engaged in a number of adaptation and mitigation initiatives to address the issues they saw as important. These initiatives were often informal and even guerrilla in form including clearing out the overgrown drains themselves when this was needed to prevent stormwater overflow. These, however, were also often caught up in the ongoing conflict with Council and were subject to multiple and sometimes contradictory understandings regarding the problem which needed solving. Some community members felt that engineering solutions were required to solve ongoing drainage and flooding issues. Others saw that poor engineering when the housing was developed had not recognised the need to work with the environment rather than controlling water flow purely though engineering solutions. This complicated conflict set up a process where community members became increasingly angry and adversarial whenever Council workers came to town and as a result Council tried to avoid the community and viewed community members as unreasonable and intransigent. As a result, any mitigation or adaptation measures put in place by Council were completed with little or no communication with the community, exacerbating their experience of not being listened to and further entrenching the conflict. From the community end, some views about development of the area and the environment were founded more in the conflict with Council than in informed knowledge about the local environment; however, there was little opportunity for negotiation. This complex context came to a head when the cyclone hit and all of the existing issues – intersecting disadvantage, perceptions of responsibility and risk being carried only by the community, lack of attention to disaster preparedness and resilience building which was responsive to community needs and resources and poorly co-ordinated climate change mitigation and adaptation – converged. The disaster made visible and amplified the issues which had been bubbling away just under the surface for decades.

How might First Nations Worldviews and complex systems thinking support a different approach to action?

Firstly, in this context there was an acknowledgement amongst community members of the ongoing custodianship of the land and of the knowledge that First Nations community members held about the Country in which this community was located; however, this acknowledgement was not integrated into community planning, resilience building or connection. In many ways the disconnection between the ongoing custodianship of First Nations communities in the area and those who moved in later reflected patterns of colonial development across Australia which disrupted connection with land and each other. This particular community, as with many in the region, had been located where it was because a developer bought some land cheaply, developed a plan for housing and a new community based on blueprints which were used on multiple sites with little consideration for the particular features which were part of this particular ecosystem. Nature was to be tamed and controlled to ensure people could buy and move into houses. Since that time, decisions had been made at a local government level which went some way to recognising the complexities of ecosystems and a conservation strategy had been put in place. The way this had been enacted however (as a simple solution to a simple problem rather than one with layers of complexity) had set up a conflict between community members who believed what the developer had told them about the future vision for the community with further development and facilities and the Council decision based on environmental considerations to prevent further development. For us, this kind of conflict provides a challenging but important opportunity to recalibrate local relationships between people and with the environment (Country). In this community, the impacts of climate change are sending a very clear and increasingly loud message. Rather than entrenching existing conflicts, work with the community and Council here requires a change which recognises reciprocal relationships as central to all aspects of community life and decision-making. This reciprocity extends also to the environment (all non-human life) where the community is located. Establishing structures and processes for dialogue, acknowledging community frustrations and acknowledging the adverse impacts of colonising development are a starting point for change. Complex systems thinking supports an understanding that the long-term conflict-based feedback loops will take time and proactive change to alter. This way of thinking also draws our attention to the often unnoticed and divergent changes which are already emerging in this community. Down on the beachfront, neighbours who are relatively new to the community meet every Friday to share a community dinner. They are working in collaboration with local young people to build capacity, knowledge and confidence in acting on climate change locally. This group supports each other in the everyday informally and as part of a network of reciprocal relationships. The group is not without tensions and moments of weariness and miscommunication, but here we can see a different loop emerging. Just as the conflict in another part of town has had impacts out of proportion with where it began (distress, isolation, flooding amongst low-lying houses with no knowledge of local conditions), this emerging moment and network will also have uncertain and non-linear impacts. Work with the community here requires an understanding of the way things are but also requires long-term support for acknowledging the reciprocity with Country and each other grounded in First Nations Worldviews and the complex entangled connections which provide a map for a different way of being. This process is neither simple nor guaranteed, but the learning from the disaster in this community made a whole lot of things visible enough to work on. Intention, knowledge, skills and investment of time and resources are required, and for us, this must be central if we want to do effective work on climate change.

Context 2– peri-urban communities on the outskirts of a capital city

The second context study is a group of what were once rural communities which over the past 50 years have had a major capital city come closer until these communities have become incorporated into that city. Housing and employment development in neighbouring Council areas as well as within the area where the communities are located is transforming the landscape, demographics and ecology of these communities dramatically. Currently a mix of suburban and rural communities are located along a large river system and into the hinterland which includes National Parks and conservation areas at the foot of a mountain range. Between 2018 and 2022, communities in this area have experienced a cascading run of disasters including drought, bushfire and two serious floods along with the COVID-19 pandemic experienced across the globe. Demographically communities are diverse across the local government area from the very affluent to first home buyers moving into new housing estates developing locally, through to social housing tenants. The area had a well-known history of flood and bushfire impacts and long-term planning and infrastructure development was in place to mitigate some impacts, particularly related to flooding. Changing population characteristics, however, with new people moving into the communities with little or no experience of the flood and bushfire history, were creating a very different level of preparedness than was present in the past.

The ways in which risk, responsibility and resilience played out in these communities in the face of regular, significant disasters reflects a number of the issues raised in Chapter 2 and examined throughout the book. In 2018, a community-led resilience building initiative was started by a small group of community members who were interested in addressing social isolation in neighbourhoods. The catalyst for this initiative was a funded project piloting different approaches to community-led disaster preparedness in a number of communities across New South Wales. We were able to work in partnership with community members over the first 4 years of the initiative as part of a Participatory Action Research (PAR) project which tracked, supported and documented learning as the initiative developed. This initiative was particularly interesting as it was genuinely led by local community members, it started before the cascade of current disasters impacted the area and it was founded on the idea that informal, relational networks in communities are at the core of resilience building. As this initiative developed through partnerships in local schools supporting children as leaders, community conversations and connecting local informal networks, momentum began to build amongst formal systems about the need for better disaster preparedness amongst community members. This momentum was driven by both the devastating impacts of the Black Summer Bushfires on local communities in the area and also a flood planning process which provided detailed data on the considerable flood risk through the entire catchment, particularly in the event of a serious flood, which had occurred decades earlier (beyond the memory of many) when the area was far less populated and urbanised.

For the community-led group risk and responsibility were both embedded in local relationships and networks, but also in formal emergency management, government and human service systems. They saw their work in strengthening local informal systems as, from experience, they knew that this was where people were supported in the long term and also in the first instance during a crisis. Here, risk was mitigated and managed through everyday relationships in streets and neighbourhoods, with formal systems sitting behind and in collaboration with these informal networks to provide back up when needed. Responsibility was seen as also shared in reciprocal relationships locally and with formal systems. To enact this process, members of the community-led initiative asked to attend the Local Emergency Management Committee (LEMC) which has carriage of decisions and operational management in the event of a disaster. This group comprises all local emergency management and related agencies and local government. Community members hoped that attending the meeting would mark the start of a collaboration with formal systems, but when they outlined the local work, they were undertaking, and their desire to work together with the LEMC, they were treated with suspicion and interrogated about their efforts in case they were at odds with the approach of the Committee. Community members left the meeting feeling relegated and with the very clear message that they were not welcome in any decision-making processes regarding local disaster resilience. The community's efforts to share risk and responsibility were not reciprocated by formal systems and as a result the community-led initiative continued on outside formal processes. For the LEMC, resilience was articulated as communities complying with emergency management orders and not making their own decisions, as these were seen as too risky. For community members, when shortly after they were impacted by fires and floods, risk and responsibility were very clearly experienced as theirs alone due to formal systems being overwhelmed and unable to provide assistance to everyone who needed it. In the face of disasters many community members, including those connected to the community-led initiative drew on the resilience created through their own informal neighbourhood and community networks, ensuring everyone they knew was safe, sharing resources such as food and fuel and assisting each other in post disaster recovery.

Following the bushfires and two floods, resources in terms of funding, government personnel and co-ordinated responses poured into the area, creating a very different kind of flood. During this time, too, we observed a number of processes where very different framings of risk, responsibility and resilience were visible and here again, community members were excluded systematically, if unintentionally. Two examples stand out quite starkly. In the first, community members who were involved in the community-led initiative wanted to understand the diverse array of new workers, projects and programs which had mushroomed in the area as part of the disaster recovery. Although the community-led group was well known in the area and was often discussed by workers and others as a positive initiative, none of the new projects or programs had contacted the group to connect or find out more about them. Members of the community-led group, themselves, contacted a number of new workers and projects to invite them to meet and connect in an effort to make sense of everything going on in the area. Workers were very happy to meet; however, it became evident that for most, it was challenging to link their work with informal community networks. In some cases, community members who had called the meeting were misrecognised by workers as clients needing assistance with the conversation dominated by workers offering a range of programs to the community members while asking nothing about the work of the now 3-year-old community-led initiative. In other cases, the worker took the lead in discussions offering to co-ordinate a meeting of services which the community-led group would be invited as a participant. In all of the meetings the ongoing role of the community-led group in working with informal systems was rendered invisible by the service system. The recovery focused service industry quickly became a self-referential system responsible for building resilience and minimising risks for the community. Attempts by community members to participate as equals, have their informal work recognised or be included as legitimate, decision-making agents in the recovery process were by-passed by services who could only recognise entities which looked like them. The second example takes this framing further. As is the case in many disaster recovery processes, the communities in this context study experienced an influx of funding from a range of sources. During a series of community conversations which formed part of the work of the community-led initiative, many community members expressed frustration about the funding application process, the structural barriers that prevented informal community groups from accessing funding and the level of bureaucratic and administrative accountabilities required if funding is received. The time, skills, administrative support and organisational structures required for completing funding applications, framing ideas in a way they can be funded and then managing funding should the application be successful, unintentionally but systematically excluded small informal community groups and favoured a range of organisations with experience and infrastructure to access and manage funding. While in some cases small informal groups were invited to find an auspicious organisation to assist them in funding processes, the number of these organisations on the ground were limited and were quickly overwhelmed with requests. Often the small, informal groups and networks had links directly with those most impacted by disaster and trusting, reciprocal relationships were in place between community members here. Many of these community members did not access formal services for a range of reasons but were in need of support which they received informally. Unfortunately, the way this structural problem played out, organisations with skills and experience in funding applications were able to secure large grants while informal community groups were left largely as recipients of support, even though they were acting as vital support systems themselves and for many others. In some cases, organisations were able to act flexibly and work with informal groups but in most cases a program or project template shaped the way funding was used with little power amongst community members to change this. At times community anger at funded projects in their areas over which they had no say bubbled over, particularly where external organisations were funded over local ones. However, this unintended but significant process of structural exclusion remains a feature of funding programs. In many ways this is a very succinct example of simple problem solving – quickly provide resources to an area impacted by disaster to assist recovery – misrecognising the complexity of the systems and intersecting contextual and structural issues which were revealed once the simple solution was applied.

The very different framings of risk, responsibility and resilience observed in the efforts of the community-led initiative and that of formal systems invite a number of possibilities for doing things differently. Learning from First Nations Worldviews here draws our attention to relationships between community and Country in this area. Successive generations of people moving into the area post colonisation have moved further and further from knowledge about and responsibilities towards the land, river systems, ecology and climate. Climate change impacts including more regular and intense bushfires and floods reveal the importance of this knowledge, which has continued amongst First Nations communities and some other community members.

Reciprocity was evident in informal community relationships and networks with community members supporting each other in a range of ways both in relation to disasters and in everyday life. For more formal systems, key learnings here are focused on the ways in which power is deployed in relation to communities and the unintentional exclusionary impacts of unequal power relations and misrecognising complex problems as simple ones, between formal and informal systems. Questions about how formal systems can more respectfully recognise and engage with informal relational systems are becoming increasingly urgent as the limits of formal systems as disaster and climate change problem solvers become more apparent.

Complex systems thinking enables us to make sense of the fluid dynamics between stable and ephemeral aspects of both formal and informal systems (informal networks emerge, disappear, adapt and change depending on context, who is involved and the focus for action; formal systems emerge, disappear, adapt and change with changing policy and funding arrangements, when workers change and through structural realignments) rather than seeing these systems in a binary opposition (formal = stable and certain; informal = chaotic and uncertain). This opens very different possibilities for collective action across systems when the more fluid aspects of each are explored. In the example above, using complex systems theory to analyse relations between formal and informal systems enables us to see the ways in which blockages such as the exclusion of community members from decision-making, rather than reinforcing stability and existing power relations, led to the emergence of a parallel set of networks and a divergence of action within the system. The capacity of the intersecting (or in this case parallel) systems divided the effort and resulted in more limited opportunities for collaboration across systems. New feedback loops were created through this disruption of relations which amplified disconnections and both parts of the system continued to diverge. This analysis provides a much more detailed picture of how networks interact and in doing this makes visible possibilities for future convergence.

Context 3 – region comprising rural, urban, coastal and inland communities

The third context in which we have seen climate change impacts made visible through disasters is in a larger region encompassing a major city, coastal communities as well as smaller towns, rural and hinterland communities. In this region the impacts of a significant and widespread storm event revealed both serious gaps in assumptions about the ways risk was managed, responsibility was deployed and resilience was enacted but also the mobilisation of creative long-term and spontaneous responses from which important learning can be gleaned. The storm and accompanying wind damage and flooding surprised everyone with its intensity, scale and direction. Communities across the region were used to storms, bushfires and floods but this one was quite different. Communications were cut across much of the region quickly, many communities lost power as well and remained without either telecommunication or power for days, and in some cases weeks. Many of those who had formal responsibilities to enact emergency management were cut off from impacted areas in the first instance due to flooding and storm damage. For many, including those in formal response roles, communication and action became limited to those you could contact face to face at a very local level. Planning and reliance on telecommunications, travel between communities and regional service provision was revealed as flawed in this context but quite quickly communities both drew on existing systems of self-organising to address risk and in some cases these systems emerged and were mobilised to address immediate needs and problems. In one community locals had a well-known system for alerting each other to rising waters as they flowed down the river. This system was completely informal and relied on neighbours contacting each other through every day (telephone tree) and creative (indicators on sheds visible to others) methods. This system worked very effectively during the storm as it included a low-tech strategy which was ideal in the context. After this event community reflection and learning led to community members working very effectively in collaboration with a local emergency management agency to map geo-co-ordinates for houses and farms. These were then displayed on the rooftops of houses and sheds to ensure flooded properties could be identified and accessed by air when streets and street numbers were under water. In this example ongoing reciprocal relationships amongst community members, local knowledge of the river system and experience in living with the natural world in the form of regular flooding were enacted successfully to manage risk and demonstrate resilience in a way which was shared and networked. Unlike the example in the previous context study, local emergency management agencies here adopted a stance of cultural humility, recognising community knowledge and self-organising and working in support of this rather than imposing a command-and-control style solution. Viewing this process through a lens of complex systems thinking, the collaboration between community self-organising and formal emergency systems made space for new ideas to emerge, a generative feedback loop to be established between the community and formal systems and risk and responsibility to be really shared in practical and sustainable ways.

Learning from emergent moments

In each of the context studies above the ways in which the emergent moments we are referring to in the chapter as disasters, the contours, relationships, networks and actions made visible through disaster events provide us with tangible opportunities to observe the patterns and consequences of particular decisions, disconnections, connections and results which are often tacit and hard to see clearly in everyday life. In this book we have examined, discussed, questioned and reflected on both the ways we understand climate change and social justice and some of the possibilities for action which are already underway. During disasters, when things go wrong, when everyday life is disrupted, critically important moments emerge when we can take stock and formulate new patterns in life and in our work. Social justice and climate change intersect in very different ways in each of the context studies and in each one patterns of exclusion did not result in dead ends. In each case, self-organising systems adapted and new ways of working emerged although the possibilities for creative and practical collaboration when different systems were able to connect (as in the last example) were quite different compared with earlier examples where disconnection and conflict shaped system behaviour.

In the next chapter of the book, we want to start imagining what a paradigm shift might look like when we infuse First Nations Worldviews and complexity into the way we design social work and human services into the future where climate change and social justice are entwined.

References

Blaikie, P., Wisner, B., & Cannon, T. (2014). *At risk: Natural hazards, people's vulnerability and disasters.* Taylor and Francis. https://doi.org/10.4324/9780203714775

Cohen, S. J., & Waddell, M. W. (2009). *Climate change in the 21st century.* McGill-Queen's University Press.

Howard, A., Blakemore, T., & Bevis, M. (2014). *Identifying risk perceptions, level of preparedness and communication channels for 'at risk' communities in respect to natural disasters.* Hunter & Central Coast Regional Environmental Management Strategy. https://www.hccrems.com.au/wp-content/uploads/2017/03/disaster-preparedness-in-at-risk-groups-final.pdf

Howard, A., von Meding, J., Blakemore, T., Heinsch, M., Allison, J., & Cavaliere, S. (2017) *Stronger for the storm: Community responses and recovery from the April 2015 storm event.* NSW State Emergency Services.

Howard, A., Rawsthorne, M., & Joseph, P. (2020a) *Hawkesbury-Nepean social housing community; resilience network interim report.* Infrastructure NSW.

Howard, A., Rawsthorne, M., Sampson, D., & Katrak, M. (2020b) *NSW get ready community led disaster pilots research report.* Foundation for Rural and Regional Renewal, Resilience NSW.

McKinnon, S., & Cook, M. (Eds.). (2020). *Disasters in Australia and New Zealand: Historical approaches to understanding catastrophe.* Palgrave Macmillan.

Rawsthorne, M., Howard, A., & Joseph, P. (2019) *Redfern Surry Hills community resilience.* Inner Sydney. Voice.

Sörlin, S., & Lane, M. (2018). Historicizing climate change – engaging new approaches to climate and history. *Climatic Change, 151*(1), 1–13. https://doi.org/10.1007/s10584-018-2285-0

Tierney. K. (2015). Resilience and the neoliberal project: Discourses, critiques, practices—And Katrina. *The American Behavioral Scientist, 59*(10), 1327–1342. https://doi.org/10.1177/0002764215591187

10

EMERGENT MOMENTS

The future

Introduction

Writing this book has been challenging both intellectually and emotionally. We have looked long and closely at the cumulative destructive capabilities of human beings, and at the results of an extractive and exploiting relationship with the planet that gives us life. At times during the process, it has been overwhelming and difficult to see a way forward and we are very aware that this feeling often leaves us in a state of despondency and powerlessness. It would be easier also to retreat back into the world of the purely social and mark out our work within the narrow parameters social impact, social policy and social service. Throughout our time spent thinking and writing for the book, however, we have regularly returned to a conversation about possibilities, about the impetus climate change provides for us to shift paradigms, recognising the complex dimensions in which life unfolds rather than framing the world as a series of compartmentalised fields. A process for re-imagining how we *are* in the world (our knowing and being), as well as how we work and live (our doing), has been touched on through the book. We consistently discussed ways of sharing information to transform our thinking about and honouring relational responsibilities to our environments.

To bring some form to our ideas about a paradigm shift, in this chapter we want to imagine social work and human services differently through a series of speculations. Everard (2016) draws on the work of Robinson (1988) when he describes this approach as *backcasting*, which

> takes as its starting point a desirable future, from which one then works backwards to chart incremental decisions, innovations, and policies that can lead stepwise towards that rather different future.
>
> *(p.47)*

DOI: 10.4324/9781003146339-10

This positions us as role-players (Ahamer, 2013) who explore different realities and create new understandings of our own place in relationship to these. It allows us to "try on" different perspectives rather than taking a fixed perspective with set adversaries. Reiterating comments made throughout the book, this places us not as neutral observers making objective judgements, but as participants, actively grappling with dilemmas that bring consequences both for ourselves and for other humans, more-than-humans and Earth herself. In re-imagining our future worlds, we aim to examine possibilities in safety via a process of speculation, in order to act ethically and thoughtfully in lived experiences as they unfold.

As we also mentioned in this book's introduction, our intention as we share our thoughts with readers is to contribute to a discussion rather than to present a completed treatise. In our thinking and writing, we have been conscious that many readers are already active in their personal and professional lives, confronting the issues that we have raised here. Further, we all do so in a world that will continue to present new challenges; some we can anticipate, and others will take us by surprise.

In this final chapter, we offer six re-imaginings, arising from our own reflections on how we might engage with the issues raised in the book in different social and human services contexts. While we share some discomfort with the way this structure flies in the face of our commitment to avoiding artificial and constraining boundaries, we take this approach for clarity, and to help readers zone in on aspects that may be most relevant to their own lived experiences. It is important to remember, however, that the people with whom we work do not live within these silos, and our work in any human service sector will connect us to people experiencing any and all intersecting categories of human experience. As we engage with this creative work, we draw on the ideas proposed in Chapter 2, and in particular, the intertwined themes of responsibility, risk, resilience and intersecting inequities. Again, we intend these reflections to be a form of invitation to dialogue. In preparing the ideas presented here, we have drawn on our own experiences in practice, research and education, as well as in our lives as community members.

As we move from the Anthropocene to a proposed Symbiocene (Albrecht, 2020; Everard, 2016; Prescott & Logan, 2017), humans are challenged to co-create a future characterised by synergies between the human, more-than-human and wider ecosystems that live in complex, messy and dynamic relationship. As Everard notes, humans will contribute to the shape of the future whether by intent or neglect. This idea provides the foundation for our re-imagining. Whatever we do, or do *not* do, we will shape the future. How might our work in social work and human services contribute to a co-created, sustainable Symbiocene? What futures can we imagine, and how might we backcast our ways of working towards them?

For each of the headings below, we highlight a range of current issues and propose one scenario, from which we ask a series of questions that will help us to explore possibilities for constructive action. For each scenario we offer, there are many others, bringing with them various levels of hopefulness and a wide range of alternative pathways to fruition. We encourage you to place yourself in the scenarios below and consider what they might mean for your own knowing, doing and being in this reimagined world. Then think beyond these starting points, ideally in conversation with others who bring diverse perspectives based on their culture, gender and life experiences. We believe that doing so will help to equip you as you move on into an emerging and as yet unknowable future, as it has helped us in the course of our discussions, which led to (and will continue beyond) this book.

Mental health

We began our discussion on this topic by questioning our own instinctive separation of mental health from health, per se, and wondered why there is so entrenched a separation between the two. There are practical reasons why this might be so – ease of funding allocations being one – however there are arguably more problems with this polarity which separates mind, emotion and body without seeing their interconnectedness. With the Commonwealth Department of Health estimating 7.3 million Australians will experience mental ill-health at some point, and increasing due to the global pandemic, perhaps we could consider the concept of health as a totality and as one connected to the environment.

Our Australian mental health system is predicated on individual pathology which creates disconnected and siloed service systems. We sit within a culture which values evidence, science and 'quick fixes', therefore often operate within medical models of health – perhaps because they offer these, perceived, answers and solutions – rather than social and spiritual models. Power sits with expert professionals – none more powerful than a psychiatrist. We seek 'cures' and this buys into the dominant discourse and, in fact, sustains, and even creates, systems which privilege diagnosis and treatment. Arguably, mental healthcare has become a self-serving and perpetuating industry, symbolised by diagnoses which bring with them hope of 'cure', access to services and funding, but also create a label by which we can define ourselves and others. Not that this is always a bad thing, but it is worth questioning this powerful position and considering other ways mental well-being and health can be defined.

Sitting alongside this discourse is an increasingly risk-averse mantle of managerialism. This system values and creates what we call 'the administrative social worker', bound by policies, legislation, risk management and mitigation, and reporting frameworks. None more so than in the mental health space which is a politically contested one, seeing services within the sector aggressively vying for resources. Yet, as social workers and human service workers, we struggle to find a free or affordable service to refer a person to which doesn't have a 2-year waiting list. The relationship between mental illness and NDIS eligibility remains vexed – the perils of not fitting neatly within a medicalised 'box'.

If we start to take a broad approach to well-being as encompassing our total environment, it is possible a relationship exists between mental health and climate change. Existential anxiety, feelings of powerlessness and a lack of optimism about the future influence our perceived ability to enact change. However, we can turn this paradigm over and wonder if seeing the connectedness between all life forms and a symbiosis, perhaps we could begin to wonder if working to improve our environment, to re-connect, could help our mental well-being.

Scenario

What if we imagine connecting pieces, rather than looking for difference? Perhaps we focus on finding similarity and use the term 'health' expansively to describe the well-being of a person, community and environment. This might involve adopting a nuanced, complex approach to mental health that is not deficit-focused, that emphasises the importance of connectedness (psychological, social, spiritual) in a way that is meaningful for the individual and beyond. It might also involve hitting the pause button for a moment before attributing a medical label to, what might be, a behaviour of difference, grief or a feeling of disquiet about the political landscape.

What is the change we suggest?

Throughout this book we have tried to take a systemic approach to the impact of climate change. The prevailing paradigm in a neoliberalist period is the individual. We employ this in the mental health space. We can work to shift this to the broader context and help to challenge the blaming that inevitably follows if an individual doesn't meet societal mores.

We can think more consciously about connections and re-connections, between people but also the health systems. The six systems we have chosen to explore in this final chapter are inextricably inter-dependent. As a participant told me in a recent focus group, it's hard to access good mental health services without money. This is not a criticism of the many skilled practitioners in that sector but a critique of what we value as a society.

What is the role of social workers and human service workers?

There has long been debate as to whether you can make change from within a system or whether you need to reject the system and work outside for change. We think both are possible through conscious critical thinking; not accepting anything on face value or as it has 'always been done'. Work to actively promote compassion, generosity and creativity at every opportunity. This serves to challenge the increasing surveillance and risk management doctrines. Others will argue the risk management frameworks are there for a purpose. And they are; to a point. Decisions made purely deontologically can still be flawed. Be creative with policy and legislation; err on the side of trust and think about the consequences of a decision you make.

Choose your battles well and your language even more so. Much of our language in the mental health sphere is de-humanising. Don't underestimate the impact this has on a person's internal dialogue. Think strategically about the change you want to make and focus there – not on minor battles along the way.

Be a voice and, more importantly, help others to find their own. Advocate individually and systemically. Employ the complexity thinking we have been talking about here and look for connections and not difference. We can challenge the concept of mental illness. Not to denude the positive impact medication and counselling have on many people but to shake-up the conversation a little and see people in the context of, possibly, poverty, housing issues, challenges with Centrelink and trauma. As practitioners and educators encourage empathy at every opportunity.

Health

While the funded health sector is a significant employer of social workers, social and human services work extends far beyond this sector. In fact, we would argue that all social workers work in "health" in one way or another. When we consider the intersecting social determinants of health, it is clear that employment, poverty, geographical and socio-economic location all play a part in peoples' experiences of health and their connection with service systems. Moreover, the social determinants of health intersect with the effects of climate change to reinforce and even to exacerbate existing social inequalities.

Having said this, we acknowledge also that the formal health sector is increasingly vocal in advocating for attention to connections between climate change and health, globally and locally. For example, the formation of a global Climate and Health Alliance in 2011 comprises an international membership of health agencies and peak bodies (https://climateandhealthalliance.org/) and provides a platform for sharing information, resources as well as contributing to policy debates. The membership of this global body includes the Australian Climate and Health Alliance (https://www.caha.org.au/). In addition, climate-related position statements such as that of the Royal Australian College of General Practitioners (2021) indicate an awareness of the connection between climate and health, articulated at the organisational level, moving it beyond a niche or "special interest group" status.

As in mental health, across the broader health system we see tension between narratives which individualise and blame individuals – locating risk, responsibility and resilience with those experiencing ill health – and those which recognise the broader social, environmental, cultural and economic factors which shape our health. The development of increasingly specialised areas of health focus have brought with them vital and life-saving knowledge but one of the unintended consequences of this process is a lack of attention to health as an integrated and complex array of relations, connections and processes. In working within systems, we wonder whether those of us in social work and human services have become compartmentalised in our thinking and practice. Climate change brings a whole of world shift along with it. Perhaps there is an opportunity for us to step back and take time to reflect on a more comprehensive and complex understanding of health as part of this.

Scenario

We imagine a world where connections between the health (broadly defined) of the planet, local ecosystems, communities and individuals are deeply understood and embedded in everyday policy and in practice. Within this re-imagination, existing power hierarchies are disrupted, to open space for new voices of knowledge and expertise and new, more collaborative, relationships. We invite a rethink of compartmentalised areas of specialty in health as the dominant organising principle. What might work look like if we moved towards an intentional shift towards building connections across the complex systems which contribute to our professional understanding of health? Even when our work is focused in specific areas connections with the broader world are very apparent in our day-to-day experience and can be in practice as well. It sounds obvious to say that people's experience of formal health systems is only one element of life and yet the tendency to view our work and our system of work as central can be relentless and often unnoticed. We imagine a scenario where work in health systems is always linked implicitly and explicitly to a recognition of a broader environment.

What is the change we suggest?

A shift in emphasis towards more networked thinking and structures which link our experience of health with our work in this field may open up very different structures and processes to the ones we can currently see. Note that we are not starting from a zero base – the groundwork has begun, although there is still much room for development of more collaborative approach. Person centredness linked to community and planet centredness move the focus on individualisation towards relationship and connection in our thinking and support the overall shift we are talking about. How might a collaborative and reciprocal form of practice change current power relations between service providers and recipients and within hierarchies in systems?

Disconnections between the formal "health sector", particularly acute health service delivery, and the world outside the institution draw our attention to possible changes in structural boundaries, in where we see *health* located and in what shapes our understanding of health and illness. In the context of climate change, very different accesses to health systems built on technology, single-use resources such as plastics and resource-heavy interventions highlight inequities in our current approach to health which will be amplified further than they are currently.

What are some of the other possible approaches to health we might imagine? If we work with the range of environmental factors impacting on health, build local, connected health systems which recognise more than medical intervention as essential to good health and if we see care and health for Earth as part of the system overall, how might we reshape what we do?

This scenario is not about naivety or pretending a range of life threatening and chronic health conditions do not impact on people, or that specialist medical care is not vital. Rather, we suggest that broadening the view and attending to complexity and reciprocity in our understanding on health may equip us to work in health more effectively as the climate changes.

Finally, our scenario asks about how we engage with cycles of life and death. Climate change brings uncertainty, impermanence, flux. How might we engage with and support cycles of life and death as part of health systems? In natural systems cycles of life and death are ever present and we wonder about how we might learn from these cycles to work in a more generative way with people in different moments of health and also when death comes.

What is the role of social and human service workers?

We suggest reflexivity is a good starting point for practice. Self-awareness of our values, thinking about choices we make and how we position ourselves in workplaces in terms of paradigms make a significant difference, e.g., resistance to individualisation, contributing to wider understandings of health, knowledge and power in these contexts. Those of us working in social work and human services work constantly within and between systems. Developing a practical understanding of complexity in health contexts help make sense of where we do our work, how to read power relations and what can be in our particular contexts to make change. We are in a position to ask questions in the everyday and at a structural level and it seems important that we have courage to do this. How might we use our voice to amplify the voices of others – not to replace but to walk alongside? How might we contribute to a paradigm where Earth health is seen as inextricable from human health, and the place of ecosystems and more-than-humans in this?

We can also engage in system redesign work in the teams where we do our work every day, in organisations and between organisations. We suggest that there are opportunities now for us to join with each other to imagine and experiment with different ways of working locally as well as connecting globally to share ideas and projects for change. Within health systems, how can you build lateral connections and networks across teams and areas? What are your relationships with broader community infrastructure and processes like and how these links be strengthened to build a more comprehensive understanding of those we work with? How might you develop knowledge of and apply complexity thinking to the work you do and the system you work in? What might you do to start some collective action locally to include conversations about climate change and its relevance in health systems?

Housing

According to Article 25 of the United Nations' (UN) *Universal Declaration of Human Rights* :

> Everyone has the right to a standard of living adequate for the health and well-being of himself and of his family, including food, clothing, housing and medical care and necessary social services. (UN, 1948)

In addition, Goal 11 of the UN Sustainable Development Goals is to "make cities and human settlements inclusive, safe, resilient and sustainable" (United Nations, 2015).

Underpinning both of these documents is a message that the right to shelter is fundamental and goes beyond physical structures to include a far broader understanding of safety, connection and well-being that incorporates not only physical considerations but also social, emotional and economic elements. In a truly just social world, then, access to shelter is a necessary starting point, not an end. The Australian Government appears to state a clear agreement with this position:

> From a social perspective, housing provides a stable base from which we can participate in society, form families, and enjoy retirement. Housing can determine lifetime education, employment, and health outcomes.
>
> From an economic perspective, housing has a significant impact upon investment, productivity and participation, as well as consumption and saving trends across the economy.
>
> Housing is also central to the effectiveness of Australia's welfare system.
>
> *(Department of Social Services, 2020)*

We do not have to speak to many people who either work in this sector or access their housing through it (or who have been unable to do so), however, to discover that the current housing system in Australia is complex, often unwieldy, and heavily bureaucratised. Housing policy connects multiple levels of government, particularly Federal and State, through funding and service agreements. In addition, in the public housing system we see a convergence of Government (social housing) and not-for-profit agencies (community housing), as well as responsibility for the provision of both housing stock and human support.

As we embark on our re-imagination of housing from our perspectives as workers in social and human services, it is useful to speculate on a range of climate outcomes: how might our vision be different if climate change is halted? Reversed? Or, conversely, continues to escalate, leading to loss of habitat and increased human migration as food sources fail, temperatures become unliveable and rising sea levels submerge whole communities. It is easy to fall into a deficit mode as we think through the future possibilities in this area.

Our role as frontline workers, as managers, as policy-influencers, and as humans in a world that encompasses the more-than-human are all inescapably affected by the future ahead of us. Thinking back to our lens of complexity thinking, though, we have cause for optimism as well as concern. We know that small changes can lead to disproportionate impacts, and that convergence of diverse elements can lead to the emergence of creative responses.

In Chapter 5 we considered the nexus between housing, climate and social justice. This case study illustrates the invidious position of people who are caught between, on the one hand, little agency in decisions made about their built environments and, on the other, a heavy burden of responsibilisation for their behaviours in response to heat, flood and other climate-related concerns. Arguments that government-funded housing is an expensive drain on the public purse, and that people provided with such shelter are "vulnerable", can lead us as workers in social and human services to feel helpless to bring about significant change. We have known and worked with colleagues who feel ground down by the relentlessness of such work and have come to rely on task-focused practice paradigms as a means of sustaining themselves through apparently insurmountable systemic challenges. We offer the following scenario as an alternate future.

Scenario

Housing that is equitable (just) and designed with climate change in mind. This means housing that protects its inhabitants from the adverse effects of weather and climate but, more than this, housing that acknowledges and counteracts the potential for housing to contribute to further climate change. We imagine that planning for housing has shifted to include dialogue and consideration of environmental impact, relationship with the natural context where it is located and different ways to live with the environment reciprocally. Housing design centres on ideas of justice for Earth and all who live here so affordability, accessibility, connection with the natural world and a small ecological footprint drive development at all level.

What is the change we suggest?

We suggest changes here need to include systemic planning and design changes which require consideration of social and environmental justice as hurdles for any new housing. Along with this we see a need for systematic resistance to propositions that such considerations represent green tape and stop much needed housing from being developed. While we see structural and policy change as essential to support this process, there is an opportunity for innovation in the provision of new community housing now. Rather than the scenario where social housing tenants can only access the poorest quality and most impractical housing for climate change adaptation, funders could reshape housing provision by establishing programs and incentives for new housing which centres social and environmental justice in the context of climate change. Modelling different and innovative housing approaches can be done without significant increases to resourcing, however, this requires bold and creative leadership at a policy level. We would like to suggest that this kind of leadership may offer a model for change in housing provision which opens new possibilities into the future.

What is the role of social workers?

Social and human service workers interact with housing issues from a diverse range of roles. Each of these brings a different opportunity to contribute to positive change, mediated by the interplay of the many elements that affect each person's unique individual experience. A frontline worker's power may be in the form of apparently small things: we sometimes underestimate the impact of showing kindness and respect, particularly when that is not what we receive in return. Managers may have more capacity to influence changes in the local workplace (from work processes to physical environments), and as seniority increases, the opportunities for social and human service workers to influence policy and practice increase.

In relation to design and innovation, housing provides a critically important opportunity for those of us in social work and human services to generate innovation by developing new structures and processes for collaborative dialogue with funders, architects and housing organisations, state and local government and community members. We are in a position to reframe and perhaps reclaim housing as a key element in social justice. In the context of climate change what might we do to connect social and environmental justice in this realm? Working across a range of fields which intersect with housing as well as housing itself, there seems to be a good opportunity to start conversations which disrupt ideas that most people have to take what they get in terms of housing, that price and profit are the only factors to be considered, and that housing provision is somehow separate from other aspects of social and environmental life. We suggest here that complexity thinking enables us to connect different questions related to housing and that in our work, it is both useful and practical to ask these questions if everyone is to have access to safe and liveable housing into the future.

Child protection

The United Nations Convention on the Rights of the Child was devised in 1989 with the intent of recognising young people as active participants in the world, having rights of their own. When we started our discussion on the emotive and, often controversial, topic of child protection in Australia we, again, looked to language and what that language constructs. The term itself (child protection) sets up a particular idea about risk and protectors. We wondered whether the term is helpful.

Currently formal child protection systems operate on a state and territory basis with some differences in policies and guidelines, however with many commonalities of purpose. They are premised by concepts of risk, power and surveillance. This led us to question what it means to be 'seen' and what it means to be 'surveilled'.

Many of you will work within formal statutory frameworks and all of you will have worked with families and children, in some contexts, as have we. As educators it strikes us very few people graduating from human services degrees and diplomas now will have worked in systems other than conservative neoliberalist ones. This matters. As practitioners we have fewer discretionary powers, a multitude of checks and balances, risk management processes and reporting requirements. Formal statutory frames are built on assumptions of untruthfulness. Children, and their families and carers, are placed in a combative relationship, irrespective of the skill and intent of the worker. Systemic power is vested in a worker in, arguably, the most influential decision-making in the life of a family.

In this context children can become commodities. This entirely negates the intent of the UN Convention. Broader than child protection systems we see this co-modification play out in family law court proceedings, income support disputes and every time we view one of our children as an extension of our hopes and wishes. This minimises children developing agency and denies them being seen as entities and a part of the world.

Scenario

Let's have a think about child 'protection' which sits outside of legislation and recognises children as developing adults. What if we dismantled the child protection system?

What is the change we suggest?

We would suggest the first fundamental change would be recognising caring for children (like caring for the environment) is every person's work. From a First Nation's perspective a tribal approach which shares responsibility and aims to have the young person 'seen'. For us being 'seen' is a reciprocal relationship based on trust. We wondered if young people, like Greta Thunberg, are demanding their right to be seen as an active participant in climate change action.

We invest a great deal of money and planning into risk assessing. In the process we can lose sight of two key things. Most parents and carers have good intentions. The second by-product of the layers of risk work is children are getting missed. Let's invest in supporting the majority – the well-intentioned parents – with resources and skills to keep them out of child protection systems. These systems are built on distrust. Then, focus our energies on the small percentage of horrific abuse cases. It's possible we are asking the wrong questions in this space.

Imagine as well, if we focused more on trust and vulnerability than risk? Risk and punitive systems inhibit trust. Can we create space in conversations for vulnerability and genuine exchange? We all say what we need to say when in a disempowered, unequal exchange.

What might this mean for social workers and human service workers?

Ironically, it means taking a risk! It might involve an unravelling of our professional identity and how we see ourselves in organisations. We suspect it will necessitate all of us entering the uneasy arena of grappling with how we wield power – with or without intent. Can we de-construct some of the boundaries we create, whilst also being an ethical practitioner working within organisational guidelines?

Don't compartmentalise these six topics in your daily work. Apply complexity thinking and look for connections.

For those of us working in education we can challenge specialist curriculum. Every time we teach a course called 'child protection' we reinforce a silo paradigm which removes caring for children from a societal responsibility. We can focus on developing generic skills as educators and students which can be applied in any setting.

Finally, we can be creative. One of the authors of this book described how, after recent flooding in the NSW North Coast which pretty much wiped out a community of resources, a nearby community decided to move the local school to higher ground. This resulted in students only losing 10 days of school. This was a creative way to genuinely protect the children.

Income support

Social and human service workers often support the most vulnerable members of society. As a result, providing support in relation to income support is a component of many roles. Some are employed within Centrelink, the federal department responsible for assessing and distributing all forms of income support, and many more in roles advocating for people navigating this huge bureaucracy, and providing support due impacts of food and housing insecurity. In 2017–2018 23% of people identified government benefits as their main source of income (AIHW, 2021). The Australian Institute of Health and Welfare report that government pension and allowances are more likely to be reported as the primary source for those receiving the lowest levels on income in the country (AIHW, 2021).

Given that up to one third of our population's primary source of income is a government benefit, let's consider how a just society would best support this. Firstly, we would suggest a level of income that provides a decent standard of living, allowing people to live a dignified life. Further to that, distributing this income without judgement or stigma. The idea of a universal basic income (UBI), that of a payment made universally to all members of a community without a means test or any work or mutual obligation attached (Ståhl & MacEachen, 2021) isn't a new one, and has been piloted in various contexts. The government response to the mass unemployment during COVID-19 effectively acted as a UBI pilot as the rate of unemployment benefit was doubled and the obligations attached waivered (O'Sullivan et al., 2020). The study 'Social Security and time use during COVID 19' identified that people used both the increased time and money well (Klein et al., 2021).

What our research has shown us, and we've outlined in this book, is healthy communities, resilient communities are connected communities. What we recognise is that connected communities don't just happen, they are often based on a whole lot of work, often by women to support that. Anyone experiencing or working alongside those who are required to fulfil mutual obligations attached to receiving unemployment benefits knows that it can be a time-consuming and stressful process. Imagine if a range of community-focused activities could be considered 'mutual obligation'. The reframing of our obligation; to our community, to our environment opens up a myriad of opportunities of how we might fulfil the current reporting requirements attached to receiving income support.

Scenario

An approach to income support that recognises people with hope and the capacity to live with dignity in turn have time and energy to work collectively in multifaceted ways that best support sustainable quality of life, including addressing climate change.

What needs to change?

A shift away from stigmatising people who receive income support as lesser, and recognition that systemic issues continue to perpetrate disadvantage. As we have discussed previously, what if we approach income support as one part of a cohesive system that supports a just and civil society. As we mention in the Mental Health scenario above, it is recognised that lack of money can impact on the ability to receive mental health support. Similarly, income insecurity directly leads to housing insecurity.

What is the role of social and human service workers?

Social and human service workers engage with people who receive income benefits across a range of roles. We all have the capacity to approach these interactions with the aim to focus on dignity and respect. We cannot underestimate the impact we can have, even in fleeting engagements. Social and human service workers can make it a priority to challenge dehumanising bureaucratic practices and advocate for respectful and collaborative engagements. Social and human service workers can aim to 'be the change' working towards roles in management and policy. We can strengthen our own professional and social networks and use our social capital to support and facilitate community engagement, interaction, enterprise and industry. Social and human service workers in policy and management can work towards reframing mutual obligation to encompass a range of community and environmental programs and projects. Earlier in the book we discussed community organising and collective action, often in times of crisis. What potential might we unleash if people are relieved of the constant stress of basic survival – food, clothing, transport – and can be proactive in this collective action?

Place-based (non-government) organisations

The concept of 'placed-based' is just the latest in a long line of terminology and is synonymous with older concepts like 'neighbourhood' or 'community' or 'community based' or 'community managed'. These are organisations – large and small – operating on a not-for-profit basis, that QCOSS (2022) argues has the following features: a focus on the local level; a shared, long-term vision and commitment to outcomes; working differently together across the community; governance at a local level; broad engagement with the community; and experimentation, prototyping and action learning. In general, they adopt community development approaches that are collaborative and long term aimed at building thriving inclusive communities. Whilst some take an environmental and social justice focus, others focus primarily on the social realm.

These organisations grew rapidly from the late 1960s in Australia from 'conversations around the kitchen table'. They often reflected disquiet with government neglect and a desire to have greater control over resources in their community. Many Aboriginal community-controlled organisations date from this early activism as did women's organisations such as women's health and women's refuges. These organisations were based on active citizenship, passion and democracy. Many commentators have highlighted the importance of a vibrant civil society (including place-based NGOs) in healthy democracies. They were formidable advocates for their local community and held government agencies accountable at the local level (Bamforth et al., 2016).

In the early days of their development most were heavily reliant on local volunteers, fundraising and local government supports (particularly through accommodation). From the early-1980s onwards we saw the development of a 'community sector', with peak organisations, specialist training and increasing reliance on state and commonwealth funding grants. We've included this abbreviated history as these organisations are nearly unrecognisable today. In 2010 the Productivity Commission estimates there are now over 600,000 not-for-profit organisations in Australia (not all will be placed based), contributing $43 billion to Australia's GDP according to the ABS (Productivity Commission, 2010). Facilitated by outsourcing of former government services, the sector grew strongly with average annual growth of 7.7% between 1999–2000 and 2006–2007 (Productivity Commission, 2010).

Placed-based organisations include (but are not limited to): family support services; neighbourhood centres; community centres; youth clubs; meals-on-wheels; not-for-profit children's services; ethnic community associations; Aboriginal Lands Councils; and local environmental organisations such as Landcare.

Scenario

The growth in the 'sector' (or what some call 'the industry') has been accompanied by a shift away from its historical roots. Neo-liberal funding regimes, whilst initially opposed by some, now dominate and shape place-based organisations. This includes pre-determined outcomes, in direct contradiction to community-driven responses more commonly supported by community development processes. These funding regimes have also facilitated rampart credentialism which has limited local people to the position of 'client', 'customer' or (at best) 'service user'. Like other aspects of 'service provision' discussed in this chapter, it has also led to a privileging of individualised case work in human services and social work practice. Government tendering processes has seen many small, place-based agencies forced into 'partnerships' with larger organisations in order to be 'competitive' for funding. Many of the largest NGOs now employ hundreds of people, are highly corporatised and very often religiously based charities with very limited engagement with the place they are 'delivering services'. Most alarmingly these shifts have been accompanied by a shift to 'quiet advocacy', with organisations self-censoring so as to not jeopardise their funding through upsetting the government (Carson & Maddison, 2017). There are of course pockets of resistance and many small place-based organisations operate under the radar and maintain a very strong connection to place and people. Local government remains committed to these organisations and unlike other levels of government understand the value of place-based organisations.

What needs to change?

We imagine a reclaiming of organisational visions, purposes and histories; a future in which place-based organisations 'have the back' of their local communities. A reclaiming of their positions as formidable advocates who hold governments accountable. We imagine a shift away from transactional and dehumanising relations with residents to one that is embedded in the everyday life of place and people. A future in which place-based organisations are seen again as part of a complex local eco-system, marked by innovation, collaboration and celebration. Organisations which understand the complexities of the convergence of environmental and social justice; organisations that take their role as stewardship for human and more than human life at the local level seriously. This means working across the boundaries of social and environmental concerns to locate fairness and well-being in ways which connect people to the breadth of challenges brought by climate change and local ways to address these.

What is the role of social and human service workers?

Those working in place-based organisations have the possibility of challenging dominant neo-liberal discourses through taking a stance and small acts of generosity. It is in the everyday that we are able to begin the process of recreating a collective, cooperative, holistic future. Cultural humility, deep listening and resistance to simple answers will all be useful tools for the place-based worker. As educators we are aware of the need to prepare students for the messiness of everyday life and to support them develop a much more complex understanding of boundaries. In this future place-based organisations would establish deep ecological roots into place, understanding that people are shaped by and shape this land.

Conclusion

So, as we look into the future, what we have suggested in this chapter and in the book overall is that social work and human services are intimately connected to and have an important role to play in acting on climate change in the space where social and environmental justice coalesce. In this chapter we have made some first step suggestions about change but they are very much a beginning. Throughout the book we have invited you, the reader, to think, ponder, question and formulate with us in making sense of how we might work in this space.

We have shaped our thinking through listening to First Nations Worldviews which centre reciprocity and relationship to Mother Earth and all who are here, and to complexity thinking which opens up possibilities for making sense of the interconnectedness of life. We have spent some time unpacking and questioning many of the taken-for-granted ideas and concepts often referred to in the context of climate change – responsibility, risk, resilience, adaptation, mitigation – as well as discussing the links with key ideas in social work and human services – care and intersections.

The ways in which we can reshape our work in social work and human services in relation to the basics of life – food, energy and water – provided us with some context and guidance in linking our role to broader climate change impacts in the everyday. We then turned our attention to the ways we might make change – from the local at home, in the office or in our neighbourhood, to the diverse operations of self-organising and collective action and then onto policy change.

In the last section of the book, we walked through some of the emergent moments we have seen already when things have gone wrong through disasters, and which we hope to see through this chapter imagining a different future is social work and human services. The final chapter of the book provides a range of case studies which contain ideas, questions and actions in context. We invite you to work through these and unpack them in your own context. We have provided some questions to guide your thinking and hope these are useful for your own work on climate change where social and environmental justice coalesce.

References

Ahamer, G. (2013). Game, not fight: Change climate change! *Simulation & Gaming, 44*(2–3), 272–301. https://doi.org/10.1177/1046878112470541

Albrecht, G. A. (2020). Negating solastalgia: An emotional revolution from the Anthropocene to the Symbiocene. *American Imago, 77*(1), 9–30. https://doi.org/10.1353/aim.2020.0001

Australian Institute of Health and Welfare [AIHW]. (2021, September 16). Income and income support. In *Australia's Welfare 2021.* https://www.aihw.gov.au/reports/australias-welfare/income-support

Bamforth, J., & Gapps, B., Gurr, R., Howard, A., Onyx, J., & Rawsthorne, M. (2016). *Planning, funding, and community action: The area assistance story.* Common Ground Publishing LLC.

Carson, A., & Maddison, S. (2017). Three reasons Australians should be concerned that NGOs voices are not being heard, The Conversation, 12 December, Retrieved from https://theconversation.com/three-reasons-australians-should-be-concerned-that-ngos-voices-are-not-being-heard-88561

Department of Social Services. (2020, December 15). Housing support. (online, accessed 28 March 2022). https://www.dss.gov.au/housing-support/programmes-services/housing

Everard, M. (2016). *The ecosystems revolution.* Springer International Publishing. https://doi.org/10.1007/978-3-319-31658-1

Klein, E., Cook, K., Maury, M., & Bowey, K. (2021). *Social security and time use during COVID-19.* Swinburne University of Technology & Centre for Excellence in Child and Family Welfare. https://www.cfecfw.asn.au/wp-content/uploads/2021/03/Social-security-and-time-use-during-COVID-19-Report-Treating-Families-Fairly-2021.pdf

O'Sullivan, D., Rahamathulla, M., & Pawar, M. (2020). The impact and implications of COVID-19: An Australian perspective. *International Journal of Community and Social Development, 2*(2), 134–151. https://doi.org/10.1177/2516602620937922

Prescott, S. & Logan, A. (2017). Down to earth: Planetary health and biophilosophy in the Symbiocene Epoch. *Challenges, 8*(2), 19. https://doi.org/10.3390/challe8020019

QCOSS. (2022). Understanding place-based approaches, Guide & Toolkit. Retrieved from https://www.qcoss.org.au/contents-page-for-place-based-approach-and-toolkit/place-based-approaches-for-community-change/

Robinson, J. B. (1988). Unlearning and backcasting: Rethinking some of the questions we ask about the future. *Technological Forecasting & Social Change, 33*(4), 325–338. https://doi.org/10.1016/0040-1625(88)90029-7

Royal Australian College of General Practitioners. (2021). *The impact of climate change on human health.* Retrieved March 27, 2022 from https://www.racgp.org.au/advocacy/position-statements/view-all-position-statements/clinical-and-practice-management/the-impact-of-climate-change-on-human-health

Ståhl, C., & MacEachen, E. (2021). Universal basic income as a policy response to COVID-19 and precarious employment: Potential impacts on rehabilitation and return-to-work. *Journal of Occupational Rehabilitation, 31*(1), 3–6. https://doi.org/10.1007/s10926-020-09923-w

United Nations. (1948). Universal declaration of human rights. Retrieved March 27, 2022, from https://www.un.org/en/about-us/universal-declaration-of-human-rights

11

CASE STUDIES

Case study: food systems, water and workers

In examining food systems and the impacts of climate change, the effects are undeniable and broad. In one such community, home to one of our authors, what is unfolding is multifaceted and complex. This small rural farming and horticultural community has, like many of its kind, seen massive changes in the way food production and harvest is undertaken. The area, traditionally founded with large and small family-owned horticulture properties, is now dominated by large corporate-owned agri-business, a theme across the industry and geographic area (Campbell, 2019). This system is part of a large integrated industrialised food system and sophisticated food chains that are strongly influenced by supermarkets (Campbell, 2019). This, along with a large contracted labour force, with lots of contention around visa status and exploitation of workers, has changed the very fabric of the community.

Water risk as plantings grow

The impacts of climate change in this area are undeniable, far reaching and intersect with competing agendas of economic growth and development. Plantings of oranges, grapes and almonds continued and increased by 25% across the district in 2020, leaving water authorities grappling with how to provide water to the crops. Dr Ben Dyer of the Murray-Darling Basin Authority told farmers this, noting that parts of the system were already relying on inter-valley trade (of water) from the Murrumbidgee and Goulburn Rivers (Kennedy, 2021).

One resident, whose decades-long career intersects with water and land management states:

The commodification of water has meant the move away from family farming to the corporate ownership we see now₄ small family farms just can't compete₄

Disturbingly, while the nation has been riveted by the crisis of the Murray-Darling Basin over the past several years, water-intensive plantings have escalated. In rural communities where growers and businesses rely on the economics of horticulture, this presents challenges and no easy answers. Again, this is not new information as articulated by this local:

The view is short sighted, season to season.

Harvest labour: challenges and responses

Horticulture differs from most other parts of agriculture in its relative labour intensity, particularly at harvest. Harvest was historically undertaken by locals and a regular influx of interstate workers, many First Nations Peoples who followed the growing season to different harvests. This has changed dramatically in the last several decades. While an accurate analysis is difficult to ascertain, harvest labour is predominantly undertaken by migrant workers and it is widely accepted that many undocumented workers are likely to be employed in harvest labour (Underhill & Rimmer, 2016). The population of this community based on the 2016 census is 3,313. However, in truth, this figure is believed to be closer to 8,000. This is largely attributed to a large migrant worker population, many who may be undocumented (RFDS, 2022). This is reflected in the recent COVID-19 vaccination hub set up by the Royal Flying Doctor service, the very aim being to provide an opportunity for undocumented workers to be vaccinated.

Most harvest labour is undertaken by contractors, who then provide the labour to properties. The impact of this on this small community has been the focus of several national television exposes' around vulnerable migrant (possibly undocumented) workers being exploited by contactors with low wages (figures such as $30.00 per day have been reported), large repayments for visas and substandard and overcrowded accommodations (ABC, 2015; Archibald-Binge, 2021; Bannan, 2021). As one local community leader articulates:

The issues are complex and everyone blames the contractors for exploiting the workers, but the growers are complicit in this too. Growers are cushioned because they say 'I've employed a contractor,' however the contractor has to negotiate the price per hour with the grower. There is no way the growers don't negotiate it down with the contractors. Covid has levelled it out a bit because there are no workers, but the minute there are enough workers, it will revert back.

Whatever the analysis of harvest labour tells us, the impacts of this are clearly visible in the fabric of the town. The main street which once held a variety of business and services now only holds a few businesses, and several produce stores aimed at the contractor demographic. Many empty shop fronts are obviously (illegally) housing workers, and a drive around the town will show many regular three-bedroom houses with mini buses outside identifying them as rooming houses.

If we again draw from complexity theory (Lorenz, 1993) to analyse this scenario, we can identify feedback loops and how they change the system in this context. If we consider the impact of migration and worker exploitation creating a cheaper workforce, we can link this to the economic growth driving increased plantings. The impact of climate change on the changing weather patterns is clear, as is the increased stress on valuable water resources. This, in concert with the reliance on an exploited workforce is creating this unsustainable cycle which appears to be in crisis.

Thoughts to consider

> As a social worker how might I navigate the competing agendas at play here?
>
> How might I reconcile the competing needs and human rights issues here?
>
> How might I, as a social worker, respond to the needs of possibly undocumented workers?

Case study: Aboriginal knowledges and community voices

We have previously discussed how greater attention is being placed on 'shared responsibility' and 'community resilience' in relation to strengthening community capacity and responses in relation to extreme weather. We have also noted how a number of researchers have drawn attention to the ways in which adopting resilience strategies without an analysis of power serves largely to reproduce and reinforce existing social and economic inequality (Ensor et al., 2018).

The following case study draws from our Community-Led Research (CLR, a process that supports community participation, community prioritising, community decision-making and community action) across three communities alongside a capacity-building project exploring how best to ensure that rural communities are more disaster resilient. We find real opportunity for learnings from First Nations Peoples ways of Knowing, Being and Doing along with community-led conversations, when open to being led by First Nations Peoples. This community-led approach relinquishes a pre-conceived idea of what 'resilience' might look like and allows us to be open to exploring and building on existing community resilience. We have found that for this to unfold, researchers/community workers must have the capacity and intention to step away from ideas of 'expert status', sit with discomfort and practice deep listening.

Like many community consultations and capacity-building projects, this one had a clear focus – that being, the strengthening of community capacity and responses and creating space for building innovation in relation to extreme weather. Like other pilot communities, this one was chosen as it had a particular pattern of extreme weather; in this case, flooding. It also had a starting point for engagement, that being response from 'key people'. So, while the initial brief was on the face of it inclusive, it was, by its pre-set parameters, pre-determined and possibly exclusionary. Meetings and consultations were initially, as is often the case, dominated by services representing agencies or particular interests.

We'd love a flood about now...

In listening to the community members, what quickly became apparent was that this was not the time to focus on floods, despite this being one of the criteria for this community's involvement. The community, like large parts of New South Wales, was several years into extreme drought. Following mention at an initial meeting looking at community coping strategies in times of flood, one participant sardonically stated, 'Flood? We'd love one about now...' Had the conversation not been responsive to this quiet comment, chances are the community would have viewed our engagement as tokenistic and tone deaf. Rather the conversation was able to evolve to encompass drought and other community challenges, while drawing on community coping skills and the transferable nature of these.

They were invited...

Similarly, the lack of inclusion of First Nations community members, if not explored further beyond 'they have been invited', could have led to a missed opportunity for us to learn from First Nations knowledges and the Community left feeling excluded. It was clear that without a move away from only engaging with services and people representing agencies, the community representation would remain limited.

This shift was made by good old community development strategies of loitering: talking to people, meeting people where they were and getting a sense of the community. What we quickly found was this community had a proud and shared history of resilience and the ability to apply that beyond the prescribed area of floods. Both the First Nations and non-Indigenous communities had strong local identification and pride. When a local First Nations community member attended a meeting in their role as an SES volunteer, we asked them (quietly, privately) for their thoughts on making the meetings more accessible to First Nations community members. Quietly and privately were important aspects of this engagement. It would have been disrespectful and othering to single out this person publicly to meet our needs and 'have all the answers'. Rather in the context of a broader personal conversation, we were able to approach this. Introductions were made and a change of venue to a culturally safe space was suggested. Through deep listening and being led by the conversations with First Nations community members this was able to be built on and supported by the project. What was shared was the already planned and discussed idea of a Cultural Trail of significant First Nations sites on Country. The idea of formalising, signposting and making this a trail accessible for all community and tourists alike to experience and learn from First Nations knowledges was not a new idea, but one that the local community had long hoped to establish. Both First Nations and non-Indigenous community members showed real excitement and commitment to this project, with First Nations community members rightly taking the lead on this development.

We know that connected communities are best able to respond to and manage crisis, such as extreme weather. We also know that climate change is driving an increase in extreme weather events. We know that real community connection must come from a place of authenticity. In creating space for innovation and resilience in communities, we can draw from and build on the resilience within communities. While building on community connection and resilience, whole of community commitment to projects such as a First Nations Cultural Trail also make a significant commitment to privileging First Nations history, culture and ongoing connection to Country.

Thoughts to consider

How might I ensure my engagement with First Nations Peoples is culturally safe and respectful?

How might I respond if there is a lack of community engagement?

How might I promote flexible and community-led approaches with funding bodies or management structures?

Case study: Knitting Nannas

'What are you knitting? – A revolution'

The Knitting Nannas delight in subverting assumptions. As they say on their website (https://knitting-nannas.com), they 'use the common stereotype of the sweet little old lady to lull the bad guys into a false sense of security'. They also subvert the notion of what activism looks like. They take pride in being playful, defusing and calming (with icy-poles and sunscreen, for example) to open spaces up where hard conversations can happen.

But don't be lulled into thinking these Nannas are just in it for the laughs; they might not take themselves too seriously, but they are deeply passionate about what they do and have a firm eye on the future they will leave for "the kiddies".

The Nannas as a self-organising system

What can we learn from the Nannas about self-organising systems? As we heard in earlier chapters, self-organisation is a feature of complex systems evolving in response to an existing or threatened change. The Knitting Nannas started out in the Northern Rivers area of New South Wales in response to proposed mining for coal-seam gas. Since then, additional groups (known as "loops", in keeping with the yarn theme) have formed all around Australia as well as in the UK, US and Europe, united through the Nannafesto. The Nannafesto sets out the Knitting Nannas' philosophy and guides action, cleverly articulating both the softness and the steeliness that characterise the movement:

> We sit, knit, plot, have a yarn and a cuppa, and bear witness to the war against those who try and rape our land and divide our communities.
>
> *(Knitting Nannas, 2022)*

The Knitting Nannas are an exemplar for systems that taken an "organic" approach to organisation. Illustrating this is the way that leadership is apparent in Nannas activities, but occurs and is sustained through an informal consensus, in the absence of either a formalised structure or process.

> I loved not having meetings bloody meetings - just a plotting session during or after a protest and an email list. ... Later I heard one of the founders[4] say proudly that the Nannas are a disorganization. I liked that, though I thought unorganisation was more the model – having just enough organisation to keep action happening.
>
> *(Knitting Nanna A)*

While the group is not limited to older women, members report an inclusivity that they may not experience in other activist groups. "As you become an older woman, it just feels more comfortable being with women[4] (meeting with experienced Nannas is like) a group of elders, reminds me of (previous experiences of) sitting around with a group of Aboriginal women in circle" (Knitting Nanna B).

Craftivism in action

"'People feel comfortable coming up and talking to old ladies sitting knitting" says Carol in the video "Nanna Power" (YouTube: 17:40/20:29). Carol's comment illustrates one of the core features of craftivism. Craftivists are often unassuming, inoffensive, even setting themselves or their crafts up for potential ridicule. As we saw at the beginning of this case study, the Knitting Nannas *use* the stereotype to *subvert* the stereotype, in what Larri and Whitehouse describe as a "strategic and tactile essentialism" (2019, p.30).

This subversion sits alongside a genuine playfulness, however, and this is evident not only in the knitted products but also in other crafts, singing and dance, which expand the inclusivity of the group while maintaining its focus. One Knitting Nanna described this as "the value of that humour and that warmth, and that imagination, sort of not letting the rage overtake you. That kind of energy empowers me" (Knitting Nanna C).

Along with this playfulness we see an optimism, a conscious commitment to a future for following generations. The Nannas Facebook page contains weekly "good news" updates. Looking at this strategy through the lens of complexity theory, we can view this as an example of feedback loops influencing the co-creation of an optimistic future. Good news stories provide concrete evidence to support hopefulness and, in doing so, challenge the demoralisation we can easily succumb to when we think deeply about the scale of wicked problems.

The importance of interconnectedness

One of the notable characteristics of the Knitting Nannas is the extent and richness of their interconnections with multiple and diverse others, both individuals and organisations. Collaborative work and networking is central to the way that the group approaches activism.

Thoughts to consider

How might I extend my practice to include opportunities for increased community interconnectedness?

How might I, as a social or human service worker help facilitate this for community members experiencing social isolation?

How might I situate activism more prominently in my community work?

Case study: urban heat sinks

Returning to the key idea of complexity, this case study illustrates the critical importance of community action working in concert with policy, infrastructure and planning initiatives. The impact of heat sinks in cities is an increasingly urgent issue as temperatures rise and sustained heatwaves become more common. Rising heat is a much less recognised climate disaster both by community members and emergency management agencies in spite of the devastating impacts, including high death rates worldwide (Australian Museum, 2022). Research in Australia has highlighted the dangerous intersections of poverty, inadequate housing, infrastructure and social isolation in relation to heatwaves (Howard et al., 2018), which along with limited perceptions amongst vulnerable population groups about how heat impacts health and wellbeing, make up a high-risk environment for many as climate change escalates.

Impacts of heatwaves

Heatwaves are of particular concern: they are occurring more often and are more intense than in the past. In recent decades more people have died in Australia in heat waves than all other natural disasters combined (Australian Museum, 2022).

It is tempting, in this context, to frame the response to heatwave impacts as a problem of technology – better housing, adaptive infrastructure, affordable energy for cooling. Policy, funding, business and technological initiatives are absolutely an essential part of any strategy to mitigate the impacts of heat on the community in general and for those most vulnerable and least able to respond due to disadvantage. The complexity of this issue, however, with interacting systems of planning and development, advocacy for green infrastructure, long-term poverty and exclusion, individualised and market-oriented resource management, intensifying urban development and fragmented approaches in urban design and social support mean that the issue of heatwave impact in urban landscapes is far from a simple problem.

Perceptions of climate change

A study by Ambrey et al. (2017) which examined green infrastructure development and disadvantage in the rapidly developing Gold Coast, Queensland provides another clear example of this complexity. They surveyed community members in a disadvantaged suburb to ascertain whether people experiencing social disadvantage were concerned about climate change, perceived green infrastructure as a positive addition to the suburb and would like to see more green initiative develop in their local area. In their results, residents surveyed did not have an increased concern about climate change and were no more likely than other population groups to view green infrastructure as beneficial. Ambrey and colleagues explain these results by highlighting two important contextual issues. Firstly, the perception that climate change is still something which will occur in the future compared to immediate problems of survival, paying bills, cost of living and daily priorities. This is important as it highlights the experience of disadvantage itself in limiting the parameters and capacity for many people to plan into the future. Daily priorities and often crises take precedence making long-term planning something that can never quite be achieved. This was also highlighted in research completed by some of the current authors on risk perceptions and disaster preparedness amongst at-risk groups, where limited resources and the pressing pressures of day-to-day living significantly impacted on disaster preparedness activities for those experiencing disadvantage (Howard et al., 2018). Secondly, Ambrey and colleagues attributed their results to a simultaneous perception of green infrastructure as expensive requiring maintenance and ongoing upkeep costs such as water bills, while links between increased heat through climate change and the costs associated with this for residents in higher energy bills were not clear due to confusing information available on climate change impacts. They conclude by recommending that any future planning for green infrastructure to address "thermal inequity" (p. 58) must attend to both community education and practical support to lower costs of renewable energy and increasing greening efforts.

Thoughts to consider

Have the extreme weather and disaster occurrences in Australia in the last three years shifted public perception regarding climate change, from the 'future' to the 'now'? If not, how can we address this?

How might I, as a social or human service worker bring this awareness to my everyday practice and activism?

How might I advocate alongside those most disadvantaged who are potentially most impacted by these impacts of climate change?

Case study: beyond the hero narrative: recognising community collective action

The floods of late February, early March 2022 in Queensland and New South Wales have had a catastrophic impact on vast areas of the natural and built environment. These extreme weather events have led to the annihilation of whole town and city areas and the displacement of tens of thousands of people. Meteorologist Ben Domensino noted that the 611.6 mm of rain that fell on Brisbane over a 3-day period was the highest since records begin in 1840. Domensino says while several features in the atmosphere combined to deliver the rain, climate change likely made the event worse. "Given climate change is a background to all weather events, it's hard to say that it does not play a role", he says. "We know the oceans are getting warmer and that puts more moisture in the atmosphere, and a warmer atmosphere can hold more moisture" (Readfearn et al., 2022).

Amid the 24-hour news cycle showing complete townships under water, cars floating down streets and other flood-caused carnage, many good news stories of heroic efforts of locals responding and helping each other emerged. This is not a new phenomenon, but rather a common media response in times of crisis. We know that accounts of heroism are 'eminently newsworthy, satisfying the thirst of a good news angle on a bad news story' (Readfearn et al., 2022).

While the rescue response of bystanders or locals is often framed as 'random heroism' (How Lismore locals became flood rescue heroes when emergency services were swamped 1 March 2022), we would suggest that this simplistic narrative is doing communities an injustice. While the behaviour is certainly heroic, it is a narrow analysis to attribute such behaviour to random responses by a few 'heroic' individuals. Eyre (2017) debunks the myth (often perpetuated by media) that disasters 'often produce wide scale, counterproductive and antisocial behaviour such as panic, social disorganisation and looting'. While not disputing these behaviours do exist, Eyre asserts that research across different types of disasters and societies has shown generally public and disaster victims respond and adapt well both during and after disasters (Tierney et al cited in Eyre, 2017).

Community in action

In considering one example (of many) reported during the recent floods at Lismore, we can draw more from the story than 'random heroism'. In this example, 45 Fijian men, who arrived in Australia just 3 weeks prior to work in the abattoir in the New South Wales town of Lismore, joined in community rescue responses. After the floods meant the men were unable to get to work due to high water levels, they put out a call on Facebook offering to help with rescue efforts. The men assisted in the coming days with rescuing aged care residents and helping at the evacuation centre (Achenza , 2022).

While the actions of these men have rightly been lauded by the community, we can also take learnings from this beyond the random hero narrative. This group of men actively reached out to the local community, posting their availability to help on Facebook, and thus connecting with local community members. Our own research in community responses in times of extreme weather and disasters tells us that well-connected communities respond best in times of disaster. Our research found that while the approaches to disaster resilience and the actions in each community were different, there were seven key factors that are critically important in community-led resilience: communication, networks, self-organising systems, decision-making, information, resources, tools and support and inclusion. In applying these factors to the above example, we can see that this group of men (networks) reached out via Facebook (communication, information) and joined current community efforts (self-organising systems, decision-making). They brought much needed person power and joined in utilising available resources (tools and support) and were welcomed and embraced by their new community (support and inclusion). We would invite you to, when reading or watching future 'random hero' stories to consider these key factors in the story.

Thoughts to consider

How might I reframe my thinking around community collective action? What other areas might this apply?

How can we all, as community members, work to strengthening these areas in our own networks and communities?

How might I support and help create opportunities for connection in all areas of practice to strengthen community connections?

How can I, as a social and human service worker, promote community connections in ways that create recognition across broader systems?

References

Achenza, M. (2022, March 1). *Fijian men pull together hero effort to rescue elderly residents trapped in nursing home,* News.com.au. Retrieved from https://www.news.com.au/national/

nsw-act/news/fijian-men-pull-together-hero-effort-to-rescue-elderly-residents-trapped-in-nursing-home/news-story/f74a95b23a5dbd101aa90918e8ed3b88

Ambrey, C., Byrne, J., Matthews, T., Davison, A., Portanger, C., & Lo, A. (2017). Cultivating climate justice: Green infrastructure and suburban disadvantage in Australia. *Applied Geography (Sevenoaks), 89*, 52–60. https://doi.org/10.1016/j.apgeog.2017.10.002

Archibald-Binge, A. (2021, December 14). *Inside horticulture's 'dark underbelly': The unseen workers propping up the farm industry.* Australian Broadcasting Corporation. https://www.abc.net.au/news/2021-12-14/australias-farm-industry-seasonal-workers-exploited-labour-short/100687182

Australian Museum. (2022). Impacts of climate change. Retrieved April 5, 2022 from https://australian.museum/learn/climate-change/climate-change-impacts/

Bannan, P. (2021, December 22). *Experts weigh in on undocumented workers issue.* The Guardian. https://www.theguardian.com.au/news/experts-weigh-in-on-undocumented-workers-issue

Campbell, I. (2019) Harvest labour markets in Australia: Alleged labour shortages and employer demand for temporary migrant workers. *Journal of Australian Political Economy, 84*, 46–88.

Ensor, J., Forrester, J., & Matin, N. (2018). Bringing rights into resilience: Revealing complexities of climate risks and social conflict. *Disasters, 42*(S2), S287–S305. https://doi.org/10.1111/disa.12304

Eyre, A. (2017). The making of a hero: An exploration of heroism in disasters and implications for the emergency services. In P. Murphy & K. Greenhalgh (Eds.). *Fire and rescue services* (pp. 113–129). Springer International Publishing. https://doi.org/10.1007/978-3-319-62155-5_8

Howard, A., Agllias, K., Bevis, M. & Blakemore, T. (2018). How social isolation affects disaster preparedness and response in Australia: Implications for social work. *Australian Social Work, 71*(4), 392–404. https://doi.org/10.1080/0312407X.2018.1487461

Kennedy, E. (2021, April 14). Sunraysia water risk rises as plantings grow in supply crisis. *Sunraysia Daily.* https://www.sunraysiadaily.com.au/farming/4119047/sunraysia-water-risk-rises-as-plantings-grow-in-supply-crisis

Knitting Nannas. (2022). *The Knitting Nannas: Saving the land, air and water for the kiddies.* Retrieved April 11, 2022 from https://knitting-nannas.com/

Lorenz, E. N. (1993). *The essence of chaos.* University of Washington Press.

Readfearn, G., Evershed, N., & Nicholas, J. (2022). *What caused the 'rain bomb'? How the unprecedented Queensland and NSW fools unfolded.* The Guardian. Retrieved May 10 2022. https://www.theguardian.com/australia-news/2022/mar/01/how-the-unprecedented-queensland-and-nsw-floods-unfolded

Royal Flying Doctor Service [RFDS]. (2022). *Vaccinating our most vulnerable.* Retrieved March 28, 2022, from https://rfds.shorthandstories.com/vaccinating-our-most-vulnerable/index.html

Underhill, E., & Rimmer, M. (2016). Layered vulnerability: Temporary migrants in Australian horticulture. *Journal of Industrial Relations, 58*(5), 608–626. https://doi.org/10.1177/0022185615600510

INDEX